TEKASHI 6IX 9INE AND THE NINE TREY GANGSTA BLOODS   COMPLEX   SHAWN SETARO   LEX

SHAWN SETARO   DUMMY BOY   TEKASHI 6IX 9INE AND THE NINE TREY GANGSTA BLOODS   MY 7

TEKASHI 6IX 9INE AND THE NINE TREY GANGSTA BLOODS   COMPLEX   SHAWN SETARO   DUMMY BOY   TEKASHI 6IX 9INE AND THE NINE TREY GANGSTA BLOODS   COMPLEX

SHAWN SETARO   DUMMY BOY   TEKASHI 6IX 9INE AND THE NINE TREY GANGSTA BLOODS   COMPLEX   SHAWN SETARO   DUMMY BOY

TEKASHI 6IX 9INE AND THE NINE TREY GANGSTA BLOODS   COMPLEX   SHAWN SETARO   DUMMY BOY   COMPLEX   TEKASHI 6IX 9INE AND THE NINE TREY GANGSTA BLOODS   COMPLEX

SHAWN SETARO   DUMMY BOY   TEKASHI 6IX 9INE AND THE NINE TREY GANGSTA BLOODS   COMPLEX   SHAWN SETARO   DUMMY BOY

TEKASHI 6IX 9INE AND THE NINE TREY GANGSTA BLOODS   COMPLEX   SHAWN SETARO   DUMMY BOY   TEKASHI 6IX 9INE AND THE NINE TREY GANGSTA BLOODS   COMPLEX

SHAWN SETARO   DUMMY BOY   TEKASHI 6IX 9INE AND THE NINE TREY GANGSTA BLOODS   COMPLEX   SHAWN SETARO   DUMMY BOY

TEKASHI 6IX 9INE AND THE NINE TREY GANGSTA BLOODS   COMPLEX   SHAWN SETARO   DUMMY BOY   TEKASHI 6IX 9INE AND THE NINE TREY GANGSTA BLOODS   COMPLEX

SHAWN SETARO   DUMMY BOY   TEKASHI 6IX 9INE AND THE NINE TREY GANGSTA BLOODS   COMPLEX   SHAWN SETARO   DUMMY BOY

TEKASHI 6IX 9INE AND THE NINE TREY GANGSTA BLOODS   COMPLEX   SHAWN SETARO   DUMMY BOY   TEKASHI 6IX 9INE AND THE NINE TREY GANGSTA BLOODS   COMPLEX

SHAWN SETARO   DUMMY BOY   TEKASHI 6IX 9INE AND THE NINE TREY GANGSTA BLOODS   COMPLEX   SHAWN SETARO   DUMMY BOY

TEKASHI 6IX 9INE AND THE NINE TREY GANGSTA BLOODS   COMPLEX   SHAWN SETARO   DUMMY BOY   TEKASHI 6IX 9INE AND THE NINE TREY GANGSTA BLOODS   COMPLEX

SHAWN SETARO   DUMMY BOY   TEKASHI 6IX 9INE AND THE NINE TREY GANGSTA BLOODS   COMPLEX   SHAWN SETARO   DUMMY BOY

TEKASHI 6IX 9INE AND THE NINE TREY GANGSTA BLOODS   COMPLEX   SHAWN SETARO   DUMMY BOY   TEKASHI 6IX 9INE AND THE NINE TREY GANGSTA BLOODS   COMPLEX

COMPLEX

PRESENTS

DUMMY BOY

TEKASHI 6IX 9INE
AND THE NINE TREY GANGSTA BLOODS

SHAWN SETARO

Kingston Imperial

Complex Presents Dummy Boy: Tekashi 6ix9ine and the Nine Trey Gangsta Bloods Copyright © 2021 by Shawn Setaro

Printed in China

All Rights Reserved. For information address Kingston Imperial, LLC Rights Department, 144 North 7th Street, #255 Brooklyn N.Y. 11249

First Edition:

Book and Jacket Design: Alex Solis & PiXiLL Designs

Cataloging in Publication data is on file with the library of Congress

Hardcover: ISBN 9781954220027

Ebook: ISBN 9781954220041

CONTENTS

Key Musical Releases   v

Sourcing   ix

Preface   xi

Part 1   1
The Rise

Introduction   3
A Troll Who Knows How To Rap

Chapter 1   5
The Story of Danny

Chapter 2   31
Treyway

Chapter 3   43
Gummo

Chapter 4   53
A Personal Hit Squad

Chapter 5   61
Where the Money At?

Chapter 6   71
Houston

Chapter 7   87
Spinning Out of Control

Chapter 8   103
The Dam Springs a Leak

Chapter 9   129
'You Could Get Us Touched'

Part 2   149
The Feds

Chapter 10   151
The Aftermath

Chapter 11   161
Lawyers, Guns, and Money

Chapter 12   171
The Big Day

Chapter 13   189
'A Jussie Smollett, If You Will'

Chapter 14   199
A Really Scary Situation

Chapter 15   203
'Do You Recognize Anyone in the Courtroom?'

Chapter 16   211
'Let's Talk About the Times When You Actually Paid Cash'

Chapter 17   221
'You Knew Cardi B Was a Blood, Correct?'

Chapter 18   233
'Did There Come a Time When You Became a Confidential
Government Informant?'

Chapter 19   237
Borderline Frivolous

Chapter 20   243
'Imma Try to Hurt a Nigga Close to You'

Chapter 21   255
Has the Jury Reached a Verdict?

Chapter 22   259
'I Don't Know If This Is a Joke Anymore'

Chapter 23   277
Extraordinary and Compelling Reasons

Conclusion   287
Over the Rainbow

Acknowledgments   291

Kingston Imperial   295

Index   296

KEY MUSICAL RELEASES

"Billy Dat" by Seqo Billy (Tr3yway Entertainment, 2018)

"Bodak Yellow" by Cardi B (Atlantic/KSR, 2017)

Day69 by 6ix9ine (Scumgang Records/TenThousand Projects, 2018)

Dummy Boy by 6ix9ine (Create Music Group, 2018)

"DWB (Dirty White Bitch)" by Schlosser and DirtyBlack (self-released, 2015)

"Don't Run" by Casanova (2xentertainment, LLC, 2016)

"For a Scammer" by Pop Out Boyz (Pop Out Boyz Ent., 2016)

"Gooba" by 6ix9ine (Create Music Group, 2020)

"Gotti" by 6ix9ine (Scumgang Records/TenThousand Projects, 2018)

"Gummo" by 6ix9ine (Scumgang Records, 2017)

"Keke" by 6ix9ine f/Fetty Wap and A Boogie Wit da Hoodie (Scumgang
Records/TenThousand Projects, 2018)

"Kika" by 6ix9ine f/Tory Lanez (Create Music Group, 2018)

"Kooda" by 6ix9ine (Scumgang Records/TenThousand Projects, 2018)

"Love Scars" by Trippie Redd (TenThousand Projects, 2017)

"Mob Ties" by Drake (Young Money/Cash Money Records, 2018)

"Poles1469" by Trippie Redd f/6ix9ine (TenThousand Projects, 2017)

"Red Barz" by Cardi B and araabMUZIK (Genre Defying Entertainment LLC, 2017)

TattleTales by 6ix9ine (Create Music Group, 2020)

"Trollz" by 6ix9ine f/Nicki Minaj (Create Music Group, 2020)

This book is dedicated to Rosie and Reuben: May you grow up to learn that "Don't act dumb, 'cause I'm dumber" is a song lyric and not a way of life.

SOURCING

All words, including curses and slurs, are spelled out in the manuscript below, rather than being starred out or redacted. This was done in order to not distract the reader with endless asterisks, and to give an accurate portrayal of what interview subjects, song lyrics, Instagram Live rants, and the like actually said.

For a complete list of sources, please visit Kingstonimperial.com/DummyBoy.

PREFACE

This book began out of confusion. The *Complex* editorial team was trying to find new ways to cover the SoundCloud rap wave, and especially to write about artists who eschewed traditional press outlets and who had either committed or been accused of interpersonal abuses. Foremost among these artists, in the middle of 2018, was Tekashi 6ix9ine. His rise was rapid and inescapable. But there were also rumors swirling around about abuse in his past. There had to be a new way into the story.

"How about looking at that Treyway guy?" someone suggested. That was the beginning. I started trying to find out everything I could about the mysterious figure who appeared by Tekashi's side at seemingly every moment. That led me down a huge rabbit hole.

And then, after several months, Tekashi, that Treyway guy, and a bunch of other people got arrested on federal racketeering charges. From the very first court hearing, I was there. It all culminated in an intense, surreal trial and an even more surreal sentencing hearing, featuring a surprise cameo from a person most folks had assumed was dead.

Much has been said, in text, via audio, and on camera, about Tekashi 6ix9ine. I've written and said no shortage of it myself, in *Complex*, on the podcast *Infamous: The Tekashi 6ix9ine Story*, and in other documentaries. *Dummy Boy* is the culmination of all of my efforts. Everything I've learned in years of reporting this story—all the interviews, all the court documents, all the side conversations, all the rabbit holes I fell into—went into this book. It gives the most complete picture of the story of Daniel Hernandez that we've seen so far. And I know, because I've been involved in most of the others. Welcome to *Dummy Boy*.

PART 1
THE RISE

INTRODUCTION

A TROLL WHO KNOWS HOW TO RAP

Rap stars are supposed to celebrate their successes and hide their failures. But when you're a rapper whose whole life is about being notorious, about making people hate you, about getting attention whether good or bad? That's not an option. All you can do is try to make your successes and your failures indistinguishable.

In the fall of 2020, Daniel "Tekashi 6ix9ine" Hernandez was, finally, a flop. He had wanted, predicted, *needed* a number 1 album, and he didn't get it. Not even close. His new album *TattleTales* debuted at number 4 on the Billboard 200 album chart. It was a disappointment, especially for an artist who spent his whole career tying his sense of self-worth to the charts. "I'm ten for ten on the Billboard" was his tagline—his first ten singles all made the Hot 100 singles chart. He was adamant that his previous album *Dummy Boy*, released days after his arrest on federal racketeering charges, was only denied its rightful top spot because of cheating by music industry insiders.

And now *TattleTales* was officially a failure, selling far less than projected. In article after article, terms like "disappointing" and "underwhelming" were used. In the face of such public misfortune, there was nothing left to do but make a joke of it. The artist videotaped himself in Williamsburg, Brooklyn glumly handing out burned CD copies of the project to anyone who would take it. And, soundtracked by the Five Stairsteps' "O-o-h Child" ("Ooh child, things are gonna get easier"), he walked up to a wall with his own wheatpasted posters and began tearing them down. Both videos were posted on his Instagram account to his tens of millions of followers.

It was a fitting way to deal with the loss. Tekashi 6ix9ine's rise to stardom began with a video. He maintained his status with endless trolling on Instagram. So attempting to make a viral video out of his defeat was the only way to go.

Three years before that day, and just two and a half miles due south, Tekashi jump-started a mediocre rap career by throwing his lot in with a dangerous street gang. It worked better than anyone involved could have imagined: thirteen months of world-beating success. But that devil's bargain, promising money and promotion to the Nine Trey Gangsta Bloods in exchange for their protection and the street cred that came with membership, exacted a high toll. It would cost Tekashi his freedom, and leave him labeled as the lowest of the low: a rat, a snitch. It would also leave many of the Bloods who protected him behind bars for years, and even decades.

"I think I'm just a troll who knows how to rap," Hernandez once told the legendary New York radio personality Angie Martinez. This is the story of how Tekashi 6ix9ine trolled us all.

4

CHAPTER 1

THE STORY OF DANNY

Locust Street looks like an afterthought. A mistake. It's a one-block stretch of Bushwick, Brooklyn that begins at the neighborhood's main drag, Broadway, and quickly dead-ends, running smack into a five-story building. It's mostly multi-family homes, three stories high, divided into apartments. There are a million streets like it in Brooklyn. But this one raised Daniel Hernandez.

Daniel—"Danny" to almost everyone—was born in May 1996, just eight years after his mother Natividad moved to the U.S. from Mexico. She grabbed any job she could: factory work, cleaning houses. Danny's namesake father was Puerto Rican, from Pueblo. He was doting but inconsistent. Using and selling drugs—the latter of which he claims got him locked up for five years—meant he was in and out of the lives of Danny, his older brother Oscar, and their mother. He had abandoned the family when Danny was an infant, and then came back nine years later only to get kicked out of the house for using heroin. That was the last time young Danny would see his father for nearly a decade and a half. For a period, Natividad even told her sons that their father was dead.

After Daniel Sr. was out of the picture, Natividad got involved with Luis Nazario. According to Daniel Sr., he and Luis had been behind bars together. Upon Luis's release, Daniel Sr., who was still locked up, gave his jail buddy a letter to deliver to his wife and kids, and their address. Luis went to visit them, and ended up taking over Daniel Sr.'s family.

Not much is known about Luis Nazario—including whether or not that dramatic story is actually true. But young Danny loved and admired him, and thought of Luis as his father. Luis coached Danny's baseball team and was, Natividad later wrote, "the backbone and biggest support to our family."

One day in 2010, when Danny was in the eighth grade, Luis asked Danny to go to the store with him. It was a question that would change everything. Danny said no, so Luis left the house. What happened next is a little murky. There are still rumors on the block about what went down, and no one was ever convicted. But whatever happened, it's clear that Luis got into an argument with someone. He was struck, fell down, went into a coma, and ended up dying. Danny found him not long after the incident, lying on the sidewalk.

His stepfather's murder sent Danny into the darkest time of his young life. He spiraled into a depression and was diagnosed with post-traumatic stress syndrome. He stopped showering, grew his hair long, and ingested almost nothing except Mike and Ikes and water. He stopped going to school. He was prescribed Zoloft but Natividad, intent on homemade remedies and healers, never made him take it.

The murder of Luis had two main effects. First, it plunged an always financially precarious family deeper into poverty.

"My jobs were not enough to sustain us," Natividad wrote

in a letter to the court when her son was being sentenced. "I applied for welfare to assist us but there were still many nights that my boys went to bed without dinner. They wore used clothes and Christmas at our house was always a sad time. We only had two beds in our home and Danny slept in my bed because we didn't have enough money to buy another one."

Even more importantly, the murder turned the moral compass of Danny's entire world upside down. Luis had been a good father, taking Danny to movies and always helping the people around him. If someone like that, a real-life superhero, could get killed just outside his home, what was the point of being good? It was better, Danny worked out, to be a villain.

Not long afterward, in 2011, Danny met Sara Molina. Like him, she lived in Bushwick but their initial connection was not in person. Danny reached out to Sara via Facebook, she recalls. "I think we know the same people," he wrote.

They began talking every day, and soon became a couple. And while Sara was supportive of whatever Danny wanted to do, even when it got wild, there was a dark side. Danny was physically abusive throughout the entire course of their relationship.

The details, save for one horrific event in Dubai in 2018, aren't public, but we do know that Danny committed domestic abuse from 2011 through 2018. We know this because, in the course of settling the punishment for his numerous other misdeeds, he had to admit his history to the federal government.

In the aftermath of Luis' murder, Danny went to work. He had to, for reasons both financial and emotional. His family was in dire straits, and he needed to help. Besides, he couldn't bring himself to go to school.

It was a wild mix of gigs: a "judge" at the Greenpoint Youth

Courts ("where the youth acts in like a band of judge, jury, youth advocate, community advocate, that type of thing," he said once when recounting the experience). Busing tables with his older brother. And then, a job at Stay Fresh Grill. This was a deli on Broadway, steps away from Locust Street. Danny did deliveries, made sandwiches (sometimes, past customers remember, with severely burnt bacon). Anything to get by.

It was at Stay Fresh that a second key event in the life of Daniel Hernandez would take place, one that would begin his transformation into the star who entranced and trolled the world. And it all started over tilapia.

Peter A. Rodgers was new to Bushwick. The Long Island native had bounced to Atlanta at sixteen, and moved to Brooklyn four years later. His younger half-brother Junius, who lived in Long Island, started to head out to Bushwick frequently to meet his brother. Peter worked at a nearby tattoo shop, and he would go into Stay Fresh to buy snacks—peanuts and tilapia, in particular.

One day (Peter recalls it as being in 2012, Tekashi in 2014), Peter took a long look at the kid at the counter. He wanted to manage rappers, to make stars. He liked the kid's voice—the sound of it, the cadence of it. And Peter was savvy: he knew that this Mexican kid was a way into the Hispanic market. That was something he and his brother, who were Black, needed some help with. The kid's look was unique too.

Danny, convinced of the importance of his villain status, had around that time taken to making and wearing clothes with outrageous slogans on them. These clothes gave him his first taste of fame. Early on, an image of him went viral, making its way onto numerous online message boards. In it, he's wearing a shirt that says PUSSY on the front and EATER on the back, capped off with a giant number 69. To match that, his shorts sported NIGGA on the front and 69 on the back.

The forums, not knowing his name, usually referred to him as "pussy nigga," after the words visible in the front-facing shot. Between those photos and the ones of him in clothes with HIV written on them, his viral fame was growing. But Peter Rodgers, who preferred to go by "Righteous P," wasn't thinking about message boards. He just had one question for the kid at the deli counter: Do you rap? The answer was no. Danny loved music, to be sure. He was into the emo and metal bands his older brother would blast. But rapping? Not on his radar.

That didn't discourage Peter at all. Danny had the right voice, the right look, and the right ethnicity. Peter would figure out the rest as they went along. Danny was into the idea. Righteous P had a vision. He wanted to make hardcore music, but have it be radio-friendly. He needed some help, so he enlisted his little brother Junius, who took the rap name Zilla-Kami. Zilla was, like Tekashi, a fan of heavy music. On Long Island, he had played bass in a punk band, and he knew every song by his beloved Slipknot. But Zilla also loved aggressive rap. He was closer to Danny's age than Righteous P was, and would come to be the new rapper's perfect writing partner and artistic foil: two young kids interested only in pushing boundaries. Zilla recognized that Danny had star power. Now all that was left was to make music, shoot videos, and ride the wave all the way to the top.

The crew used the name "Scumlife 69" or "Scumgang 69" —often shortened just to "Scumgang"—to refer to themselves. And it fit. The crew took the extreme aesthetics from the heavy music they loved so much, and they had explicit lyrics from the get-go. ("She suck my dick until she choke" was the opening line of the group's very first collaboration).

The division of labor was this: Righteous P chose the beats and wrote the lyrics, sometimes assisted by his brother. Another member, "Scumbag" Chad Foster, was the style guy. "His natural aesthetic is in the DNA of the whole shit," says one friend. "It's just him, naturally." Chad was also the biggest anime fan of the bunch, a love that worked its way into the crew's videos. Danny's job was to rap.

When this all got started, Danny hadn't even settled on a rap name. On the crew's first song, "69," he refers to himself as "Wallah Dan"—though by the time the video for the song came out, he'd have a new moniker: Tekashi 69, with the latter pronounced "six-nine." The "69" was for his crew, and the "Tekashi" was from a Japanese tattoo artist Danny knew, though that guy spelled it the more standard way, "Takashi." Takashi captivated Danny because of his combination of artistic expression and addiction. "He expressed his art through drugs, and I always thought that was mad cool," Danny later told a radio interviewer. "For a person that was caught up in drug abuse, he was really artistically inclined, and I fell in love with that."

Scumgang's style was, as Danny later derisively described it, "more of, like, a rock and roll rap." The crew's focus, even more than on their songs, was on their videos. That was where young imaginations could really run wild. The more explicit, the more boundary pushing, the better. Their first effort, "69," announces its intentions from the opening seconds.

The clip opens with the camera lingering on a table littered with half-drunk beer, candles, and cigarettes. It moves up to reveal Danny receiving oral sex from a topless girl. He's drinking and smoking, and simultaneously having his hair braided by a second woman in her underwear. He takes a call, in Spanish (surely intentional, given Rodgers' initial interest in using Danny to get a Hispanic audience), from a dope fiend who needs "a few bags." Danny, wearing one of his now-famous outrageous homemade shirts, reading "STD'S"—he was now thinking of it as a clothing line, "69 Scum Cartel"—films the girl giving him oral sex, with the intent to put the footage on the internet. "Do it for the Vine, do it for the Vine," he says.

Outrageous clothes and faked oral sex weren't the only ways the crew went all out. They got access to a yellow Lamborghini and drove it around, with Danny hanging out the window. This delighted the folks on Locust, who were ecstatic to see one of their own doing big things.

"The neighborhood was excited," remembers one local resident. "You're talking about two hundred thousand dollar imports. It had to be a big, beautiful thing for them, because he got to do it on his block, and everyone on the block got to be there and participate. You can see that he had that idea from the beginning, just to bring everyone into it and make everyone a part of it."

Danny's early videos didn't set the world on fire. But they did catch some attention in a surprising place on the other side of the globe. Danny was always savvy about the internet, so it was natural for him to check who exactly was watching his videos. He saw that a disproportionate number of people who saw one of them were from Slovakia. Unbeknownst to Danny, they were sent there by a member of a popular "new wave" rap group from there, who shared the clip on Facebook. ("New wave" was basically the region's name for the Sound-Cloud rap explosion). After asking around online, Danny quickly discovered that when it came to new rap in Slovakia, a label called "I Love Party Productions" (soon renamed into the edgier "Fck Them,") run by a guy named Yaksha, was the biggest game in town.

Danny reached out via Instagram.

"His look was crazy, and I felt a lot of energy from him," Yaksha recalls of seeing Danny's early videos, which he laughingly calls "very amateur."

But that amateurism didn't dissuade Yaksha. His label's flagship group recorded a track with Danny called "Rollin Stones." It was released in December 2014. From the very beginning of "Rollin Stones," it's apparent that Danny is making a play to cement his new audience. "Slovakia, what's good?" he yells in the song's opening seconds. "We out here."

Danny and Yaksha talked and they formed a plan: they would make Tekashi 69 famous in Europe first, and then piggyback off that to get him known in America. It was a plan that was just crazy enough to work. "Rollin Stones" took off in Slovakia and the neighboring Czech Republic. Meanwhile, Yaksha's YouTube channel was turned over to Danny so he could release his videos directly to his new overseas fans. "I remember when Danny had eight thousand followers, and five thousand of them was from Czech," one friend remembers.

But while things were building up on the other side of the world, Danny and his Scumgang crew had some issues at home to contend with. "Scumgang" was a catchy name, and it perfectly captured what the edgy crew was up to. There was only one issue: other people were already using it.

Back in late 2007, a crew of friends in Flatbush, Brooklyn, long inclined to pull pranks on each other, started referring to those hijinks as "scums"—a low-key way of insulting a former crew member, whose name sounded similar to the word "scum." That practice quickly transformed into the whole crew—a mix of aspiring rappers, dancers, and promoters, some with ties to the Crips—calling itself "Scumgang."

Seven years later, when some wild kids in Bushwick started using that name too, there had to be a reckoning. The Flatbush crew's co-founder, Scumlord D!zzy, was out of town. So it fell on a younger member to broker a meeting. Danny and Righteous P made their way out to Flatbush and met him at a neighborhood Chinese spot. Over chicken wings and french fries, they worked out their issues. They decided, as D!zzy remembered later, to be "under one umbrella, but two different branches."

Righteous P, as the manager, did most of the talking for Danny during the meeting. But the young Flatbush scum did want to know why Danny wore all these crazy "HIV" clothes? The answer was simple.

"Every single time I post it, everybody has something to say about it," he recalls Danny saying. "So, the fact that they run to talk about it, and I feel no type of way about it, I might as well."

When it came to career goals, rapping was not high on Danny's list. He said, "I want to direct videos and I want to make movies."

It wouldn't be long until that wish would get him in some very real trouble. Trouble that would place his burgeoning rap career in serious jeopardy, and ultimately destroy his relationship with his Bushwick buddies.

On February 21, 2015, Tekashi 69 (or 6ix9ine, a variation he started using more or less interchangeably) was ready to party. He was at a studio in Manhattan and he met a rapper named Tay Milly and his crew. Tay invited Danny to come hang in Harlem. The guys seemed cool, and looked like they had a bunch of money. Why not?

They all hopped in a car and went uptown. Danny, who

had never been in Harlem before, knew vaguely where he was, but not exactly. Not long after they arrived at the spot, Tay said he was going to call a girl "from last night." She came over, and that's when things got ugly.

Less than two weeks after that night, Tekashi recalled what happened. "When she came in she asked me how old I was and I told her I was eighteen and I assumed she was older."

What happened next was caught on video. The girl was penetrated simultaneously by two of the men. While this was going on, Tekashi was touching her breasts and smacking her butt. And Tekashi, in a scene straight out of one of his videos, could be heard on the tape saying, "This is how we do. This is how we rock."

As the night went on into early the next morning, videos—of the "this is how we do" moment; of the girl, dressed only in underwear and a bra, sitting on Tekashi's lap—were put on Instagram. Tekashi was tagged in the clips and, using his account "Tekashiiii69," reposted them. Why the letter *i* four times on his account name? Well, his accounts were frequently taken down for posting edgy content. Posting that material was important, he once said, for "shock value." Outrageous pictures helped you get famous and go viral. It was all an act, he insisted—a "scumbag persona." But this time, the act would have serious real-world consequences. The girl was just thirteen years old. And her mother was about to see the video.

The next day, February 23, the girl's mother saw the videos on social media. On March 5, Tekashi was arrested. He gave a statement to Detective Maureen Sheehan. Sheehan was a veteran. She'd joined the NYPD in 1992 and was a part of the made-famous-from-television Special Victims Unit. She was just three years from retirement, and had seen it all, from sex offenders to men who choke out and rob old ladies (as happened in one 2008 case that briefly got her name in the newspapers). With that history, it's doubtful that an eighteen-year-old guy caught red-handed on video presented much of an interrogation challenge. Danny's statement to her was given at a police building on East 123rd Street, not far from where the incident happened. At 9:15 PM, Danny told her his story.

He started out with the basics. "I grew up without a father," he told her. "He died when I was thirteen. I live with my mother and brother." And then, a statement of identity. Just six months after releasing his first video, he knew who he was. "I am an artist."

He copped to a history of creating and sharing explicit pictures and videos under his "Scumbag69" hashtag. But, he insisted, not everything in his music videos or on his IG was as it seemed.

"The girls that are in the pictures, I don't do anything with them," he said. "It's a photo shoot. I never touched them. A lot of times when I do the pictures, my girlfriend is there with me, taking the pictures."

When they got to talking about the night in question, Tekashi identified Tay Milly and the girl. But, he insisted, "I didn't have sex with her. She was doing what she was doing."

Danny was no longer Tekashi 69, #Scumbag69 image-maker. When he was faced with consequences for his actions, he became Daniel Hernandez, a scared kid who had been led astray by some older guys. It was a move he would resort to in later years, again and again.

Danny was worried about Tay Milly, who was rumored to have jumped out of a window because he feared getting picked up by the cops. ("Is Tay still alive or is he in a coma?" Danny asked Sheehan). Danny also said he wanted to apologize to the girl. But most of all, he was worried about himself.

"I'm going to go to jail for fifteen years and be a registered sex offender," he told Sheehan. And worst of all, it was happening just as he was starting to make something of himself. "That hashtag is legit now," he exclaimed.

Danny was sent to Rikers. His bail, those close to him remember, was set at $100,000. Righteous P and Zilla hit up their friends to get the money. It wasn't easy, but they managed to scrape it together. They had the distinct impression that Danny would pay them back. But when Danny came home from Rikers that summer, he had a whole new challenge. Sara was pregnant. He was going to be a father.

First and foremost, Daniel Hernandez had to put the night of February 21, 2015 behind him forever. So, on October 20, he pled out. For a charge as serious as "Use of a Child in a Sexual Performance," it was a pretty sweet deal. Sentencing would be put off for two years. During that time, he'd be put on interim probation and would have to fulfill a bunch of other conditions. He couldn't post "any nude, semi-nude, or otherwise sexually explicit images of women or children" on the internet. He couldn't post any images "depicting violence against women or children." He would have to visit a mental health clinic, and go to therapy if they told him to. He had to write a letter of apology to the girl and her family. He'd have to do three hundred hours of community service. So far, so standard. But there were a few final conditions that would ultimately prove problematic. He'd have to get his GED. And he had to stay out of legal trouble. It was the wording on this one that would come back to haunt everyone involved. It said that he "may not commit any crime or violation during the two-year adjournment."

If Danny did all of that, he would hit the jackpot. No prison time, and he wouldn't have to register as a sex offender. He would just have to serve another three years of probation. But if he slipped up, he would have to spend one to three years in state prison.

Danny didn't pay his friends back. That was a big source of tension. And with a child on the way, Danny was having doubts about whether he wanted to rap at all. Maybe he could be a cameraman or director. Maybe he could help other artists, the way Righteous P helped him.

Danny briefly stopped rapping and instead began looking for other artists to write songs and make videos for. He even had one who was a "girl Tekashi 69," remembers one artist and producer who was helping him in that period.

But once Danny's daughter Saraiyah was born—just nine days after her father's guilty plea—he redoubled his efforts toward his own music career, and toward his outrageous image. "When he had the kid, that's when he turned into 6ix9ine," recalls that artist and producer, Justin Rose.

This new determination meant that Danny started spending more time with Scumlord D!zzy, leader of the original, Flatbush-based Scumgang. D!zzy was older, and an experienced rapper. And, even more exciting to Danny, D!zzy had ties with the Crips.

"I became the big bro and the one that he knows really knows about the streets," D!zzy says now about their early relationship. "He was a kid. He doesn't know the ramifications of being involved with a gang. So, he just wanted to be that."

At first, D!zzy was patient. He tried explaining that, in the rap world, if you could avoid dealing with what he called "street people," you should. Success in hip-hop already meant lawsuits, problems with women, and tons of other drama. No need to drag gangs into that.

Danny kept pushing. Everything finally reached a head

when he was putting together plans for a video shoot. He wanted to buy a bunch of blue bandanas, so that everyone in the video would appear to be Crips. D!zzy demurred, but Danny was insistent. Finally, D!zzy said no firmly.

"I made it very clear: 'You're not swindling me. I know you're trying to manipulate me to get people in your video that make you look a certain way, and I'm not doing that.'"

But Danny was sure of one thing: to be a successful rapper, you need to be affiliated with a gang.

Throughout 2015 and 2016, Danny was releasing videos at a slow but steady pace, averaging out to one every two or three months. The clips stayed pretty on brand, minus some of the explicit sex once the plea deal took effect. Danny was still wearing his grill. He was still sporting his homemade clothes, scrawled with things like HOE; and still bringing expensive cars to Locust Street. He had several duets with ZillaKami (written solely by Zilla) that showed a real chemistry between the two. Yaksha's label was putting out the videos, guaranteeing a growing overseas interest. On top of all of that, Tekashi made a friend.

Danny, whose biggest viral claim to fame thus far was a video of him pulling a wrestling move on a twerking girl in her underwear (a clip many people referred to as the "pedigree Vine," after the wrestling move's name and the video's native platform), found a perfect companion in Christopher Schlosser. Schlosser, as nearly everyone calls him, had a knack for creating outrageous viral videos as well.

Danny and Schlosser met through their mutual friend Drew, who shot and directed a number of Tekashi 69 videos. One day, Drew suggested that Schlosser meet an artist he'd been working with. Schlosser was surprised to see it was the guy he'd seen in the pedigree Vine. They met and discovered, as Schlosser remembers, that "our styles was kind of the same."

The pair got along from the start. Schlosser remembers the studio session for their first collaboration "All Night" as "one of the funnest I ever had."

Schlosser, the jovial, ever drunk, dreadlocked guy from the Bronx; and Tekashi 69, the wild Mexican kid from Bushwick, found they had a whole lot in common. Both were always up for an adventure. And they got one that was about to lead to the biggest opportunity of Danny's career so far.

It was March 8, 2017. Adam Grandmaison was in New York, and he needed something to do. Grandmaison is known to an entire generation of rap fans as Adam22, host of the *No Jumper* podcast. He has a preternatural ability to find young rappers right before they blow up. As a result, by 2017 he was an important tastemaker in the burgeoning field of SoundCloud rap—a blanket name given to young rap artists who avoided traditional record industry channels, preferring to post their music directly on the internet.

This scene grew out of southern Florida, and tended towards harsh, aggressive, rock-influenced delivery. At concerts, artists were far more likely to start mosh pits than they were to kick a freestyle. The artists were young and, to stand out, they began to look wilder and wilder. Colorful hair and face tattoos were the rule. Danny played right along. His hair was likely to be green, orange, and yellow; or pink and yellow, depending on the day you caught him. As for tattoos, he had dozens, including a giant 69 on his chest.

Adam, who is based in L.A. but had lived in Brooklyn years before, was on the East Coast for music industry meetings. He hung for a while with Az Cohen, son of famed music industry bigwig Lyor Cohen, and they listened to unreleased

Migos and Young Thug collaborations. And they smoked a lot of weed.

The month before, Schlosser, who had no previous relationship with Adam, had sent him a message on Twitter. It was a still from a video Schlosser had shot for his song "DWB"—an initialism for "dirty white bitch." The still showed Schlosser with a woman whose back was to the camera. They were both in a tub, and the tub was filled with pints of Lean, the codeine drink that began as a favorite of Houston rappers but spread nationwide. Schlosser is holding a Lean bottle with one hand, and the other hand is in the girl's crotch. Adam shared the photo on Twitter, saying, "this guy likes my podcast I must be doing something right." Schlosser, inspired by Tekashi's outrageous homemade clothes, had already had tote bags made with the image on it. So he sent one to Adam. Just as Schlosser expected, Adam tweeted out a picture of himself holding the bag, captioning it, TOTEBAG OF THE CENTURY. The influential podcaster's trip to New York was just days later.

Adam and Schlosser remember the next part differently. In Schlosser's telling, Adam hit him up: "He's like, 'yo, I'm in New York. What's your number? I know you got bitches.'" Adam, for his part, told an interviewer that Schlosser was the one to reach out first. Either way, it led to quite a night. In fact, *Oh What a Night* was the title of the vlog Adam would make about the experience.

Danny hadn't originally been part of the plan. But that afternoon Schlosser had, as usual, been at Drew's house, and Danny was there too.

"Yo, the *No Jumper* nigga tryin' to chill today," Schlosser said. "Let's go chill with him. I'm gonna get these two girls that I know." So, Danny came along.

They met Adam in Manhattan late at night, after Adam

finished hanging with Az. As Adam was leaving, he told Az, "I'm about to go meet up with the motherfucker from the tote bag." Schlosser was already inebriated, having imbibed, as he memorably puts it, a "big dick" bottle of Jack Daniels.

The five of them—Adam, Schlosser, Danny, and the two girls—walked down the streets of the West Village, with Adam filming. Schlosser mugged for the camera: "I'm Schlosser from the Bronx, nigga. Fuck the Bronx. Fuck New York."

They stopped for beer at a bodega. The girls wanted to drink, and Schlosser wanted to *keep* drinking. By the time they get where they're going—a hotel room—Danny has told Adam that he's not just a random hanger-on. He's a rapper, and one with about 20,000 Instagram followers. He showed Adam some videos, including "69."

"His videos were really good," Adam said, looking back. "On top of that, his voice sounded pretty good, and I was looking at him visually like, damn, there's definitely something going on here. But I wasn't fully sold at all."

One of the main reasons? Among the videos Adam saw was "DWB." The clip was as explicit as the tote bag. The hook of the song, yelled throughout, was "I only fuck with white bitches 'cause they suck dick." It left Adam confused. *Was this a joke?* He wasn't sure. Either way, it was bad. *Really, really bad.*

Regardless, everyone had a good time: Schlosser and Danny joked about being the "STD Gang." Adam, often befuddled, caught the whole thing on video. The girls, for their part, seemed unimpressed, occasionally chuckling at jokes but mostly just checking their phones, albeit while dressed only in their underwear.

Danny and Schlosser left with a connection, however tenuous, to Adam22. Adam tweeted a photo of the five of them the next day, girls facing backwards with Schlosser licking one of their crotches (over the panties), captioned, WHAT DID I GET MYSELF INTO LAST NIGHT. Danny was left with a determination to get on *No Jumper* again, this time for real.

The only way to get on *No Jumper* was to go to Los Angeles. Later that same month, that's what Danny was determined to do. But he needed some company, so he asked Schlosser to come along.

Danny, Schlosser, and Drew scraped together money to get the plane tickets. *Where would they stay?* "Fuck it. We'll sleep on the beach," Schlosser remembers Danny saying. Schlosser found that attitude inspirational and motivating.

At the airport on the way there, Schlosser and Danny decided to up their trolling game and post what they thought would be a funny photo. "Yo, let's take a picture of us holding hands," Schlosser suggested. "It's gonna get mad likes, and we'll laugh about it."

When they arrived in L.A., Adam seemed uninterested in having them on the podcast. But they ended up not having to sleep on the beach after all, due to some new friends.

Danny had previously connected via the internet with a rapper named Trippie Redd. There are differing versions of exactly how that got started. But the two young rappers definitely liked each other's music.

Once Trippie had become aware of Tekashi 69, he and his pal Chris King, an older rapper who was a friend and mentor figure, began to formulate a plan. Trippie and Chris knew there was tension in the ranks in Scumgang. ZillaKami and Danny were at odds, largely over Danny's failure to pay back his bail money. Trippie came up with a plan. He would do a song with Tekashi, and then Zilla and Tekashi would reconcile. Scumgang could then become a part of Trippie's burgeoning 1400 crew. They could form a SoundCloud rap supergroup.

Now that Danny was in L.A. without Zilla, the timing was perfect to put the plan in motion. Trippie hit Danny up to hang out and go to the studio. Schlosser was down with the idea, mostly because he liked Trippie's music.

The first meeting was at Trippie's manager's place. There was no recording yet. Just them talking, vibing, freestyling a little bit, and feeling each other out. Pretty soon, though, they recorded for real. Using beats from the producer Pi'erre Bourne, they did a song, "Poles1469." The beat came from a pack of three the producer had intended for Trippie. A second, finished in New York not long after, became "Oowee/Thots." There was one left over, and Tekashi took it back to New York with him.

Trippie's manager pushed everyone to make a video for "Poles" before Danny and the crew went home. So the day of their departure, everyone got up early and went out to the desert to make a video for the new song.

The clip featured Danny, Trippie, and Chris King riding four-wheelers and setting off guns that, instead of bullets, shot out colorful plumes of smoke. Speaking of colorful, by this time, Tekashi's look had really begun to stand out. His hair was fully rainbow now for the first time. (He ran out of colors, he explained, so he just decided to do every color at once.) The gun waving in the clip went along with Danny's screamed threats: "If a nigga try and test me, I off him/Put a hole in his head, he a dolphin."

Schlosser was on site, but is mostly MIA in the video, unable to resist the lure of a car full of sexy girls. The video shoot lasted a few hours, and the New York crew then headed to the airport and returned home.

The resulting video came out on April 27, 2017. It was a key moment for Tekashi 69, and for Trippie. Tekashi was leaving Scumgang behind. He was collaborating with better-known artists. And whatever you thought of his lyrical shout-outs to dolphins, you couldn't ignore Tekashi 69's charisma on camera, and his intensity on the mic.

Trippie's plan of re-uniting Scumgang under his auspices never came to fruition. By the time of the LA trip, the breaches in Scumgang had become irreparable. Danny believed that Zilla and Righteous P were negotiating with Epic Records behind his back, promising to rid him from the group—a belief that led him to a profane Instagram rant in June 2016. (As a reality check, a producer who was around the crew at the time remembers early talks with the RCA-affiliated Polo Grounds label that petered out once Danny was arrested in 2015.)

"P, you a bitch. Zilla, you a bitch," Danny yelled into his phone while walking down the street. "None of you niggas is Scumgang. *I'm* Scumgang, nigga. Niggas know me 'cause of me. That's the only reason niggas know Scumgang. They was gonna sign a deal with Epic, but they know they didn't have no control over me. So [they said], we gonna drop Tekashi, and we gonna start fresh with Zilla."

This rant didn't come out of nowhere. It was exactly the type of move Danny had been making all along. It was second nature to him to say or do any outrageous thing to get attention—wearing clothes with PUSSY and HOE written on them in giant letters; body slamming girls in their underwear. Even his relationship with his best friend Drew began over internet insults. The more extreme you were, the more attention you were likely to get. So, any problem, any beef, he approached with the same full steam ahead tactics.

Zilla seemed to essentially admit the substance of Danny's attacks in a response video. Saying that Danny stole money from him, presumably referring to the bail money for the 2015 case, he asked, "how we supposed to trust you in a contract? I'm writing your lyrics, bro. What are you gonna do?" Zilla also claimed that Danny "snaked" the crew's camera equipment and attempted to shoot other rappers' videos, keeping the money for himself.

Regardless of the state of Scumgang, "Poles1469" had its intended effect. Putting Tekashi 69 next to Trippie helped both rappers' stars rise. And thanks to his friendship with Yaksha, Danny followed up the video's release with a short tour of Eastern Europe. The song also got Danny on the radar of the head of Trippie's label, a young, aspiring record executive named Elliot Grainge.

Elliot Grainge was born in the United Kingdom in November, 1993, making him not even three years older than his future star artist. His father Lucian was a music business lifer who, by the time of his son's bar mitzvah in 2006, was the chairman and CEO of Universal Music Group International—a position he flexed by having Take That (the most successful boy band in UK history) and Björk's original group the Sugarcubes perform at Elliot's 200-person celebration. By 2011, Lucian was chairman and CEO of the entirety of Universal Music Group.

Elliot wanted to go into the music business, like his dad. He started out by putting on concerts in Boston while he was in college at Northeastern University. A few years later, in 2016, he started his own record label called Strainge Entertainment ("strange" spelled with an extra "i" to mirror his own last name). The company, under legal threat from a long-established record label called Strange Music, home to the rapper

Tech N9ne, would change its name in 2017, first to Elliot Grainge Entertainment and then to 10K Projects.

Shortly after Trippie moved to Los Angeles, his manager (though he now prefers the term "business partner") Milo Stokes introduced him to Elliot. Stokes and Grainge had originally met because Milo was working at a new business called Create Music, and wanted to build a relationship with Elliot's dad's company.

"Once we established a business relationship with Create and UMG, Elliot said he was starting a label," Stokes recalls. "At the time, I was running around with Trippie. We ended up taking a meeting with Elliot, and the rest was history."

Grainge's family tree certainly helped ("He was a very connected individual," Stokes says, understatedly). But the budding mogul's youth and ideas also weighed heavily in his favor. Trippie signed to Elliot's label.

In the summer of 2017, Trippie was performing in New York City for the first time. So it only made sense to have Danny come out to perform his verse from "Poles1469." Before the show, Danny met up with Grainge for pizza. The brash rapper and the young executive got along great. At the show, Danny was a sensation. The crowd went nuts, feeding off the rainbow-haired rapper's hyperactive energy. There was a real sense that something special was going on.

Grainge wasn't going to waste any time. He wined and dined Danny out in L.A. as they negotiated a record deal. And on July 28, 2017, just days after Danny finally appeared on *No Jumper* for real (and spent much of the time complaining about ZillaKami), he signed to Strainge Entertainment, LLC. His advance payment was modest by big record contract standards, but it was a lot of money for Elliot and his still-new venture. The prospect of Tekashi sharing a record label with his pal Trippie may have seemed thrilling at the time. But things were about to go very, very bad.

In August 2017, the simmering tension between Danny and ZillaKami exploded. Zilla posted a photo from the 2015 incident. It was shocking. There had been rumors about this arrest swirling around for a while, but almost no one had any idea what actually happened. There were rumors about an underage girl. Zilla aired it all out. The photo Zilla posted online showed Tekashi shirtless, with his arms around a young girl, who was wearing only a bra.

"Don't play games with us. She thirteen, and we got paperwork," Zilla wrote.

He followed it up by posting a screenshot of court records showing Danny's guilty plea. "Y'all wanted proof now SDFU and look at the proof," Zilla continued. "Tekashi69 pled guilty you bitch. Thought we wouldn't find it. Ya done where my 100K." Zilla took pains to tag Adam22 and *No Jumper* as well as, for some now-lost-to-history reason, Adidas Originals. The "100K" was a reference to Tekashi's bail money, the original cause of their split.

Danny did his best to seem unfazed. He responded by jumping on Snapchat. He sarcastically claimed to be a "happy rapist" through a filter that made his voice preternaturally high and gave him cat ears.

At that point, Trippie jumped in and decided to distance himself from his collaborator. He recorded a video dissing Danny. "I'm sorry brozay," he said. "1400 don't promote pedophiles... If we give niggas clout, we give niggas clout. It was an accident."

Trippie's pal Chris King was there when Trippie recorded the clip. To him, it wasn't a big deal. "We was just laughing about it," he says now. But to the hip-hop media, it wasn't a joke at all. All sorts of websites began picking up on the clash and the accusations being thrown around. What started as a joke would soon become a violent feud.

But at the moment, it was fine. Actually, better than fine. Trippie insulting Danny gave the aspiring rapper Tekashi 6ix9ine a storyline. It gave him an obstacle to fight against. Adversity to overcome. This was the stuff all great artists had to deal with—people trying to take them down, to get in their way.

At the same time, Danny was writing a song using that one remaining Pi'erre Bourne beat from his trip to L.A. He and Drew worked on the lyrics for weeks. The song was originally supposed to be a diss track. ZillaKami's friend Sosmula was mentioned by name at first. But cooler heads prevailed. However, one name remained in the final song. The song, "Gummo," contains an oblique diss to Trippie Redd, via a mention of his bodyguard KB: "No KB, you a loser, nigga/Up that Uzi, nigga."

"If you don't have KB watching over you, you will lose somebody," is how Danny later explained it.

Drew and Tekashi wrote the song with a new approach in mind. Earlier that summer, they'd sat down and had a heart-to-heart talk. They'd taken stock of what Tekashi 6ix9ine had accomplished so far; and they thought about their goals. *Were they going to keep on their current course, making punk-influenced music that was slowly building them a cult following in Eastern Europe?* That way didn't seem to be making them any money—Danny had taken home all of $2,000 from his tour over there.

There was another option. They could make music that people actually *liked*. Music that was listenable, enjoyable, playable. Not aggressive and challenging, like Scumgang. Tekashi and Drew could create something that would get them a lot of fans; and make them rich. This, they decided, was going to be the path from now on.

And Christian Ehigiator was going to help them on the path. Chris discovered Danny back in May, 2017, shortly after the "Poles1469" video. Chris was a Brooklyn native, young and hungry, on the lookout for new talent. He'd caught the music business bug in college, along with his two best friends, one of whom would later go on to discover and manage XXXTentacion.

In the beginning of 2017, Chris was already managing the third member of his college trio, a singer-songwriter. And he was setting up rap shows at local clubs. Plus, he'd started managing the rap career of his childhood buddy, who rapped under the name Seqo Billy. By that spring, Chris was sure he had cracked the code of hip-hop success. He went to Seqo's neighborhood every day, with the same pitch:

"Somebody give me a mixtape. Somebody give me a single. Give me something. I know what to do. I could make an artist pop." And then, Chris got a recommendation.

Chris heard from a rapper he knew who wanted to recommend his cousin, Drew. There was one issue, though. Chris had already met Drew, and didn't like him. At a video shoot some time before, Drew had shown up late, on a skateboard, reeking of weed—a terrible first impression. But that turned out not to matter at all. When Chris and Drew finally met again, in May of 2017, Drew actually talked down his own music. "I'm just a cameraman for Danny," Chris recalls him saying.

That meeting was in front of a Starbucks in SoHo. The "Danny" whom Drew had been referring to was there. Chris was struck immediately, before hearing a note of music or a bar of rhymes. It seemed like Danny was going through something serious.

"He was looking over his shoulder, trying to be fake tough, like he had something on his mind," Chris recalls. "I think he just came from the hospital—his mom was in the hospital or something like that. I feel like I saw some type of pain or something in his face."

In their short conversation outside the coffee shop, Danny made reference to a bunch of rappers Chris didn't yet know, like Trippie Redd and ZillaKami. "I feel like he was trying to get clout points," Chris says now. Regardless, Chris wanted to see and hear more from this sad-eyed kid who'd walked all the way from Brooklyn to SoHo just for this meeting. So a few days later, they reconvened at a studio in Greenpoint.

Seqo, who waited inside the Starbucks during the initial meeting, came late this time to listen and give opinions. They were both surprised by Danny downplaying his music while talking up the videos, as was his habit at the time. But as he thought about it, Chris ended up respecting the honesty of an artist who said things like, "my music is not that good, but I got fans."

As they listened to the music and watched the videos, Seqo and Chris started to hatch a plan. Chris was in love with Danny's backstory: a high school dropout with a murdered father, a mother who spoke no English, and a series of dead-end jobs. Seqo honed in on a different idea. If they could get this crazy-looking Mexican kid love from the hood, they'd be unstoppable. And Seqo knew just the people to make it happen.

CHAPTER 2

TREYWAY

The rap moniker "Seqo Billy" was more than something slick to say on a record. It had a hidden meaning. "Seqo" was a shortened version of his first name. But "Billy" wasn't meant to be a name. It was a descriptor. "Billy" was short for "Billy Bad Ass." Attaching "Billy" at the beginning or end of your nickname was a way of announcing that you were a member of the Nine Trey Gangsta Bloods street gang.

The Nine Trey Gangsta Bloods were formed on July 16, 1993 in New York City's notorious Rikers Island jail. Back then, the Hispanic gang the Latin Kings were a powerful force in the jail, and they would often gang up on Black prisoners. In self-defense, two prisoners, Omar "O.G. Mack" Portee and Leonard "Deadeye" McKenzie, banded together to form the United Blood Nation. One of the UBN's original subgroups, or "sets," was Nine Trey, named for the year of the UBN's founding, 1993. Nine Trey were meant to be the UBN's enforcers, the muscle.

The United Blood Nation was named after the Bloods gang that began in Los Angeles decades before, but UBN had no real connection to the Bloods in California. In Rikers, Nine Trey's main purpose was to defend Black prisoners against the Latin Kings, as they began engaging in what *The Village Voice* described as a "vicious turf war."

By the fall of 2017, Nine Trey had long since spread all up and down the East Coast. They were well known to law enforcement. Their two main leaders, Pedro "Magoo" Guiterrez and James "Frank White" Braxton, had been taken down as part of a giant bust by the feds in North Carolina earlier in the year.

Nine Trey, as one of the original East Coast Blood sets, is steeped in rules and codes. OG Mack and OG Deadeye originally wrote thirty-one rules to keep their organization together. So the number thirty-one took on an almost mythological significance for them. As an initiation, you had to fight multiple members of the gang for thirty-one seconds, a practice known as "shooting your 31." Monthly dues for the gang are often $31 or multiples of that amount.

Organizationally, Nine Trey is divided in half. The more important half, the ones who give the orders, are known as the "World Wide Lineup," sometimes called the "Prison Lineup" or the "G-Wall." These are the members in state prison. The gang members who are free and carry out those orders are known as the "World Wide Lineup in the Town," or sometimes the "Street Lineup."

The two sides have an identical rank structure: Godfather at the top. Then High 020, and Low 020; then generals from five-star down to one-star. The most inexperienced members, below even the one-star generals, are sometimes referred to as "scraps."

Within the Street Lineup, there are separate organizations determined by geography or friendship. Each one of those follow the ranking conventions. Those would, confusingly, also be referred to as "lineups," or sometimes just as "lines." It isn't unusual for petty beefs to break out among members, so a single region sometimes has multiple lineups. In fact, at the height of Danny's involvement with Nine Trey, his single Brooklyn crew splintered into *four* separate lineups, all running simultaneously.

What exactly does Nine Trey do? Well, by the time Danny first encountered them, drug dealing was a big part of the gang's activity. Marijuana and cocaine were popular choices. But in Brooklyn in the late 2010s, there was one option that was bigger than the rest—heroin. Or more precisely, a mixture of heroin, fentanyl, and plain powder sold as heroin. Here's how it worked, according to Nine Trey member Kristian "CEO Kris" Cruz, who became a cooperating witness in Danny's case:

A Nine Trey member would buy a kilo of fentanyl (or sometimes fentanyl analogue) online for around $6,500, usually from China. Then they would get a kilo of "cut"—just plain powder—for about $1,000. Then a kilo of heroin for $55,000. Then they would mix it all together. The result would be three kilos of something that was one-third of each substance. The gang member would sell those three kilos for $47,000 each, claiming to the buyer that they were all heroin. It was easy to find buyers at that under-market price. And the buyers, usually fellow gang members who intended only to break up the kilo and sell it, didn't look too hard into what they were selling. If they had any inkling it was cut with fentanyl, which they sometimes did, they didn't care. Boom: a profit of $78,500 per kilo of heroin. Kristian Cruz alone sold eighty kilos of heroin using this method, making millions of dollars in the process.

In addition to drug dealing, violence was embedded in the Nine Trey way of life. War with other gangs, war with rival Blood factions, war amongst themselves—it all happened, and frequently. As Tekashi gained fame and beefed with other rappers, he would often find himself clashing with their affiliated Blood sets. There was the Untouchable Gorilla Stone Nation, colloquially known as the Apes, the group to which Brooklyn rapper Casanova claimed allegiance; there was the Five-Nine Brims, with which Trippie Redd was affiliated. Beefing with a rapper frequently meant a de facto war with their entire set.

The Brooklyn faction of Nine Trey that Danny was about to join was particularly fractious, even before his involvement. As early as 2015, there were already two separate street lineups, two hierarchies among Nine Trey members in the same neighborhood. One was led by Jamel "Mel Murda" Jones, and one by Aljermiah "Nuke" Mack.

Mel and Nuke hated each other because Mel Murda had once told Nine Trey head honcho Magoo to suck his dick. Nuke first joined Nine Trey at the age of eleven, and was a true believer. To him, insulting the leader of the all-powerful Prison Lineup was unthinkable. In the following years, the violence between them was intense. Shootings, either by Mel or Nuke themselves, or by proxies, were not uncommon.

The faction of Nine Trey that Seqo Billy belonged to, and was about to usher Danny into, was in its way a tight-knit crew, violent internal rivalries aside. Many of the key members were in their thirties, and had known each other for years. Some were even related. For example, Seqo's aunt was Mel Murda's half-sister. And many of the members had been in Jim Jones's orbit for years.

Jim, the "capo" of Harlem's Diplomats rap crew, started

his career in the music business in the 1990s via his friend Cam'ron. While he stayed relatively low-profile at first, over the years Jim began moving more and more into the spotlight. As he did, so did his gang ties. Jim shouted out Nine Trey on his records. Around 2009, he started bringing in gang members, including his close friend Mel Murda, to rap in his spin-off projects like the group Byrd Gang. ("We related," Jim once joked about his bond with Mel, punning on the fact that they share a last name, Jones. "We *blood* related.")

Another Nine Trey member who was around Jim Jones during that period, though never as a rapper, was Kifano Jordan. Jordan, known as "Shotti," kept to the background in his days with Jones. You can see in one video of the crew that he has a hoodie pulled far up over his head, and he's constantly ducking out of camera range.

But by the time he met Tekashi 6ix9ine, Shotti was no longer so shy. He was a full-fledged Nine Trey "big homie," an influential and feared figure, with a long criminal past behind him. Shotti would become Tekashi's mentor and protector, his shortcut to street credibility. And ultimately, in Tekashi's mind, his biggest betrayer.

Kifano "Shotti" Jordan, like many of his future Nine Trey brothers, had a complicated beginning. He was born on April 14, 1982 in Trinidad. His father Fitroy Cambridge was married to another woman and already had half a dozen children when Kifano's mother Suzette Jordan became pregnant, first with his sister Sasha and then three years later with Kifano. Suzette's mom, not a fan of this situation, was an American citizen, so a plan was hatched. Suzette, Sasha, and Kifano moved from Trinidad to Brooklyn. Suzette found work as a nurse, but she had to put in long hours. That left her two kids free to run the streets of their new home city. It had a devastating effect on a young Kifano.

Kifano's half-brother Wally-Emmanuel Cambridge spent a lot of time with his sibling before Kifano left Trinidad.

"He was always full of life, quick to make you smile and laugh," Cambridge wrote in a letter to a federal judge years later, remembering his younger half-brother's "easy going nature." But when the brothers reconnected after Kifano's move, it was a different story.

"The bright-eyed little brother had changed... He was more jaded, street smart and cynical," Cambridge recalls, "but his broad smile and comforting nature were still there."

What had happened? A whole lot. Jordan and his family moved to Crown Heights, Brooklyn. His junior high school was just across the street from the Albany Houses projects.

"It was a scary situation because there were a lot of times we witness[ed] violence," remembers one longtime friend.

Kifano was a smart kid who went to a middle school for gifted and talented children. Even by those standards, Sasha remembers, his grades were stellar. He once said that he was accepted into Hunter College High School, an elite school that accepts only the top one-quarter of one percent of NYC students. But being smart in his neighborhood meant you were picked on and bullied. And a young Kifano figured out there was only one way to respond: you had to be tougher and crazier than the person picking on you.

"When I was coming up, it was either you roll or you get rolled over, bottom line," he said once during a rare interview. "I was never about getting rolled over. That shit's about doing things that the other guy wasn't doing."

Among those "things that the other guy wasn't doing" were a number of crimes that caused run-ins with the police. There was an incident involving a gun in December 2003, when Shotti was just twenty-one. And another five years later when Shotti, riding a dirt bike, was alleged to have led police on a high-speed chase through Brooklyn streets. For that one, he pled to Reckless Endangerment and got time served. There was an additional case in 2009, and then a case of alleged assault six years later. For that last one, Jordan pled to Disorderly Conduct, and agreed to a two-year order of protection.

But all of that was just a warmup for the wildest case yet. May 27, 2016 was a day that would establish Shotti's bona fides as a man willing to do just about anything if his safety was at stake. And it would have effects that would last well into his next phase as a music business mogul.

Shotti (or "Kareem Harvey," an alias of his at the time) was living in Trenton. On that day, he was driving down Route 78 West, coming up on Exit 17, in Clinton Township, New Jersey. In the car were two other people: a twenty-year-old woman named Neja and a twenty-three-year-old man named Kasheem.

As they were driving along in a white 2002 Chevy Tahoe, a patrolman was behind them, about to exit the highway. But he reported noticing that the car was odd. There was some kind of huge camera bracket obscuring the Tahoe's license plate—you couldn't see the state (it was, he later saw, from Maryland). There were dark tail light covers. And the driver's view of the rearview mirror was obstructed because there was some kind of tag hanging from it. The cop turned on his siren and pulled over the car.

The car had, the patrolman wrote in his arrest report, "a strong odor of raw marijuana" coming from inside. Kasheem, despite the loud siren, was asleep in the backseat, with no seatbelt on. Shotti, the driver, had no seatbelt either. But that was only the beginning. He also didn't have a shirt on, and his pants were unbuttoned. When asked where he was coming from, he was vague. "North Jersey," he replied.

Another cop arrived on the scene and the first one filled him in. When the pair walked back to Shotti's car, they said they could tell that someone had sprayed air freshener in an unsuccessful attempt to cover up the smell of weed.

The original patrolman made Shotti get out of the car. Shotti insisted that the weed smell was there because he had smoked earlier, and the smell lingered on his clothes. No, said the cop. That was *raw* marijuana I smelled, not burnt. Even as Shotti stood there away from the car, the smell was still there.

Kasheem was high. The cops could tell from his red eyes and cottonmouth. But when the second cop talked to Neja, things got weird. She was nervous, and her eyes kept darting over to Shotti. That cop quickly sussed out that she wanted to talk to them alone. When that finally happened, she informed them that Shotti told her to hide a bag of some kind of substance "inside" of her. She hid it in her vagina. But after talking with the cop and telling him the deal, he allowed her to go back inside the heavily tinted car to remove the bag and put it on top of the center console. It turned out to be twenty-five grams of heroin packaged together with sixteen grams of another white powder.

Once that cop got Neja's story, that was all she wrote. It was time to handcuff Shotti and bring him in. But Shotti could sense something was up with the car. He kept looking at it, nervous, as the other cop was talking to him. And as the cop went to put handcuffs on, Shotti took off running on the shoulder, crossed the exit ramp, and leaped over the rail. He ran down the embankment, went straight for a few more feet, and climbed a fence. He kept going, until the cops lost him in the tree line.

About five minutes later, a third cop saw Shotti walk into a building. The police caught him coming out of the second floor bathroom, where he had tossed a plastic bag of marijuana in the garbage. Back in the car, they later found a weed grinder and, far more dramatically, an eighteen-inch machete.

Once the cops got Shotti, he claimed he was having an asthma attack. Not wanting to take any chances, they gave him oxygen and took him to a nearby medical center, and from there to jail. He was given $35,000 bail and a court date of June 3.

And then he went on the run.

His not showing up to court had spillover effects. An arrest warrant was issued that September, and on October 15, 2016, Kifano Jordan was named Hunterdon County's Fugitive of the Week. And he remained a fugitive for the entirety of Tekashi's 2017-18 rise to the top of the rap world, right up through his own arrest on federal racketeering charges. But, true to his brash ways, being a fugitive didn't stop him from appearing on social media, on stage, on record, or even on television. It didn't even stop him from *living in New Jersey*.

Running from the cops wasn't the only thing keeping Shotti occupied around this time. He also helped to run a cosmetics company started by his then-girlfriend. Dollhouse Cosmetics was a small operation in Bed Stuy, with another location in New Jersey. But even a Nine Trey big homie is not immune from getting his feelings hurt, and the couple split not long before Tekashi came on the scene. So Shotti's plate was empty when the opportunity presented itself to get involved in the career of Seqo's new discovery.

Someone else in Nine Trey who was ready and willing to

help out was Anthony Ellison. Ellison, usually known as "Harv" or sometimes as "Hollywood," was in many ways Shotti's polar opposite. Shotti was loud and brash; Harv more reserved. Shotti, five years older than Harv, played fast and loose with gang rules, even occasionally stiffing fellow Nine Trey members on drug deals (welshing on what you owed came to be called a "Shotti move" among some members of the gang). Harv was a stickler for Nine Trey order. "Growing up all I wanted [was] to be a gangsta the right way," he texted Shotti once. "Neva look up to nothing else." Harv didn't like that Shotti ranked higher in Nine Trey than he did, and there was always a rivalry between the two over who was tougher.

This particular subset of Nine Trey was based in Bedford Stuyvesant, Brooklyn, or "Red Stuy," as members sometimes referred to it due to their Blood affiliation. It has a tight-knit feel, and many families have lived there for generations.

Among those was Seqo's. His aunt's grandfather owned a brownstone on Madison Street, and it stayed in the family. The house, which they called "Maddy" after the street name, became a clubhouse and a meeting place for the crew. Seqo's aunt had a nickname: Ms. Tr3yway.

The nickname was a case of art imitating life. It all started with Garland Tyree. Tyree was a Staten Island based Nine Trey Godfather known as "S.I." He was convicted on a weapons charge in 2004, and sentenced to ten years in prison. While there, he had a tendency to end up in solitary confinement. During one of his stints in solitary, he had a brainstorm. "I just jumped up and started writing," he once told an interviewer. "No typewriters, no nothing. It was all hand-written on typing paper."

The resulting book was a fiction, sort of. It told the story of the 5-Trey Gangsters, a group whose name, codes, structure, and activities were virtually indistinguishable from the gang to which Tyree actually belonged.

In August, 2015, a few years after self-publishing his book, Tyree violated the terms of his parole. The U.S. Marshals pulled up to his door. Tyree went to Facebook and posted, "Today I die." He set off a smoke bomb and started shooting. He wounded a firefighter, and was shot and killed. Tyree never lived to see the full impact of his novel. In it, the hero, 5-Trey leader B-Right, is pursued relentlessly by a federal prosecutor and his "pack of cowardly informants." The title of the book? *The Trey Way*.

Garland Tyree's book had some big fans in Red Stuy. When Seqo was recording a song, he used "Treyway" as an offhanded ad-lib. His aunt liked the name. They decided to give it to a record label they were talking about building. Shotti was brought into the conversations too.

This was where everything stood when Seqo Billy first met Tekashi: a longstanding Nine Trey crew with deep interrelations, and some deep structural tensions; Tr3yway Records on the verge of being created; and a meeting place on Maddy. That was the kindling that would ignite the fire of Tekashi 6ix9ine's viral fame.

CHAPTER 3

GUMMO

In the fall of 2017, Tekashi 6ix9ine had a record label, a manager, and a new direction. He was giving up on the rock-influenced sounds of his Scumgang days, and was ready to go commercial. The first salvo in this direction was "Gummo," the song he'd labored over with his friend Drew.

But for an artist as visual as Tekashi 6ix9ine, a song was nothing without a video. And this was where Seqo Billy came into play. Seqo had an idea. He wanted to, as he says, get Danny "in tune with the urban community more." And Danny was thrilled to have a real-life gang member on his side. He even shouted out Nine Trey in the lyrics to "Gummo." "In the hood with them Billy niggas," he rapped.

So, when it came time to make the video for "Gummo," Seqo and Danny's desires melded into a plan. They would shoot the video at Maddy, with real life Nine Trey members there to lend credibility to the rainbow-haired rapper.

Maddy was owned by Ms. Tr3yway's mother, who still lived there. She appeared in the clip and later, after its world-beating success, was teasingly called the "'Gummo' grandma" by some of her then-coworkers at the Department of Corrections.

The idea of the video was to play up Danny's Mexican heritage. Just like Righteous P had, Danny's manager Chris realized that his heritage could be advantageous. Donald Trump was president, and "build the wall" sentiment was everywhere. So announcing Mexican allegiance loud and clear, as Danny did in the video by wearing a Mexico soccer jersey, would surely get attention.

There was just one issue. There was no way a bunch of guys in Red Stuy, Nine Trey members or otherwise, were going to show up en masse for a video shoot for someone they didn't know—especially someone from Bushwick. Some subterfuge was called for.

Seqo told everyone around to come to a video shoot—for *him*. They were going to shoot a clip, he said, for his own song "Billy Dat." And a number of Nine Trey guys showed up. Danny bought a whole bunch of red bandanas. Chris, nursing a hangover from the previous night, skipped the shoot.

Almost immediately after arriving, Seqo took Danny over to Shotti, who was at the top of the stairs outside Maddy. If Nine Trey was going to represent this rapper, the gang's big homie needed to know who they were repping.

"What's up, homie?" Shotti said. "We here for you. Whatever you need, we here. Couple of the homies gonna show up in a little bit. In the meantime, you need anything?"

"I'm good," Danny replied. "You need anything?"

"Get a bottle of Henny and something to eat for the guys."

Danny bought two large bottles of Hennessy and brought them back to Maddy, fuel for the shoot to follow. The video shoot got started in the mid-afternoon, and only took a few hours. It was a block party. They played songs from Seqo, from

Danny, and from the Pop Out Boyz, another local crew who were tight with Seqo. Members of the group and their affiliates had been arrested back in 2016 for credit card fraud—an incident that became national news because they rapped about that very practice on a song called "For a Scammer."

When the police showed up, Ms. Tr3yway sprung into action. She got everyone to pull a grill out and act like they were just having a cookout—not an uncommon early fall outdoor activity in that neighborhood. All in all, the crowd of about forty had a great time drinking Henny, mugging for the cameras, and dancing to the music. At one point during the day, Danny tried to convince Shotti that he was destined for fame. Shotti was posted up at the top of the stairs, and Danny said, "Yo bro, this shit is gonna be huge."

After it was all done, Seqo called Chris. "Yo, you'd be so proud of your boy," he said. "He brought bandannas for the homies. He bought two bottles of Hennessy—the big joints." Altogether, the video cost around $150.

Less than a month after that filming, the video was ready to go. Danny gave it to Yaksha to release on Fck Them's YouTube page—a sort of final thank you, since he now had a record deal, a real manager, and other business ties. He wasn't yet authorized to release the clip through his label, so this was the quickest way to get it out into the world.

The response was instantaneous. Danny's friend Schlosser wasn't a fan of the track originally ("I was there when he first ever heard the beat, and I was like, 'This shit sucks.'") But he saw the mania firsthand. Even before the full video came out, when just a teaser was available, people were going nuts. Schlosser recalls hearing a car drive by, blasting just the few seconds of the song that was then available on a continuous loop.

"Energy-wise and visually what he did was powerful," Schlosser says now. "Because we never seen that. We never seen a fucking rainbow-haired Blood. Fuck if he was Black or anything. He just broke the whole barrier."

Not long after the video dropped, Schlosser and Danny were at the Applebee's in Times Square.

"Some weird dude ran up to us and got on his knees like, 'Oh, 6ix9ine,' and was kissing his shoes and shit," Schlosser remembers. That was when Schlosser realized that everything had changed. His friend Danny had really turned into Tekashi 6ix9ine, rap star.

What made "Gummo" work was exactly the incongruity that Seqo, Chris, and Tekashi sensed. Who was this rainbow-headed, rainbow-grilled Mexican kid? Why was he around all these hard-looking guys flaunting their Blood affiliation? Was he friends with them? How? Was it a joke? Was it serious? Whatever the answers to these questions, people couldn't look away. In fewer than three months, the video garnered over seventy million views.

Elliot Grainge, Tekashi's new label head, was blown away. Within weeks, he called Chris. "How the fuck is this doing so many numbers? This shit is gonna be huge," Tekashi recalls him saying. As the view count clicked ever-higher, Shotti took notice. And he called Seqo.

"This little nigga knows what he's doing," Shotti said. "I thought all that rainbow-hair shit, he was bugging for that, but he know what he's doing. Tell him to stay in touch."

Tekashi did. By the time he was ready to record a follow-up song just a few weeks after "Gummo" was released, Shotti was in the studio with him, making sure to appear on camera in their very first interview.

By then, Tekashi already had his patter down. And he

would use it for the rest of his rise to the top. Just like when he said that his Scumgang crew members Righteous P and Zilla-Kami went behind his back with Epic Records, this time he was yet again the victim. But instead of the perpetrators being his friends, it was now unnamed "haters." He was channeling their antagonism and using it to make himself successful. It's all there in the very first sentence of his first interview.

"First of all, I want to say to all my haters that, you know, I really appreciate y'all 'cause two weeks ago, nobody was jacking Tekashi 6ix9ine, but y'all niggas made me relevant."

Tekashi's beef with Trippie Redd was still going strong. In the interview, he crowed over the fact that "Gummo" was on the verge of gaining more YouTube views than Trippie's popular track "Love Scars."

The follow-up song Tekashi had just finished while giving that interview was called "Kooda." It was named after one of his friends whom he called on FaceTime during the recording session. The song was inspired by the questions and disbelief around "Gummo." The song's aggressive posture is obvious from the opening lines: "Niggas running out they mouth, but they never pop out."

"A lot of people didn't understand it," Tekashi once explained. "They didn't understand how a kid with rainbow hair could be affiliated with the Nine Trey Bloods, and it just didn't mix."

Tekashi was spending more and more time at Maddy, so gang nomenclature worked its way into the lyrics of "Kooda." He made sure to say that he was "on fifty," which was Nine Trey slang for "on point" or being aware. And he threatened to pull up on his rivals "on *sangre*," the Spanish word for blood—"on Blood" was a popular phrase of affirmation among the crew. By early November, before "Kooda" was even complete, they were ready to shoot the video. And Tekashi knew what he had to do.

"After we shot 'Gummo,' I knew we had a formula," he explained. "The gang image... That's what people like. It was just a formula, a blueprint that I found that worked."

So, they pulled up near a housing project in Brooklyn, just over a mile from Maddy. It was colloquially known as "Smurf Village" because of the buildings' short stature—only two stories.

For the shoot, Tekashi was all about his newfound Blood ties. He wore a red jumpsuit and an oversized red bandana. Next to him were Blood members wearing their telltale red beaded necklaces. But there was a conscious attempt to show Tekashi's growing street cred by including other gangs as well.

"Yo man, do you think you can get some Crips there?" Tekashi asked his new DJ, Pvnch, while planning the shoot. Pvnch was happy to oblige.

It was a brilliant move. Unlike on the West Coast, where Crips and Bloods are enemies, gang dynamics in New York City were more fluid and complicated. So it would *look* to the outside like Tekashi was bringing warring factions together, but that wasn't really the case at all.

"What people don't really know is that Crip and Blood don't really have beef in New York," Pvnch says now. "They [both] have beef with some other people." So having Crips and Bloods together in the same video? "It looks crazy aesthetically, but they're all friends."

Plenty of Crips showed up, along with Bloods. The video was shot at night, in the parking lot of a strip mall with a Boost Mobile store, a supermarket, and a few other businesses. Expensive cars were brought out. Everyone involved made the most of it.

"We good with everybody," Tekashi brags in the behind-the-scenes footage.

"Big gang members in here," Shotti agrees. "We bringing back Dipset."

"Niggas co-signing this whole movement," a Crip visitor yells, with his arm around Tekashi for emphasis.

The Nine Trey members who showed up already seemed to know the deal: Tekashi was the star, and they were there to hype him up. All the other gang members got the memo as well.

"Who says 6ix9ine ain't the homie?" they asked the camera. "Who says 6ix9ine ain't Blood?"

They were luxuriating in each other's company, the free-flowing Hennessy, and the chance to be in a music video with a hot artist—one who they hoped would lift their own profiles and finances. By this time, the Bloods had already given their star rapper a new nickname: "Bix" or "Bix 9ine." It was "Six" but with a *B* for "Blood" swapped out for the initial consonant.

Later in the shoot, everyone moves down into the Utica Avenue train station. Tekashi is angrily shouting the words to the song and getting shoved around by dozens of dudes in the background. But those dozens of dudes are a backdrop, there to provide street cred and co-signs. Tekashi is front and center, a rainbow-haired, rainbow-grilled star.

At the end of the night, Pvnch debriefed with Shotti and a few others. The DJ called the shoot "a packed parking lot with nothing but gang." It wasn't an exaggeration. The massive gang turnout also succeeded in responding to haters who thought "Gummo" was a joke or a fluke. Tekashi really was, to use Pvnch's favorite word, "outside"—he was around, and cosigned by, real gang members. And Tekashi's success?

"That puts everybody in a position to gain," Shotti said.

As the "Kooda" video was being readied for release, Tekashi was beginning to do up-and-coming rap star things. He made appearances at strip clubs, like Angels NYC in Flushing, Queens, which he visited on November 13, 2017.

It was a wild night. Even though the "Gummo" video was only about a month old, the song got the crowd into a frenzy. The DJ ran back the intro over and over again. When he rapped the song along with the record, Tekashi put special emphasis on the shoutout to his new Nine Trey friends: "In the hood with them Billy niggas," he screamed.

In addition to strip club appearances, there were also live shows. Not full-fledged concerts just yet—after all, Tekashi only had two songs at this point that went along with his new gangster image, and the second one hadn't even been released. But club appearances where he would perform his two tracks, usually a bunch of times in a row. The very first one of these was less than a week after the visit to Angels, at Haus in Manhattan's TriBeCa neighborhood.

It was November 19, 2017, a Sunday, so the club was having "Industry Sunday," with Pvnch as the DJ. The night promised a "surprise special guest," but the rainbow-colored diamond grill image on the flyer gave the surprise away.

Pvnch played hits from Future, Drake, 21 Savage, and Lil Uzi Vert. Shotti was there, having a blast, jumping up and down. Tekashi spent most of the night in the back, standing next to a pretty brunette in a white turtleneck and hoop earrings—a brunette who was *not* Sara Molina.

When Pvnch put on Seqo's "Billy Dat," Tekashi and his crew went nuts.

"Gangtivity!" Shotti shouted.

Even Drew, who was still involved in videos and song-writing but stayed pretty far from the gang stuff, was throwing up Nine Trey hand signs in excitement.

"Red Stuy's where we really at," the lyrics boomed. "Billy up, Billy dat."

Eventually, it was Tekashi's turn.

Pvnch led the chant. "Six!" he yelled.

"Nine!" the crowd responded.

Tekashi got on the mic. He already knew that, before he did anything else, the gang demanded loyalty.

"Treyway!" he yelled. The would-be label name had been adopted as a catchphrase, a way of promoting the gang without saying the name outright. Tekashi handed over the mic to his gang sponsor, his big homie, Shotti.

"Whole city, we got this," Shotti screamed. "Turn up for us. Come out, baby."

This time, Tekashi was actually on something that resembled a stage. One arm around Seqo, he tore into "Gummo," his confidence noticeably improved since the strip club event just days prior. And this time, his vitriol was aimed squarely in one direction.

"Shout out Trippie Redd," he rapped. "But I fucked that nigga's bitch."

There was a reason for the hostility. Just days before, Tekashi flexed his gang connections for the very first time, to attack Trippie.

CHAPTER 4

A PERSONAL HIT SQUAD

On November 11, 2017, Tekashi was eating breakfast with Chris when they got a phone call from Trippie's manager. Trippie was in town to shoot a video, and wanted to know if they could put this beef behind them. After all, they were all on the same label, and the whole thing was pretty silly. Why didn't Tekashi come to the video shoot, hang out, and take a picture with Trippie to demonstrate that the beef was done?

"Nah, I don't want to squash the beef with him," Tekashi replied. Trippie had, in Tekashi's mind, already gone too far.

"Well," the manager said, "if you change your mind, here's the address." It was in Red Hook, Brooklyn.

Tekashi knew just what to do, now that he had Nine Trey at the ready. He reached out to Shotti, and said that he wanted something done about Trippie. Shotti, never one to miss a hint when it involved violence, responded, "Say less."

Tekashi and Shotti pulled up to Maddy, and went from there to the site of the video shoot. But they didn't go inside.

Instead, they hung out near the sprinter van that they knew would later be used to transport Trippie back to his hotel. They were trying not to be seen. They were joined in their mission by Harv, who was driving a four-door coupe.

After a while, Trippie and about a dozen other people climbed in the van and took off. Tekashi, Shotti, and Harv followed along in arguably the most boring car chase in history—ninety minutes in heavy traffic on the highway, from Red Hook to the Gansevoort Hotel in Manhattan.

When the sprinter reached the hotel, Tekashi's crew parked a little way away to avoid surveillance cameras. Shotti got out of the car, telling Tekashi to stay put. Harv and three friends joined Shotti.

Chris King, who was there with Trippie, recalls what happened next this way: A bunch of guys were just hanging out in the lobby, claiming to be Bloods. One of them went to shake Trippie's hand, and then punched him. Then a big rumble broke out, and the assailants ran away. The whole thing took about a minute and a half.

When he got back to the car, Shotti was exultant, screaming, "It's fucking Treyway! It's the fucking mob! I love my niggas!"

Harv punched Trippie dead in the mouth, Shotti explained. Harv, true to form, wasn't happy about all of Shotti's yelling. He didn't even seem to know who Trippie was. He just walked in, got Trippie pointed out to him, and did his job.

That wasn't the end of it, of course. In this new age of rap beef, nothing was real until it was on social media. Trippie, enraged (and perhaps hoping to get out in front of the story), hopped on Instagram Live. He admitted that Tekashi had "Nine Trey niggas" waiting for him at the hotel.

"As soon as I walk in the building, hit right in my mouth, nigga." He pulled down his bottom lip to show a cut on the inside of it. But afterward, he said, "My niggas beat his niggas' asses, and they ran." Chris King, in the background, called Tekashi a "rainbow-haired faggot."

Tekashi recorded a mocking response, pretending not to know who was behind the incident. "I don't know what's going on, but I feel really bad about it," he said.

"Chin is bruised up. You just can't be out here calling people gay, bro. Can't be supporting false accusations... You should put some ice on that chin. Bruised up. I feel bad, bro. You can't just start snitching and say, 'It was the Nine Trey.' You can't do that, bro. It's not gangster." Tekashi ended by saying to Trippie, with the sarcasm dialed up to eleven, "I just want you to be my friend again."

The incident was a tipping point for Tekashi. It was the first time he went beyond using the gang as window dressing for videos, and began using them as what a federal judge would later call a "personal hit squad."

And Shotti was at the center of it. He grew closer and closer to Tekashi, and as a result started yet another internal rift in the Nine Trey family. One day, Ms. Tr3yway ran into Tekashi, and was surprised to find out that he'd been told he couldn't go over to Maddy anymore. Ms. Tr3yway never said anything of the sort. She suspected this was part of Shotti's master plan. He was going to push everyone away from Tekashi now that he was a star. There was another part of the dynamic too. Seqo and his aunt didn't like Tekashi's constant trolling and antagonizing. Shotti, on the other hand, was all about it.

But Shotti didn't just take a friend away from Seqo and Ms.

Tr3yway. He took their name. Ms. Tr3yway had asked Shotti months prior to register the trademark for "Tr3yway Entertainment," but he'd never done so. Now, he had Tekashi screaming out "Treyway" at every show, on every social media post. Some people even thought that Shotti's name *was* "Treyway" because of how frequently he and Tekashi used the term. As Ms. Tr3yway saw it, the idea was to make the world believe the term belonged to the loud rap star and his big homie protector, and not to the people who'd come up with it in the first place.

That wasn't Shotti's only power move. He was beginning to play a manager-style role as well, pushing the publicity-shy Chris Ehigiator out of the picture.

After the incident with Trippie, Harv and Tekashi grew close, and Harv became the rising star's bodyguard. When Tekashi was in trouble—when people were threatening him outside a T-Mobile store; when a rogue Nine Trey affiliate named Snow Billy seemed like he had nefarious aims—Tekashi called Harv to straighten things out.

The video for "Kooda" hit the internet on December 3, 2017. By that time, "Gummo" had tens of millions of views. The follow-up was a hit as well. As his fame and YouTube view counts grew, so did Tekashi's desire to become an actual member of Nine Trey. Sure, being *around* gang members was cool. But the logical next step was to become "real right" or "double r"—100 percent, real-deal official. So right after "Kooda"'s release, he started bugging Seqo and Shotti, working in his newly learned slang.

"Yo, let me shoot my 31," he'd text. Or he'd be on the phone with Shotti and say, "I want my 31."

Tekashi, as a burgeoning celebrity, didn't have to fight anybody in order to get in the gang. After bugging Seqo a number of times, the elder Blood just started referring to Tekashi as a full-fledged member.

But life as a rising star wasn't all gang wish fulfillment. It came with increased scrutiny. And the rumors swirling around Tekashi since ZillaKami released the paperwork from the 2015 arrest needed to be addressed. So, in mid-November, just before the release of "Kooda," Tekashi sat down for an in-depth interview. For his interlocutor, Tekashi chose DJ Akademiks, a YouTube personality who delivered hip-hop news in chatty, fast-moving videos.

Because Tekashi was still new enough that no real reporting had been done on his case, he could paint his own picture. And he did. His lies were all tiny, small enough that to call him out on any individual one might seem pedantic. But as a whole, they presented a very different, and far more exculpatory, picture of what happened in that Harlem apartment than what Tekashi had told Detective Maureen Sheehan.

First off, he lied about his age. He described himself as a "seventeen-year-old kid," when he'd been eighteen at the time. He told Akadamiks that the girl had said she was nineteen, which was different from "I assumed she was older," as he'd told the detective in the immediate aftermath.

But the biggest lies had to do with sexual assault. He said he never touched the girl when the video showed him smacking her butt; and her sitting in his lap—the latter was the image ZillaKami shared at the height of their beef.

Tekashi explicitly told Ak that "No one had sex with the girl," which was a lie contradicted by the videos from that night. He also said that he'd written a letter of apology, but he neglected to mention that it had been court-mandated. Tekashi did tell the full, unadulterated truth about one thing, though. He had shared the video, he said, because "I wanted to go viral."

That was one wish which was coming true with stunning regularity. People couldn't keep their eyes off of the rainbow-haired kid who was constantly surrounded by gang members. But in order to keep his momentum going, Tekashi needed another song, quick.

Instead of finishing something new, he decided to re-work an old one. Back in March, a pre-Nine Trey Tekashi put out a song called "On the Regular." So, for a follow-up to "Kooda," he just took that instrumental and hook, added some new words, and got the rappers Fetty Wap and A Boogie Wit da Hoodie to add guest verses. This was a big step. Tekashi was finally popular enough to get established artists on one of his songs.

There was another milestone too—a big one. Tekashi had his first hit song. In late November, he got the official word. On the Billboard Hot 100 chart—the ultimate arbiter of a song's status—for the week of December 2, "Gummo" entered at number 58. It stayed on the chart for twenty weeks, peaking at number 12.

When it came time on December 20 to make a video for "Keke," as the revamped "On the Regular" was now called, the standard formula was followed again. Tekashi was surrounded by a bunch of gang members, but this time in a new location: A Boogie's Bronx neighborhood of Highbridge.

The most amusing moment of the whole shoot occurred when Tekashi struggled to climb on top of a basketball hoop for a dramatic aerial shot. He got lifted up high enough to grab the rim, but he couldn't pull himself upright from there. For long seconds, he struggled, legs around the inside of the hoop, hands desperately grabbing the outside, his back dangerously dangling toward the ground, only being held aloft by a supporting set of hands back on earth.

Eventually, a Nine Trey member had to climb up from the other side and reach around the backboard to help. He reached over the top of the backboard to grab Tekashi's hand, and the young rapper steadied himself. The crowd yelled, half in admiration and half-mocking. It was a perfect metaphor for Tekashi's career so far. Nine Trey members were elevating him, to the audience's admiration and bemusement. But from the outside, it all sounded like cheers. And in the end, it would look to the world like Danny Hernandez got to the top all by himself.

Meanwhile, Tekashi's rapid-fire release plan was having its intended effect. He would play a snippet of an upcoming song on Instagram to build anticipation (as he did with "Keke," releasing in-studio footage of him, A Boogie, and Fetty Wap dancing along to a part of the track). Then the entire track would mysteriously leak in advance of its official release. And then, the video. Each step in the process resulted in a new round of shares on social media.

The plan worked like a charm. Just three weeks after hitting the Billboard Hot 100 for the first time, Tekashi now had two songs on it: "Gummo" was at number 13, and "Kooda" debuted at number 61. He was starting to turn internet infamy into actual stardom. And he was changing as a result. A month before shooting the "Gummo" video, Tekashi did an interview with *Mass Appeal* where he decried the need for designer clothing.

"I came from nothing," he said. "I didn't have the Jordans on...I didn't have all this shit. I couldn't afford it. I wanted it, but I couldn't afford it. But now that I got money, do I want it? It's cool...I have nothing against these brands. But if I couldn't afford it then, I don't need it now."

Just months later, that sentiment had disappeared. On the set of the "Keke" video, Tekashi wasn't wearing Jordans. But on his feet were fancy, revered-in-Japan Reebok Instapump Fury sneakers.

CHAPTER 5

WHERE THE MONEY AT?

By the end of 2017, Tekashi was starting to make real money. It was time to pay the piper. In December, he made his first major, five-figure payment to the gang. What was the money for? When asked in court in 2019, Tekashi didn't mince words.

"So they could buy guns and stuff like that."

He made payments to both Shotti and Harv. The big homie and the bodyguard. The situation quickly became untenable. Control over the flow of money, and by extension over Tekashi, needed to be established quickly.

So, around the top of 2018, Shotti, Harv, Mel Murda, and Tekashi all met up at Shotti's cousin's house on Long Island. They gathered to determine what was going on with the money Tekashi had been giving to the gang so far, but also to figure out who was going to guide things from here on out. The gang members chatted for a while sans Tekashi, and then Mel called him in. Mel Murda, as the highest-ranking member of Nine Trey, would be making decisions. Mel attempted to put the rapper at ease.

"Yo, you do everything good. Don't trip." He wanted to reassure the gang's meal ticket that he wasn't in any danger. They just had some things to figure out.

"Who you gave money to?" Mel enquired.

"I gave money to Harv, and I gave money to Shotti," Tekashi responded.

"How much you gave?"

Tekashi explained. He'd given Harv $25,000 at that point. And he'd given Shotti $30,000—an amount that he was supposed to share with Harv.

"Yo, where the money at?" Mel asked them.

Shotti was defensive. His rank in the gang was high 020, just one level under Mel.

"I gotta take care of the homies," he explained. "Homies gotta eat. I got shit to take care of." That included buying weapons. "We don't got no guns out here," Shotti continued. "We need to equip ourselves."

Then Shotti got angry. "I'm the high 020. Fuckin' niggas asking me what I did with the money." In fact, he reminded Mel, "I gave some to you."

Mel knew better than to ask Harv to defend himself. Harv didn't explain himself to anybody, Godfather or no. It was time to make a decision. Mel decided that Tekashi's career should be in Shotti's hands, not Harv's.

While Tekashi was having major decisions made for him within the Nine Trey structure, his rapidly increasing stardom meant he could begin to take back his power in other ways. He would frequently not bother to pay the people who accompanied him on club dates—something many of them took as an insult, since they viewed themselves as security. He would also take deposits for performances and then not show up at all.

Tekashi was driven by a single need—to get attention.

Every time he performed "Gummo," it was an excuse to mock Trippie Redd. There were other pranks as well. A few days before Christmas, he posted a video to Instagram that he'd shot in a hospital, where he went in the aftermath of an asthma flareup. In the clip, he's lying on a gurney with a white sheet over him, letting the audience think he was dead until the very end, when he abruptly sits up.

Shortly afterwards, Tekashi's second major rap beef began to brew. The Brooklyn rapper Casanova was affiliated with a rival Blood set, the Apes. And he had issues with Nine Trey: a Nine Trey member had tried to rob him some time before, and the rapper had mocked the failed attempt in his 2016 song "Don't Run."

But Tekashi's DJ Pvnch was close to Casanova, and tried to link the two Brooklyn rappers. Pvnch suggested to Casanova that he appear on a remix of "Kooda," but was rebuffed. Tekashi was concerned, and he tried to reach out in an attempt to smooth things over.

"Yo bro, get Casanova on the phone," he'd demand of Pvnch. "Let me talk to him."

"Cas refused to get on the phone," Pvnch says now. "I feel like, because he knew that Tekashi was like a viral kid, [he thought] Tekashi would probably try to yell at him and record it, and try to make Cas look bad."

It was a fair assumption, but one that would have long-lasting consequences. With no direct conversation, hostility and rumors blossomed. Finally, Tekashi decided to strike. At a late December gig at Club Freq in New York City, Tekashi worked Casanova's name into a performance of "Gummo."

"Shout out Casanova, but I fucked that nigga's bitch," he rapped. The music ducked out, leaving the diss hanging in the air.

Days later, Casanova released a video for a new song called "Set Trippin." Pvnch is adamant to this day that it was not originally intended as a diss towards Tekashi, but was only taken as one because of the heightened context. Regardless, the song was soon rocketing around YouTube with "(6ix9ine Diss)" appended to the name as if it were an official subtitle. It's easy to understand why. The song has lines like "see you with that red flag on, what that be 'bout?/Punch you in the face, motherfucker, I knock ya teeth out" and "How you tryna rep the hood? You ain't even gang"—lyrics that play into the perception of Tekashi as a fake gang member, someone who doesn't really belong in the world of Nine Trey.

Whether the song was intended as a diss or not, Tekashi definitely received it that way. In a group text just days after "Set Trippin" came out, he wrote, "YO WE GOT TO RUN DOWN ON CASONOVA WHEN I GET BACK."

Harv already didn't like Casanova, whom he viewed as a "bitch-ass nigga." But Seqo was skeptical. Tekashi was going viral with regularity. He was already the hottest dude in the rap game. Why make trouble, especially with someone who could actually cause real problems for the Billys? And Seqo heard some troubling things about Casanova's Blood set: there was an order out among them to shoot at any Nine Trey members they came across.

"There's a kite out saying if any apes happen to cross ya path to fire on you or anybody around you ... smarten up my nigga."

Harv was skeptical about Seqo's intelligence, and didn't seem to care even if it *was* accurate. True to form, he was ready to take on all comers, no matter the odds. "They don't want to war with Billys," he replied.

Luckily for everyone involved, cooler heads prevailed.

There wouldn't be a full-fledged war between Tekashi and Casanova in the aftermath of "Set Trippin."

At least, not yet.

Right around the time "Set Trippin" was released, Shotti began to take even more control over the term "Treyway." He approached a New Jersey entertainment lawyer with one question: "What can you do for Tr3yway?" Shotti was determined to make Tr3yway Entertainment—a version controlled by *him*, not Ms. Tr3yway or Seqo Billy—the biggest thing in the music business. This despite the fact that Ms. Tr3yway was the one who trademarked the term "Tr3yway" and who registered "Tr3yway Entertainment Inc." as a business with New York State. Shotti completely disregarded, or was unaware of, the fact that she owned the name legally. If he owned it in the court of public opinion, that would do.

The entertainment lawyer came to Shotti with an idea.

"We have to brand Tr3yway."

Days later, they had an hours-long brainstorming session, trying to come up with ways to get the world to say the term.

Shotti, a felon on the run from the law, didn't have a social media presence. But to become a mogul, he had to get one. It was a necessary sacrifice. So at the top of 2018, as part of the plan, he got a logo and set up an account at @tr3yway_ent— using the same *3* for *E* stylization that Ms. Tr3yway used. Shotti took full advantage of the star whose career he was helping to guide, having Tekashi shout "Treyway" on camera at every opportunity. Shotti and the lawyer continued to talk almost daily, formulating plans to have the world screaming out "Treyway."

The reason for promoting the company was simple. Even Shotti could see that Tekashi was unstable, that he couldn't be relied on to have a long career. He was going to crash soon, and it was going to be hard. Shotti needed to have options outside of his star if he was going to continue on the music business gravy train. Also, having the name everywhere served as a constant subterranean commercial for Nine Trey itself.

As 2017 rolled over into 2018, Nine Trey's role as Tekashi's defenders ramped up. Seemingly everywhere he went, a violent intervention was necessary. Not all of them made the headlines. But one that did was Yams Day.

Tekashi was invited to perform at the annual Yams Day concert on January 18, 2018 at the New York Expo Center in the Bronx. The concert was held to celebrate the memory of Steven "ASAP Yams" Rodriguez, the co-founder of Harlem's influential ASAP collective. Yams had helped launch two of the crew's members, ASAP Rocky and ASAP Ferg, to stardom before dying in 2015 at just twenty-six years old. But this concert would be remembered for something a lot different than paying tribute to a beloved figure.

Shotti, arriving late, attempted to get backstage after Tekashi finished performing. The security guards didn't recognize him, and, depending on who you ask, either shoved or hit him. One Nine Trey member told the rest of the crew what was happening—he said, "they jumped Shotti"—and they, along with other affiliated folks, started fighting back.

"We retaliated because they were swinging first," a rapper named Flee Kevo who was on the scene remembers. "Fifty against fifty. It was wicked. Sticks flying, fire hydrants. It was crazy."

Crazy indeed. One Nine Trey member was caught on tape stabbing a security guard. Harv got hit in the face with a stick, but then got control of the stick and started beating the guy with it. When it was all over, Tekashi fell back on an old trick —he lied.

"For Yams's family, this had absolutely nothing to do with me," he said in an Instagram video, using his best somber voice. "I got into no altercation, no fight. Nothing happened... Stop making up stories. That had nothing to do with me. Can everyone please stop saying it had something to do with me?" But even in that video, he still couldn't help but mention all the haters who were wishing ill on him. Even in his public relations coverup moment, his true motivation—proving the haters wrong, at all costs—shone through.

As the incidents kept piling up, Tekashi continued getting hotter. He'd do something outrageous, and it would spark anger. For example, before his first trip to Los Angeles, he made sure to insult "D**K SUCKIN SCARY WEST COAST CLOUT CHASIN RAPPERS" on social media. People would do something violent, like an audience in Minnesota who threw bottles at him. Tekashi would respond to *that* with even more provocative language, spurring more hate, and more headlines. All the time, he was releasing songs as fast as he could make them.

It wasn't fast enough. After "Keke," Tekashi and Drew buckled down and worked on recording enough songs for an actual project. By late February 2018, Tekashi's first project *Day69* was ready to go. But the speed at which everything was done meant that controversy was just around the corner.

One day after the album's release, a Tumblr user claimed that the project's cover artwork was stolen from him. The artist who did the cover effectively copped to the theft by posting on Instagram that his art was "based on" a drawing done by the Tumblr user. Eventually, the art was changed.

The incident may seem small, but it's emblematic of the lack of organization in Tekashi's career, especially as Chris Ehigiator was getting pushed out. Stealing work, whether it was an album cover or a song ("Gotti," also on *Day69*, originally belonged to a Miami artist named PACkmaN), was an easy way to keep things moving, and they could always deal with the repercussions later.

In February 2018, right around the release of *Day69*, Tekashi was at a video shoot in Crown Heights, Brooklyn. When he was there, he met someone who would change his life. Jorge Rivera was in his early thirties, and was an undocumented immigrant in New York City. He'd paid a coyote to transport him across the Rio Grande from Mexico in 2004 as a teenager to find a better life for his family.

Fourteen years later, he was working at his uncle's tire shop, and starting to drive for a car service in Brooklyn. The service got a call from someone who said they needed a ride to a music video set. Jorge was not impressed. *You can do whatever you want*, he thought, *as long as you pay me*. The customer told Jorge that the artist shooting the video was a young Mexican guy. Jorge took note. When he arrived at the shoot, he talked to Tekashi.

"That's good that you're doing this. I'm also Mexican, just like you," Jorge said. He had this guy, who was apparently a big deal rapper, sign a little Mexican flag sticker.

A few weeks later, at around one AM on a Sunday morning, Jorge got a call from the Mexican rapper. He found this odd, because he hadn't given Tekashi his phone number. But still, a client was a client. Tekashi (who liked that Jorge was driving a new, $60,000 Chevy Tahoe) had a request.

"Hey, can you come tomorrow to pick me up right here on Long Island? I have to do a couple of interviews. Can you bring me around?"

Jorge picked him up at seven AM, just a few hours after the phone call, and drove him around until later than one AM the next day. They went to the radio interview, and they went to a barbeque place in Times Square for dinner. Jorge's normal rate was $35 an hour, but he gave his countryman a bulk discount ("Like on the subway," he explained). He charged $390 for that first day.

As March turned to April, Jorge was becoming the regular driver for Tekashi. He was running errands as well—buying food and the like. And he discovered who the real boss was. When Jorge turned in his hours at the end of the day—his regular rate eventually settled down at $500 a day—Shotti was the one who signed the receipts.

Jorge noticed an interesting dynamic. Shotti was a tough guy. But a major part of his job seemed to be to keep Tekashi in a good mood. If Tekashi was happy, they could do business, spend money, and generally keep everything moving. So, the laughing, joking, and teasing between the two was near-constant.

After only a few weeks of being Tekashi's regular driver, Jorge started to put something together. At first, he would wait outside the houses he was driving Tekashi, Shotti, and their friends to. But after a while, he would have to use the bathroom, or get hungry. When he went inside, he would see guns and drugs.

Right around when Jorge first started driving for Tekashi, a big change happened inside Nine Trey. It was a change that would cement Shotti's control over Tekashi's career, and his money. A Nine Trey member named Roland Martin, known as "Ro Murda," had been released from prison that February. A Nine Trey member since his teens, with a record of gun and drug busts dating back to 2002, he was coming off nine years in state prison for a drug conviction—years during which he was still involved with the drug dealing end of Nine Trey, communicating via phone calls.

Ro's move from the prison to the street side of Nine Trey meant that it was time for some reorganization. By virtue of having earned his stripes behind the wall, Ro had Godfather status in the gang. So, the lineup of Nine Trey that contained Shotti, Harv, Tekashi, and Mel Murda was "dubbed"—gotten rid of. And a new lineup, headed by Ro, was instituted. Mel remained a Godfather technically, but retreated from being involved in the gang's day-to-day operations. Harv was falling out of favor with Shotti, and Tekashi was distancing himself from Harv as a result. So, Harv aligned himself with Seqo Billy and the original Maddy crew.

Ro had known Shotti since the Jim Jones days. And Ro brought in people loyal to him, who shared that history. As a result, Shotti was now beginning to gain even more control around who Tekashi was seeing every day. Shotti's habit of unpredictable and often violent responses to any slight was becoming more and more normalized. And soon, there would be plenty of slights to choose from.

CHAPTER 6

HOUSTON

Tekashi was setting himself apart in the rap world not just because of his rainbow hair or his countless tattoos, or even because of the endless hatred he engendered. It was also because of his willingness to take on seemingly impossible foes.

It was an approach that meshed with his style, and Shotti's worldview. But it was also one forced on them by necessity, at least at first. Tekashi's take-no-prisoners attitude meant that he clashed with the family of the most feared hip-hop figure in the city of Houston, and arguably in the world: the notorious J. Prince, founder of Rap-A-Lot Records.

By 2018, James Prince had been a mythic character for decades. Equally loved and feared, he took on everyone from the U.S. government to championship boxers to his own artists, and somehow remained on top through a combination of mystery, business acumen, and occasional rumored violence. He even managed, through his son Jas, to maintain a stake in the career of the biggest hitmaker in all of music, Drake, who implicitly paid tribute to the elder Prince on his

2018 song "Mob Ties"—a catchphrase Prince and another of his sons, J. Prince Junior, frequently used.

It was this son, J. Prince Junior, who set the whole thing off. On March 10, 2018, Tekashi was in Houston, and was invited to a sneaker store by the shop's owner. Once there, the owner pulled Tekashi aside and told him that J. Prince Junior was coming. Prince entered the store with a whole slew of people, and everyone shared the store for about thirty minutes.

J. Prince Junior's birthday party was the next day. So he texted Shotti, and invited him and Tekashi. There was one caveat, though: arrive by 12:15 AM, no later. Shotti responded that the time was unrealistic, but they would be there.

Tekashi and Shotti didn't think anything of it when they pulled up to the party after 1 AM. But J. Prince Junior and his brother Baby Jay took the late arrival, as well as Tekashi's overall lack of deference to the Prince family, as a form of disrespect. When Tekashi and Shotti got to the door, the word had come down from on high: "Junior said no."

"Whoever with 6ix9ine, go that way!" someone yelled as they pointed towards the exit.

The following Wednesday, J. Prince Junior posted video of the incident on Instagram. He added some commentary: "First off @6ix9ine_ , don't think that u can go to other people's city and not show them the proper respect that's due, we've earned that and demand it! Although I might not condone in a bunch of the moves you've made, I don't know u and I know that your young and new to this so u have a lot of learning to do... not for one second do u get it misunderstood that u can get away with the disrespect in my city the way you've shown in others." He hashtagged the post "#MobTies."

On Tekashi's group text afterwards, everyone talked about what happened.

Chris Ehigiator jokingly weighed in. "NIGGAS GOT VIOLATED IN HOUSTON?" he asked sarcastically.

Tekashi defensively explained what happened: He and Shotti went to a party and got asked to leave because they hadn't "checked in" with J. Prince. Checking in was standard procedure when you visited a town that wasn't yours. It consisted of an out-of-town rapper paying respect and homage (and often some money or a gratis guest verse) to a powerful person when on their home turf.

Harv, at this point majorly disenchanted with Shotti and feeling like he was on the verge of being pushed out, responded by taking a shot at the would-be Svengali.

"Why nigga didn't shake no barricades and scream they the mafia," he wrote, a mocking reference to Shotti's frequently belligerent behavior at strip clubs.

Tekashi tried to wave it off. It wasn't a big deal. Nothing had happened, really. But Harv just couldn't let it go.

"Gangsters don't pick and choose there [sic] beef," he wrote. "Same way you are at [Club] lust should be the same way you are everywhere." If you're going to yell and scream at a few overworked nightclub bouncers, you should be willing to do the same to the Don of Houston.

To Tekashi, this was ridiculous. Fighting back when it's a small crew versus an entire party full of people? With cameras rolling? That's a sure way to be embarrassed even further—to end up on the internet "with mad knots on ya forehead."

"You sound pussy," Harv replied, reminding everyone on the chain that he had been shot before and had the bullet holes in his body to prove it. Being scared of getting some knots from a few punches? That was ridiculous.

How did he get violated, Tekashi asked Harv. It was, again,

a simple situation: It was a birthday party, they got there late, and the birthday boy didn't want them there. So what?

Harv wasn't impressed. He laughed at the idea that someone would tell them to arrive by 12:15. "That's a demand," he wrote.

Tekashi was feeling the pressure. "Ya all waited for this moment to gang up on me," he typed. "How is my own niggas hating[?]"

But Harv, one of his "own niggas," didn't see things that way. He wasn't hating. He was just telling the truth: Tekashi looked like a pussy for refusing to stand up to the Prince family, party full of people be damned. He was picking and choosing when to be a gangster. To Harv, that was the ultimate crime. It didn't matter that there were hundreds of people at the party, and only about seven people with Tekashi. If you were a real gangster, a real Billy, you fought back. Tekashi was the type, Harv thought, to be a Blood only when it was convenient. If he was in jail with a bunch of Crips, he would even disavow the gang. He and Shotti were both not following the codes.

"Nobody on your side tough tho they may think they smart," Harv wrote. "[N]iggas kno who the real rights are... Stop pushing Billy...get security and live your internet life."

Tekashi was still trying to argue logically: He didn't get touched. Let the Houston guys talk if they want to. Who cares? But he also picked up on another dynamic in the conversation. This whole thing wasn't about him at all. It was about Harv and Shotti. Everyone knew they didn't like each other.

"Man... this some beef between you and shotty and ya using me to to voice that," Tekashi wrote. "That shit wack."

Then the breaking point came. Tekashi tried one last time to mollify Harv.

"We not your goons," Harv said.

Tekashi wanted to agree, despite the fact that he ordered Harv to punch someone in the face just months prior.

"I respect it," Tekashi wrote.

Harv's response changed everything.

"Respect this dick."

That insult was the nail in the coffin for the already-ailing relationship between Tekashi and Shotti on one side, and Harv on the other. Harv was ready for war. He sent a video of himself on a plane, headed for Austin to meet Tekashi.

"I made up my mind today," he said. "I want smoke. It's lit."

Harv and another Nine Trey member headed out to Austin to meet Tekashi, who was scheduled to play a show there. It was an unofficial showcase at the same time as the city's famous South by Southwest music festival. In the runup to the show, Harv called one of the guys with Tekashi. He was so threatening that the guy broke down in tears.

Harv arrived in Texas on the evening of the show. He texted Tekashi when he arrived, upset that the famous rap star hadn't booked hotel rooms for him and his friend.

Tekashi was shocked. After how aggressive Harv had been, he was demanding a hotel room? That was, to Tekashi, being treated like a hoe.

"I thought you was my brother," he wrote. "You tranna play mind games with me."

To Harv, none of that mattered. He was left stranded, and that was an insult.

"You really violated," he texted.

When he showed up at the Summit Rooftop Lounge for the show, Tekashi was not surprised to see Harv was right up front, waiting for him. As act after act went onstage before him, Tekashi noticed Harv wasn't the only one. J. Prince Junior and about 50 of his closest friends were right there, barricading the stage.

In the middle of all the tension, Chris Ehigiator remembers, he got on the phone with Tekashi and gave his usual spiel, which normally served to calm the rapper down.

"It's your thing," he said, emphasizing the rapper's control. "You can fire whoever you want to fire."

As Chris remembers it, Tekashi handed the phone to one of the guys organizing the show, who said, "Danny said he don't even want you here." It was the end of the line for Chris. He was out, and Shotti was in. Tekashi's last connection to the world outside Nine Trey was severed.

Except that this time, Shotti wasn't actually around. It was only Tekashi, Drew, and Drew's friend. They decided to cut their losses, forfeit about $10,000 that they were supposed to collect after the performance, and jet.

J. Prince Junior took the cancellation as a victory. "Niggas talk a lot of shit, but won't even show up to they own show," he taunted on social media. "Goddamn, you don't want your back end, nigga?"

"I got a question to ask everybody," Prince Jr. continued. "Where 6ix9ine at? He ain't show up to his show."

Things were at a low point. J. Prince Junior and his pals were taking celebratory laps around the streets of Austin. And Tekashi, after a meeting with an entertainment lawyer, was convinced that Chris Ehigiator had stolen $300,000 from him during their time together. In Tekashi's memory, he fired Chris the day *before* the unofficial SXSW show, after discovering the alleged theft. Chris says now that the idea of him stealing from Tekashi is "preposterous." He chalks up the accusation to Tekashi's "divisive" nature.

Back home, Shotti did his best to save face. He recorded

threatening messages defending Tekashi, and taking on J. Prince Junior. "[Tekashi] got the best protection in the world. Treyway, nigga... J. Prince Junior, what you ever did, nigga—come out your father's nuts? You fuckin' faggot. What you ever did?" He claimed Prince originally asked him if Tekashi could perform a few songs at the now-controversial birthday party.

"You dick-sucking nigga," Shotti continued. "Because he came late, y'all mad? You don't run shit. Y'all niggas ain't got no mob ties. We *are* the mob, nigga!"

The video wasn't only notable because of its graphic language, or the fact that Shotti was positioning himself against the Prince family. It was part of a trend. Shotti was becoming more visible, more on camera, more of a public personality. He was no longer the guy who lingered in the back in Jim Jones DVDs, hoodie pulled up high over his face and struggling to stay off camera. Instead, fugitive status be damned, he was developing a public persona of his own, and no small amount of Tekashi's fame was rubbing off on him. Tekashi? Well, he was quickly falling in love with the idea of becoming an untouchable, reckless gangster, just like Shotti. And in response to all of the drama with J. Prince, Tekashi was about to do maybe the most reckless thing in his life to date.

The need for retaliation against J. Prince and Rap-A-Lot was clear. But that was hard to do. J. Prince was based in Texas, and going against him on his home turf was, as Tekashi had learned firsthand, a losing battle. Insulting J. Prince over the internet was fine in the short term. But something more dramatic and visible was needed. Something that would embarrass J. Prince the way that the party and live show videos embarrassed Tekashi. That would come soon, and in an unexpected way. But in Houston, Shotti and Tekashi had learned that it was important to respond to someone not checking in with you with the threat of force.

They would put that lesson to use just a few days later. On March 20, 2018, Trippie was set to perform at Radio City Music Hall, opening for the Bay Area rapper G-Eazy. They gathered up a crew to pay Trippie a visit. Promoter Fluff Jonez, who had booked some early Tekashi performances, was there. He remembers seeing lots of police outside the venue, but Shotti being undeterred.

"Yo listen, we gonna fuck this nigga up, bro," Fluff recalls Shotti saying.

They never got a chance. The crew stayed outside Radio City for hours. But for all their trouble, they only ran into a few members of Trippie's camp who, Fluff claims, told the police about their presence.

But while Tekashi, Shotti, and company were outside the venue, they noticed something strange. The rapper Frenchie BSM, who was affiliated with a different Blood set, the Pirus, was there with Trippie. The Nine Trey members were enraged. Trippie was checking in with the Pirus, but not with Nine Trey? Perhaps inspired by their recent run-in with J. Prince, Tekashi and company decided to prove that Trippie couldn't get away with that. Something had to be done. If they couldn't get to Trippie, they'd get to Frenchie instead.

So when Frenchie drove off at around 8 PM, two cars of Nine Trey members followed him. Tekashi and Ro Murda were in a black Benz, and Shotti was in a black Maserati. Tekashi, exhausted, fell asleep. When he awoke two hours later, they were somewhere in Queens.

Shotti, assault rifle on his lap, was screaming, "I got him! I got him! Now he's mine. I know where he at. He in the towers"

—a nearby building complex. He drove off in search of Frenchie.

"I got to go home," Ro said. It's not that he didn't want a part in the revenge. But he had other concerns. "I'm on parole." He had just gotten out of prison, and didn't want to go back.

Later on, with Ro safely ensconced at home and not at risk of a parole violation, the chase continued. Shotti heard that Frenchie was at Quad Studios in Manhattan—the same studio where 2pac infamously got shot in 1994, the inciting moment of the East Coast-West Coast rap wars. Shotti, in the Maserati, sent a video of Frenchie to Tekashi's car, which promptly met him there.

Both cars waited outside the studio, for what they assumed would be Frenchie and Trippie together. But when Frenchie came out, he was with someone else entirely, the California rapper Joe Moses. The duo ran to a nearby sprinter van. Tekashi's car ate a red light and pulled in front of the sprinter, waiting to see where it would turn. Seeing that the sprinter was stuck at the red, Shotti's Maserati pulled up to the van on the driver's side. Shotti stuck his hand out of the car and fired at the van five or six times. Amazingly, no one was hurt.

As Tekashi's fame increased, his former mentor Scumlord D!zzy was watching closely. He didn't like what he was seeing. Tekashi was still claiming Scumgang. Not only that, he was taking sole credit for it. To the man who began the whole thing, this was unforgivable. Right after the release of "Kooda," D!zzy recorded a diss song aimed at 6ix9ine, called "Scummo."

"6ix 9ine played himself when he went under the radar, abandoning his 'brothers' from Bushwick to portray himself as A Blood from Bedstuy," D!zzy wrote in a statement to accompany the song's music video. "He took his fraud activities to the next level when he went on major platforms misrepresenting the S.C.U.M G.A.N.G Brand & Lyfestyle which started in Flatbush from a band of REAL BROTHERS. But he committed career suicide when told the world HE STARTED S.C.U.M G.A.N.G."

But Tekashi didn't heed D!zzy's warning. He continued claiming that Scumgang was all his. That's what he told Fat Joe in a February 2018 interview: Scumgang was "my shit." Then came the *Breakfast Club*. The *Breakfast Club* is the popular morning radio show on New York City's hip-hop radio station Power 105.1. Tekashi's first appearance on the show was in March 2018, and it quickly became their most popular interview ever. In the middle of it, he dismissively referred to D!zzy and his friends as "some group."

To D!zzy, that was not okay. But there was a chance for revenge. D!zzy's friend KD connected him with some people who were looking for him. Some people from Texas. A publicist who went by "Skyy Lyfe" or "Skyy Daniels" reached out to D!zzy through KD. They were coming to New York with a Texas rapper named Junya Boy who had some affiliation with Rap-A-Lot, and they were ready to tell the world the truth about Tekashi 6ix9ine. They wanted D!zzy to spill everything. He was ready.

They decided to do an interview on April 3, 2018 with DJ Thoro at This Is 50, 50 Cent's outlet. The office was right in the heart of Midtown Manhattan.

The night before the interview, D!zzy was up for hours, planning what he was going to say. On the way there, he went live on Instagram. "Rap-A-Lot, what's good? J. Prince, what's good? We cleaning this shit up. We about to go to This Is 50 right now. We about to shake shit up in the city... I was lining everything up. Now it's time to let niggas know what campaign we on. We on that get-our-throne-in-order campaign."

He took a shot at Tekashi, who had lately been calling himself the King of New York. "I let the nigga run around saying king, 'cause I was taking care of real king shit." At one point, D!zzy showed off his backpack, with "SCUM" written on it. "Ay yo, my bag is waterproof," he said, bending down so the camera could catch it. "Scumbag waterproof. The money don't get wet."

When they arrived at the office, D!zzy, Junya Boy, Skyy, and Skyy's assistant went inside. In the interview, Junya Boy talked about how it was messed up for Tekashi to come to Houston and disrespect J. Prince. D!zzy talked about the true story of Scumgang. They wondered why real gang members like the Nine Trey guys were co-signing Tekashi. The interview was going well. Everyone seemed happy. D!zzy's plan for revenge was working out great.

But as the interview was happening, someone heard about it and called Tekashi's camp. It made sense. The ties between Tekashi and 50 Cent's crew ran deep, and in many directions.

So, when a couple guys started insulting Tekashi, right in 50's office? And Rap-A-Lot was involved somehow? Faheem "Crippy" Walter, a pal of Shotti's who had been moving into Tekashi's inner circle and was now acting as a bodyguard, got word quick. He called Shotti, who was with Jorge and Tekashi at Tekashi's place.

"Yo," Crippy said. "J. Prince, Rap-A-Lot, they in the city. They got an interview at This Is 50."

It wasn't actually J. Prince who was in the city, of course. It was a rapper who had some kind of loose affiliation with him. But those details weren't crucial. This was the chance for revenge that Nine Trey was looking for. It was on *their* turf this time, not J. Prince's. They'd have a chance to embarrass him the way he'd embarrassed them. Tekashi hurriedly got ready, and they jumped in the car to drive to Crippy's place. They went inside and made a plan.

They had to hurry in order to get to This Is 50 before D!zzy, Junya Boy, and the crew left. So, they gave Jorge the address and went over in two cars. In one was Shotti, Tekashi, Crippy, and Jorge. In the other, Ro and two other Nine Trey members. When they arrived, Crippy got on the phone with his contact inside of This Is 50, who fed him updates on the offenders' locations. At last, they reported, "they're coming down now."

Shotti loaded and cocked his gun, and Tekashi pulled out his phone. He was going to tape the whole thing and put it out on the internet. It would be what J. Prince Junior had done to him at the party, times a million.

Shotti, Ro, Crippy, and one more Nine Trey member ran into the lobby of the building from outside as Junya Boy, Skyy, her assistant, and D!zzy entered the lobby from the elevator. Jorge remained behind the wheel. Tekashi, too famous and too much of a Nine Trey cash cow to be participating in an armed robbery himself, was responsible for filming the whole thing.

So, he stayed in the car. He moved up one row, from the way back to the middle, so he could get a better view. He started filming, but it was wet. The raindrops on the car window were blocking his view. He opened the car door and continued filming. The guys, making sure their guns were showing, walked into the lobby and started screaming and cursing.

Skyy saw them, and they saw her. "Bitch, get on the ground!" they yelled. All of a sudden, guns were pointing at her from all directions.

I'm going to die, she thought. *This is the end. I'm never going to see my kids again.*

Suddenly, miraculously, someone opened the door and Skyy ran out—but not before the robbers got her backpack. On it were hard drives that had client information and an in-progress memoir. Fifteen years of memories down the drain. There was also, ironically, a video camera. She got in her car, frantic, and headed to the airport, eager to get out of there. Her assistant got robbed of $1,500 cash and a gold chain.

None of the robbers bothered to wear masks. The whole point was for the Rap-A-Lot guy, whoever he was—and by extension for the J. Princes, senior and junior—to know who robbed them. And for everyone else to know it, too. There was little danger of getting turned in to the cops. No one would report being the victim of a robbery like that. It was too embarrassing.

D!zzy saw everyone come in. When no one started shooting immediately, he knew he'd survive. "I'm from the hood," he remembered later. "This shit is regular, you know what I mean?"

The Nine Trey guys had no idea D!zzy was going to be there, and Tekashi didn't either. They robbed him regardless. And months after the fact, he was still angry about it.

"Once I felt like my life wasn't in danger, I really was upset that when they came in I was looking at the [gun] and he was able to snatch my bag out my hand."

You can see this clearly on the surveillance video—the exact moment where D!zzy gets his bag snatched. Later, he reconstructed his thought process.

"I don't got my bag. I got my ID and shit in it. That's what I'm thinking about. At first, I'm tight. My little shit that I need, I had a flight, no ID. How do I fucking get on my flight now?"

So he talked back, argued some, started pushing. While all this was going on, a man actually walked up to the building and opened the door, blithely unaware that he was about to stumble into the middle of an armed robbery.

Tekashi's wasn't the only camera filming that day. Surveillance cameras in the lobby caught everything as well—D!zzy pushing back, peoples' outfits, the guns. It was all there.

After the robbery, Crippy and Shotti got back in the car with Tekashi and Jorge. They started driving away. There was one problem, though. They were in Midtown. At rush hour. The car got all of twenty feet before they hit a red light. And then—sirens.

"Nah, I ain't going to jail today, Blood," Shotti muttered. Despite his newly high profile, he was still a wanted man. An arrest might bring his fugitive status into the light.

Jorge tried to calm Shotti down. "We're not going to jail. We're fine. You're paranoid. Relax." Jorge knew a thing or two about paranoia. He kept his car wired for sound and video at all times.

"I ain't going to jail," Shotti said again. He needed to get rid of his gun. It was the only way out of this mess. So he threw the gun on Tekashi's lap.

"Yo Bix, get the fuck out of the car."

Tekashi tried to talk sense into Shotti. He was famous. He couldn't walk around Times Square with a loaded gun. Everybody knew what he looked like. He was wearing a hoodie, so his famous rainbow hair could be covered up. But his face tattoos would definitely give him away. Shotti wasn't hearing it.

"Bix, get the fuck out of the car."

There was no way to argue with Shotti when he was like this. He was scary. So, if he told you to take his gun and get out of the car, you took his gun and got out of the car.

Defeated, Tekashi stuck the gun in his hoodie and hopped out. He decided to get on the train to get back to Brooklyn. Then he realized how insane that was, and left the station. How was he going to ride on the subway, carrying a gun? All of a sudden, he saw Crippy, who had also been kicked out of the car, across the street. Crippy knew that even in insane circumstances like this, his job was to keep the star safe.

"Shotti's buggin' back there," he said to Tekashi. "Come on. We're gonna go home."

How? The obvious choice was to hop in a cab. At least that way they'd be around a lot fewer people, and have less of a chance of getting stopped by the police. They tried to get a cab, but failed. It was wet outside, and it was rush hour. Finally, they went back to Tekashi's original plan: the subway. There was one issue, though. The famous rap star still had a gun. Crippy, like any good security guy, knew what he had to do.

"Get chest-to-chest with me," Crippy said. They stood facing each other, hoodie to hoodie. Tekashi passed the gun to Crippy.

"Go buy us a MetroCard and swipe us home. Keep your head down and pull the strings on your hoodie."

Tekashi did as he was told and pulled his hoodie strings tight. They got on the A train. Miraculously, no one recognized the rapper with two of the top 100 songs in the country. They made it all the way to their destination with no problems. From there, it was about a fifteen minute walk to Crippy's place.

Tekashi followed through on the next part of his plan. He sent the footage of the robbery to DJ Akademiks. Akademiks, the same person who had given Tekashi the softball interview about his 2015 case, had grown very friendly with the rapper.

Ak posted the robbery footage, coyly not saying where he got it from.

"Allegedly," he wrote, "this is footage of a 'Rap A Lot' artist being robbed today in New York while headed to an interview w/ thisis50." He added parenthetically, in case viewers were missing the point, "In the video u can hear someone say 'rap a lot.'"

J Prince Jr. jumped in immediately in the comments. "I advise u to have your facts right before u try to tarnish my families name," he wrote. That was of course followed by a threat: "Your too accessible!"

But it was too late. The footage was already shooting around the internet, with Akademiks' Instagram handle running through the middle of the screen. The video showed up on YouTube with titles like "6ix9nine goons allegedly rob rap a lot affiliate." It was a clear-cut victory for Tekashi.

Everyone eventually ended up back at Tekashi's place. They took D!zzy's backpack and threw it in the closet of Tekashi's house. It was an awkward, unintended trophy.

CHAPTER 7

SPINNING OUT OF CONTROL

J ust eleven days after the robbery at This Is 50, Tekashi's branch of Nine Trey would be involved in another robbery which was again committed for the purposes of bragging on social media. But this time, both perpetrator and victim were gang members. The rivalries inside of the always fractious crew were beginning to spin out of control, helped on by Tekashi's stardom.

On April 13, Tekashi wanted to enjoy his newfound celebrity status at a Mets game. He took along a date, an Instagram-famous woman who had leveraged her online fame into gigs tending bar at strip clubs (a position known as a "startender"). Also along for the ride were Jorge, Shotti, Tekashi's brother, and the brother's girlfriend.

Things started off well. Fifteen minutes before the opening pitch, Jorge took a photo of Tekashi and Shotti posing with Mr. Met. Tekashi's on the mascot's left; Shotti's on his right. Mr. Met doesn't seem to notice that both are throwing up Nine Trey hand signs.

Early in the game, Shotti got a disturbing phone call

telling him that Ro Murda had been robbed. We have to leave, he told Tekashi. The situation had to be dealt with.

Danny, his date, Shotti, and Jorge split, leaving only Tekashi's brother and his girlfriend to enjoy the Mets' ultimate 6-5 triumph over the Milwaukee Brewers. The crew headed to a house in Queens. They were going, Shotti said, to get a gun. When they got there, Shotti searched around inside a closet until he found a black backpack. Inside was a long black assault rifle, broken into pieces.

With the gun secured, Shotti moved on to his next priority. He wanted to protect his asset, to keep Tekashi out of trouble. Take Danny and the girl back to Danny's place, he told Jorge. But Tekashi wanted to be right in the thick of the action.

"I want to go with you guys," he insisted.

They headed to the house of a Nine Trey member who had taken part in the This Is 50 robbery. Shotti and Tekashi went inside, while Jorge and Tekashi's date stayed in the car. She had no idea what was going on, but she knew one thing—it was time to get out.

"I want to leave," she kept saying.

Jorge went inside.

"Danny, listen," he said. "The girl wants to leave. What do I do?"

"Don't worry about it," Tekashi said. "We're almost out of here." And a few minutes later, the three of them left.

But that was not the end of the night for the rest of Nine Trey. They discovered who robbed Ro. And they discovered it because the robber told them, and everyone else too. Ro hadn't been the original target. He was *supposed* to be the robber. One Nine Trey member, Nuke, was trying to enlist Ro to rob a second member.

The intended victim had been a successful drug dealer, the

brains behind the gang's heroin-mixed-with-fentanyl scheme. He was flashy, and had aspirations of being in the music business. His brand was "Always Paid," or "AP." The intended victim was friendly with Ro Murda—he even let Ro wear his AP chain on occasion. And when Ro got out of prison, the dealer had been right there to welcome him back with some money.

That night in April, though, Nuke intended to use the friendship to his advantage. He wanted to rob the drug dealer. It was a win-win proposition. Nuke would get some money, and increase his status in the gang. So, he approached Ro Murda that night. He was drunk and riding with Ro in Ro's black Range Rover.

Nuke's proposition was this: Ro should set the dealer up, and rob him. And if Ro wasn't down for that, how about setting up Tekashi or Shotti?

"Give me somebody," he demanded.

The newly freed Ro wanted no part of the deal.

Nuke wasn't pleased. He pulled a gun on Ro and demanded the chain Ro was wearing instead. Ro, seeing he was cornered, went to pull over the car. As soon as he did, he jumped out and ran, leaving so quickly that he abandoned his Rolex watch on the car's center console.

Nuke celebrated his victory by taking a video. The clip starts with footage of the front of the Range Rover.

"This the Range!" someone yelled celebratorily. "This the bad boy right here!" Nuke, wearing a green hoodie with white laces and a green hat, hopped out of the car.

"Ro Murda, what up?" he cried, rubbing Ro's face in the fact that he, Nuke, had taken Ro's car. And not only his car.

"Can I see the wrist? Can I see the fuckin' wrist?" the companion continued. Nuke scratched his head, intentionally exposing his left wrist to the camera. On that wrist was Ro's Rolex.

"Ro Murda, what up?" he repeated.

That kind of behavior couldn't be left unpunished. Shotti already had issues with Nuke, because of Nuke's long-running beef with Shotti's close friend Mel Murda. Shotti, Ro, and a few other guys went in search of Nuke. They found him, still drunk, in front of a barber shop. They tried to get the window of their vehicle down to fire a shot at him. But they didn't lower it fast enough, and succeeded only in shattering the window of the car and destroying the side mirror.

Nuke gloated about the robbery online. When he posted the video on Instagram, he captioned it with a mocking nod to Ro Murda's rap crew, called the Jakkboyzz.

"How da fukk the Jakkboyz getting Jakked out here?" he asked.

Privately, he was bragging to people as well. He DM'd a friend on Instagram that he "booked" Ro—slang for robbing. "Took his truck," Nuke wrote. "Sunstroke Ro. Yesterday," he wrote to another Nine Trey member, using a different word for robbery.

Nuke continued bragging about the incident long after-wards, laughing it up with a friend over a month later about how Ro had run out of his truck like he was Usain Bolt. But he also felt justified. "Helped Ro out so much n [he] went against me," Nuke texted Ms. Tr3yway.

Nuke's spur-of-the-moment robbery had reverberations throughout Nine Trey. News of the incident made it all the way up to the gang's top leader, Frank White, who sent word that Nuke should be kicked out of Nine Trey.

The whole incident was a funhouse mirror reflection of the robbery at This Is 50. It was the exact same dynamic. You rob someone not because you need the proceeds, but to embarrass them, and to advance your own status. You put proof of your guilt on video, because how else will people know you did it? With Tekashi, his audience was the whole world. With Ro and Nuke, it was a handful of Nine Trey members in a few neighborhoods in Brooklyn. But eventually, both robberies would end up in the same federal courtroom.

Just because Nine Trey infighting and the J. Prince beef had both escalated to armed robbery didn't mean that other beefs were cooling down. On the contrary. Tekashi's ongoing issues with Casanova were about to reach a whole new level. In the beginning of March, Tekashi released the song "Billy." It was his response to Casanova's "Set Trippin," the song everyone took as a diss.

In "Set Trippin," Casanova had rapped, "Y'all don't bleed like I bleed."

Tekashi, firing back, had Shotti do an intro on "Billy" where he responded, "We don't bleed. We *make* niggas bleed, Blood." It was easy to miss if you weren't clued in to intra-Blood beef, but it was a big deal. A Nine Trey big homie was issuing Casanova a direct challenge.

Meanwhile, Tekashi was graduating to genuine celebrity status. As a result, he started doing genuine celebrity things, like walking a boxer to the ring in a big fight.

The relationship between rap and boxing has been historically strong. In both, the stars are primarily young men of color. Mike Tyson alone has been a muse for everyone from the Notorious B.I.G. and 2Pac to the famously PG-rated Will Smith, who once wrote a comical song called "I Think I Can Beat Mike Tyson."

So it wasn't a surprise that Adrien Broner wanted a hot rap star by his side when he squared off in a catchweight fight against Jessie Vargas on April 21 at Brooklyn's Barclays Center. And who better than Brooklyn's most controversial rapper?

Tekashi handled the pre-fight publicity in his own inimitable way, orchestrating a multi-step beef with Broner. He even pulled in Shotti to insult the fighter on Instagram: "He gonna get knocked out, Blood," he taunted. "That's why Mayweather don't fuck with you, Blood."

It was all for show, a way to get attention for the big reveal that Tekashi and the fighter would be arriving together, and Tekashi would perform a song for him.

The day of the big fight, Tekashi, Shotti, and a female rapper Shotti had befriended and was promising to sign to his Tr3yway Entertainment label decided to go shopping in downtown Brooklyn, near the arena. They brought Jorge along to drive.

They began the day by getting money from the bank, and then by getting some food. As the crew began to get back in the car, two guys in a beige sedan noticed Tekashi. They pulled up alongside the car, pulled their phones out and started recording. Then one of them decided to show off a little bit.

"Fuck 6ix9ine," he said. "Yo, 6ix9ine, you pussy."

Shotti was sitting in the backseat right behind Tekashi. When he heard the insult, it was almost like a switch flipped. He couldn't just let it go by. He had to retaliate.

"Go ahead," Shotti barked. "Say again what you just said."

"Fuck 6ix9ine," the guy repeated.

Shotti grabbed a gun from his waistband. He opened the door of the guys' car, and pistol-whipped the guy who was recording.

"Say it again, you pussy!" Shotti demanded.

Jorge took off, as the stunned victims started yelling for

Shotti to meet them at a nearby intersection, in hopes of revenge. When Jorge got to the next corner, he ignored the red light and turned right in an attempt to escape any potential problems. But trouble was following from two directions. From behind, the guys Shotti attacked were following them in a car. And in front, a giant garbage truck was blocking their way.

Shotti got angry. He cocked his gun and said, "These niggas think I'm playing?"

And then he showed how he'd earned his nickname. He got out of the car, got down on his knees, and fired two shots at the guys in the car. Amazingly, he didn't hit anyone.

But they were still trapped.

"Move! Move!" the female rapper screamed at the garbage truck. And the truck did. Everyone got back in the car, and they drove back to Tekashi's place.

Later that night, everyone showed up at Barclays for the big fight. Tekashi's crew had only been given fifteen passes, and they'd brought a lot more people than that.

They narrowed it down to about fifteen, including Tekashi, Shotti, Jorge, Ro, and Fuguan "Fubanger" Lovick, a good friend of Ro's who'd recently started hanging around. That crew took an elevator to the arena's lower level, in order to meet up with Broner and his manager. To get there, they had to walk through a hallway. It was long and narrow, with a mural of athletes and musicians on one side and some mirrored glass on the other. They were led by a few people, and behind them were two uniformed NYPD officers.

All of a sudden, at the other end of the hallway, they hear yelling and people coming towards them. A giant crew of Casanova and dozens of his friends came bursting through the door, shouting. It's hard to tell how big their posse was from the video, but it's a ton of people—estimates from those on the scene range from thirty to seventy.

In the video, as the crew approaches, Tekashi falls back and the Nine Trey members around him step forward. Since they're vastly outnumbered, Shotti responds in the same way he had just hours before. Except this time, he's not the one who fires the shot. Shotti tells Fubanger to pull out his gun. Fubanger, panicked, shoots it in the air in a desperate attempt to disperse the crowd. Shotti grabs the gun and hides it in his coat pocket.

The warning shot has its intended effect. Everyone scatters, mostly running back in the direction they'd come from. After a few seconds, a few brave members of Casanova's crew, including the rapper himself, start moving more tentatively back towards Tekashi's crew.

Tekashi, by contrast, ran away. He, Jorge, and Ro hid in a closet for a few minutes. Jorge ended up with Shotti's jacket, which held the gun Fubanger just let off—a fact that Jorge didn't yet realize. The cops started questioning and searching everybody. Luckily, Jorge happened to know the cops who were searching him.

"What are you doing with *those* guys?" one of them asked.

"They're paying me to drive them," Jorge explained, still unaware that he was holding a coat with a gun in the pocket.

The cops went to do a perfunctory search of Jorge. He raised his arms, and the coat swung a little and hit his leg. It was only then he realized what was in the pocket. He somehow managed to keep cool, and left the arena with the weapon.

The rest of the crew attempted to get into the fight, but the cops weren't having it. Shotti, true to form, actually went live on Instagram while talking to the cops in the immediate aftermath of the shooting. One of Tekashi's crew argued that they should be allowed into the arena. "It's over, man," one cop said. It was time to go. So, they left, with the plan of watching the fight from their car parked nearby.

But on the way out, Tekashi couldn't resist taking another shot—a figurative one, this time—at Casanova. Walking out of the arena, he went on Instagram and recorded a video aimed directly at Casanova, where he basically explained exactly what had just happened.

"This how the fuck we mob, man!" he yelled as he exited, arena behind him, surrounded by his crew. "Treyway shit, man! Jakkboyzz shit, man." He made sure to point out his location, just in case the viewer couldn't tell from the video: "We at the fucking Barclays, stupid."

And then came the part aimed at Casanova. He quoted one of Cas's own songs, "Don't Run"—the song that had originally been aimed at Ro. Except this time, Tekashi re-purposed the words, using them to point out that Casanova *had* run, from the gunshot Tekashi's crew had just let off.

"'Fuckboy don't run,'" he quoted. "Where you going?" He repeated Cas' "*Boom boom boom*" gunshot sound ad-lib from "Don't Run"—effectively bragging about the real-life gunshot just minutes before.

"Niggas started running and shit," Tekashi continued, telling the outside world exactly what happened. "His whole squad hit the floor. Everybody hit the floor, Blood." He continued quoting from "Don't Run," just in case the point was missed.

The media response was immediate. TMZ published a story on it the next day, and it got picked up by a number of other outlets from there.

The police initially zeroed in on Shotti as their main

suspect, and he was briefly booked by Essex County, New Jersey police as a person of interest. But by early May, the cops had given up on that theory and were focusing on Fubanger instead.

While bragging about a shooting in its immediate aftermath would eventually have serious repercussions for both Tekashi and the shooter, in the short term it was just more PR. The more controversy he was in, the more people listened to his music and watched his videos. The success built on itself. Song after song hit the Billboard Hot 100. "Gummo" went gold (500,000 sales equivalent units) in January, and platinum (1,000,000 sales equivalent units) in March. "Kooda" went gold in February. Even the album, the last-minute hodgepodge *Day69*, reached number 4 on the Billboard album chart.

Tekashi was well aware he had discovered a formula. Gangs, beefs, and outrageous behavior rocketed him straight to the top, seemingly overnight. No more $2,000 tours, no more flying cross-country to beg Adam22 for an interview. And with Shotti at his side, ready to commit violence at the slightest provocation, there seemed to be no danger of losing street cred anytime soon. There was no need to back down from anyone.

So Tekashi thought nothing of it when he started hanging out with Cuban Doll. Cuban, a young woman from Dallas, had started her career in 2012 as a model and social media personality. Four years on, she'd made the natural progression into music, and begun releasing songs.

In April 2018, she was headed to New York City. Tekashi, ever on the lookout for a pretty girl, hit her up. "You in my city? We better link," he said. Otherwise, he joked, he held so much sway that she wouldn't be able to get past the airport.

Cuban had just seen Tekashi for the first time in a funny

Instagram post. And she knew "Gummo." So, she decided to meet up. She'd be at a club with the rapper Lil Yachty, she told him. He could meet her there.

Tekashi was on his best behavior that night. He was polite. He opened up doors for her, introduced himself to her team. He was, she remembers, like a "sweet puppy." Cuban and her crew went to dinner afterwards, and Tekashi and Shotti came along. That was when Tekashi started demonstrating his newfound street cred. He talked about Shotti's role.

"This how I'm good in the city," he explained. "I can go anywhere I want because of this dude. Nobody gonna touch me. That's why I talk crazy. That's why I do whatever I want, because of him."

"So Shotti official?" she asked.

"Yeah, he official." And then, Tekashi offered Shotti's protective services to Cuban. "You coming to the city, he's gonna make sure you're straight."

The next day, Tekashi and Cuban linked up again and went to the studio. They stayed in touch and, on May 5, after a long Instagram Live spat with Trippie Redd, Tekashi got on Live with Cuban for a debrief. It was a lighthearted, friendly conversation where Cuban half-seriously interviewed Tekashi about his history with Trippie.

But someone else noticed that Tekashi and Cuban were getting along. The rapper Tadoe was Chicago rapper Chief Keef's cousin and, though a tight-lipped Cuban now denies it, Tadoe was reportedly dating her at the time.

Tekashi got Tadoe's phone number from a rapper Shotti was working with. The rapper only gave it up with the promise that Tekashi wouldn't record the call. It was a promise he broke. Tekashi recorded the call and put it on the internet. The video shows a call that quickly developed into a yelling match.

"Lose this number!" Tadoe yelled. "I kill people."

"You do not kill nobody, nigga," Tekashi responded.

Tekashi's Instagram caption poked fun at Tadoe's cousin's most famous song, "I Don't Like": "Niggas like this I don't like," he wrote. "@cubandasavage keep your head up I got love for you."

The exchange became a media sensation. But there were rumors of a darker undertone, rumors that Tadoe beat up Cuban as a result of her friendship with Tekashi. The next day, Cuban appeared to confirm those rumors. She went on IG Live again, this time from a hospital. She had bruises on her face, covered up with a big yellow hoodie. She complained, using no names, about what happened.

"This nigga talk to all the bitches, but be mad when I talk to anybody," she explained. For the initiated, it was obvious what she was implying. "Look where I'm at," she continued, moving the camera around to make it clear. "The hospital. My hip is broke."

A few days later, Cuban headed out to Hawaii with Tekashi and a few other people. Footage made its way around the internet of them playfully celebrating his birthday. But that was far from the end of the story.

Tadoe leaned into his newfound infamy, recruiting Trippie Redd and Chief Keef for a song inspired by the experience called "I Kill People." Tekashi ratcheted up the tension too, recording a video (with a very uncomfortable-looking Cuban Doll in the background) where he unloaded on a ton of Chicago rappers, not just Tadoe.

"Fuck Chief Keef, fuck Lil Reese, fuck all them niggas," he said.

It was a big statement. Keef was the rapper who first popularized Chicago's drill music movement—a movement so tied to actual real-world street violence that the genre was named after a slang word for murder. Tekashi was no longer beefing with a sole Chicago rapper. He was now taking on the whole city.

His revenge against Chicago didn't end at a video. He knew that Keef was coming to New York City to perform at a launch party on June 1 for an issue of the magazine *High Snobiety*. And he knew what to do.

Tekashi was going to be in California, so he couldn't do it himself. But he knew someone who could. He called up Kooda. Tekashi offered his friend $20,000 to shoot at Keef when he was in New York. Kooda agreed.

At midnight, as June 1 turned into June 2, Kooda and some friends left an apartment on Christopher Avenue in Brownsville. They hopped in a van and slowly moved to Times Square. Keef was staying in the area's W Hotel. By 4 AM, Kooda was in place. And, incredibly, he was recognized. Not by an enemy, but by a fan. Someone stopped him and asked if they could take a picture together, and Kooda obliged.

At 4:17, Kooda got on the phone with Tekashi.

"I got eyes on him," Kooda said. Keef was at a nearby papaya-and-hot-dog spot.

"All right."

At 4:36, Kooda called again.

And then, five minutes later, when Keef was standing in front of the hotel, the shot came from someone in Kooda's crew. It missed Keef, as intended, and hit the outside of the building.

Kooda and the crew hopped back in the van. It headed down the FDR, over the Williamsburg Bridge, and back toward Brownsville. Kooda called Tekashi from the van at 5:06. They arrived back at the apartment building at 5:28.

The next day, the news exploded with stories about the shooting. TMZ was on it early. They mentioned the beef between Chief Keef and Tekashi, but pointed out that Tekashi was in L.A. at the time of the shooting. They weren't the only ones. Every single article about the shooting mentioned the beef between Keef and Tekashi—surely as Tekashi intended. The next morning, Tekashi poured fuel on the fire. He all but admitted to being behind the shooting in a mocking interview with TMZ.

"We don't play with guns," he smirked. "It's all rainbows and peace." He couldn't resist smiling. "I'm a big fan of Chief Keef," he continued, tongue firmly in cheek. "How much you think a feature costs from Chief Keef?"

Three days later, he revisited the theme: "I guess Chief Keef—you know, he's a gangsta rapper. He promotes violence. I guess he has a lot of beef in these streets. I don't know who he beefing with that wants to hurt him, but, it's definitely not me. I'm actually a fan."

Meanwhile, behind the scenes, Kooda was ready to get paid. He met up with Tekashi and Shotti on the evening of June 3. Tekashi had well over $20,000 in cash on him, enough to pay Kooda in full. But Shotti stepped in and pulled a power move. Kooda's crew only fired one shot, and in the air at that. He hadn't earned the full amount. Shotti counted out $10,000.

"That's enough," he said. "Take that."

In the aftermath of the shooting, Tekashi continued his trolling of Keef. He went to Chicago, where he filmed himself giving out food to people on the street because "these other Chicago rappers don't give back." He also recorded himself going to Keef's neighborhood, the notoriously rough area known as "O Block."

"I should call this shit No Block," he trolled. "It's ten

o'clock. Where the fuck are y'all niggas at?" Tekashi posted a photo of himself standing outside a gate in O Block, throwing up a Nine Trey sign. "Hi CHICAGO. I'm here on O Block but it has a gate," he wrote, adding a broken heart emoji. "How do I get in? There's a police in the booth."

Keef conducted his own public, but unsuccessful, search for Tekashi in his neighborhood, documenting it on social media. But his efforts were no match for Tekashi's finely-honed sense of trolling.

Tekashi contacted Aareon "Slim Danger" Clark, the mother of one of Keef's children, and flew her out to New York City for a (filmed) shopping spree at the Gucci store, getting her $75,000 worth of product.

It was money well spent. Clark appeared in a video on Tekashi's Instagram account, wearing his jewelry. In case anyone missed the point, she introduced herself to Tekashi's millions of followers.

"What's up? This Slim Danger. This Chief Keef's baby momma. I'm out here in New York. And guess what? That nigga don't do shit for his fuckin' kid."

CHAPTER 8

THE DAM SPRINGS A LEAK

One day right around the time of the Keef shooting, Shotti called Harv and suggested a meetup at the house that Nine Trey used as a meeting spot. Tensions between Harv and Shotti were running high. Harv drove up in his white Range Rover, bumper dragging on the ground. Tekashi, Ro, Crippy, and some other folks were there. But Shotti was nowhere to be found.

"Go behind the gate," Ro told Tekashi. Rule number one was to keep the meal ticket out of harm's way. They all knew Harv didn't show up to have a friendly chat.

Harv got out of the Range. He was wearing red Lees and holding a black pistol. Tekashi went back inside.

"Yo, yo, where the gun at?" Crippy asked. He was frantically looking for weapons for himself and the crew.

When Tekashi and Crippy went back outside, the whole crew debated: Should they go and shoot Harv? They decided against it. It was a fortuitous choice. Just a minute later, the cops showed up, and everyone scattered. Harv dropped his gun on the ground and got away. But the cops picked up someone else—a member of the crew who had the bad luck to be wearing jeans that were the same color as Harv's.

Harv's violent plans didn't work out that day. The next time, he'd be better prepared.

This was right at the time Jorge dropped out of sight. Tekashi didn't immediately notice, due to a European tour that kept him out of the country for a good chunk of June and July. What no one knew was that the driver had been picked up by ICE agents at the end of May. But they hadn't seemed interested in his immigration status, except, perhaps, as a means to an end.

Jorge's arrest was a dramatic scene. He'd been out driving for Tekashi until 5 AM one morning. Finally relieved of duty, he made the five-minute drive from Tekashi's house to his. He miraculously found parking right in front. *It must be my lucky day*, he thought.

He went to his room and went to sleep. Only a few minutes later, ICE agents knocked on the ground floor of the building. The floor was occupied by the landlord, who promptly let them in. The agents went upstairs and knocked on Jorge's door. His wife opened up.

The agents went back to Jorge, dressed only in his boxers. He quickly threw some clothes on and went with them to get processed in Manhattan. The authorities offered him a deal: help them with the investigation into Nine Trey, and they'd let him out. And maybe, just maybe, his cooperation would mean that at the end of everything, he'd be able to walk free *and* remain in the country.

The federal investigation into Nine Trey was at that point just beginning to gain steam. Their first real break was when a drug dealer for the gang, Kristian Cruz, was caught with fentanyl, heroin, and guns. Facing the prospect of a long prison sentence, he began to cooperate. In May 2018, he mentioned to the feds that all the drug dealing he'd been doing was under the auspices of Nine Trey. They found that very interesting. They were in the early stages of looking into a case against the gang, and Cruz's information could be a big help. Ultimately, he would become a confidential informant.

Jorge had no choice but to do the same. So, on July 2, Jorge Rivera's life as a confidential informant began. He had a special program installed on his phone so that it was recording all the time. His truck already contained two cameras with audio and video, and the government gained access to those recordings as well. He got a handler.

Meanwhile, Tekashi's disorganization was beginning to affect Jorge's pocketbook. He was not getting paid regularly, and was owed tons of money—about $36,000, by his estimate. But he couldn't quit. After all, working for Tekashi was the only thing keeping him *out* of prison and *in* the United States. So, after a long day of driving Tekashi around, Jorge would work a second shift in order to have money to live. It was crushing work for months on end, with little sleep and less time to spend with his young son. He had Shotti breathing down his neck on one side, the government on the other, and an estranged wife and son to support. Things got bad enough that he actually attempted to kill himself by driving into a wall, reasoning that the life insurance money would help his family. Luckily, he survived.

During the time Jorge was locked up by ICE, Tekashi pulled one of the biggest stunts of his career. Summer Jam is the annual concert put on by the New York City radio station Hot 97. It has been going on for decades, and has played host to countless historic hip-hop moments from artists like Jay-Z, the Notorious B.I.G., and Kanye West. The show features a mix of iconic veteran rappers and new hot ones. In the summer of 2018, no one in New York was hotter than Tekashi.

But the station wasn't going anywhere near him. One DJ who was an early supporter tried to raise the idea early on and had been shut down. Plus, when the station bigwigs met with stadium personnel and the state police to plan the show, they explicitly said no Tekashi.

Tekashi did not take this slight lying down. He insulted the station during a chat with Akademiks. And then he let this drop:

You know I'm coming out on Summer Jam regardless, right?

The plan was hatched. Tekashi would pull up to the venue in disguise (which meant covering up his face tattoos with makeup). Then, he and his crew would beg, borrow, or steal passes to get inside. When they arrived, they reached out to the DJ they were friendly with, who turned them down flat.

He didn't end up getting in, but Tekashi still managed to be the star of Summer Jam by capturing every headline with his stunt. But even while staging a prank, he was still attracting violence. While heading towards the entrance, he and his crew came across another rapper, a Brooklyn Crip with whom he'd been trading social media barbs for months.

"Yo 6ix, what's crackin'?" the rapper yelled. Tekashi had his whole posse chase after the rapper. That event was captured on tape. A fight was averted, because the whole thing happened just steps from cops and venue security. The run-in just served to get Tekashi more headlines, more videos, more clicks, and more attention.

That summer, the pressure of being in public all the time was getting to Tekashi in new ways. He brought a new DJ on his European tour, a woman named Blue Diamond whom he'd met in early 2018 at a club in Connecticut. Once they were on the road, she noticed something unusual: Tekashi was exercising. *A lot.*

"He was trying to lose weight, so most of the time he spent in the gym and resting," she says. "I don't know who told him he was fat, [but] he was very concerned about losing weight."

It might not have been any particular person. Tekashi was frequently shirtless, both onstage and off. It was the perfect way to show off his ever-increasing number of tattoos. But any exposure like that invites mockery. Combine that with sudden access to money and the attendant gluttony it can inspire, and the result was a star who by the summer was extremely stressed about his weight. And his response to the worry was obsessive.

"On tour, he would eat salads all day and drink water," Blue Diamond remembers. "His snacks were fruits and lime and water, that's it. He wouldn't really eat much. He would eat a salad for breakfast and then snack on fruits throughout the day, and be in the gym. He was on a very, very strict diet and he was determined to lose that weight." It worked. He lost the weight and "got really skinny," she remembers.

Something else was on Tekashi's mind that summer, too. Some time earlier, he had befriended the controversial Florida rapper XXXTentacion, real name Jahseh Onfroy. The connection came through X's manager Solomon Sobande, who was college buddies with Tekashi's former manager Chris.

X made music as intense and passionate and volatile as his personality. Despite the deep links between his camp and Tekashi's (Sobande was at the original SoHo coffeeshop meeting between Chris and Tekashi), it wasn't exactly smooth for X and Tekashi in the beginning.

"At first, Jah didn't like Danny because some stupid rumor was going around," Sobande says. "So, I was a little reluctant for them to meet. Also, I knew Jah. He was very volatile. So I wanted to kind of be very strategic on how they met."

Eventually, the two rappers connected and grew close, mostly talking over FaceTime. X, despite being the younger of the two, acted as a mentor. His advice to Tekashi was to stay out of trouble, and to stay independent. XXXTentacion and Tekashi had similar, controversy-dogged career arcs. X, like Tekashi, had pulled off a number of outrageous publicity stunts. And for most of X's career, he'd been dogged by reports alleging he abused women.

So, when XXXTentacion was murdered on June 18, 2018, in the middle of Tekashi's European tour, Tekashi was shaken. He started looking over his shoulder all the time, Blue Diamond remembers, because "he thought somebody might come for him, too." He insisted both publicly and privately that he would stop trolling.

Tekashi's paranoia was understandable. Just two days prior to his murder, X sent Tekashi a DM reading, "BE SAFE, OKAY? NEVER LET YOUR GUARD DOWN."

In the immediate aftermath of the murder, Tekashi took to social media and recorded a short video where he seemed to be working out his response in real time, in front of the camera.

"Sometimes I just feel like I do too much trolling," he said, hand on his chin. "Sometimes I feel like I just do too much. And tomorrow's not promised, you know what I mean? And I feel like someone might get the wrong image of me. You could be here today and be gone tomorrow."

"X spread nothing but positivity," he went on. "He always called me on the phone: 'Danny, are you okay?'" X had encouraged him to leave beefing behind, Tekashi explained. So how could someone like that, someone so committed to positivity, be murdered? Tekashi was aware that he wasn't exactly spreading love and light himself. "There's probably like a hundred million thousand people out there trying to kill me," he said.

But his resolve to stop trolling didn't last long. A week and a half after X's murder, Tekashi enlisted Blue Diamond for a skit poking fun at the Chicago rapper Juice WRLD, who had led a chant of "Fuck 6ix9ine!" at a recent concert.

The change of heart didn't come as a surprise to Blue Diamond. She'd noticed from being around him that Tekashi had one primary concern: the need to stay on top. And he knew exactly how to do it.

"He didn't want to fall off," she remembers. "He came up from nothing and he just got all this money so fast, and he was really scared to fall off. So his everyday thought was, 'How can I go viral?' That's all he would think about all day.'"

Enlisting Blue Diamond for a skit mocking Juice WRLD's emo music got some attention. But the thing about being on top by going viral is that the stakes need to constantly be raised. There's no time to take off, to mourn the murder of a friend, or to think about your own safety. And when you add that dynamic to the high-pressure world of hip-hop, plus a street gang that is violently splintering, things can begin to spiral out of control really quickly. And they did.

During that same European tour, Tekashi was putting together a song called "Fefe." He wanted a special guest on it. He sent the song to Nicki Minaj, and they hopped on the phone to talk about it. Five minutes after the conversation, she sent him a voice memo with a large chunk of what would become her verse.

In July, once the song was complete, Tekashi went out to

Los Angeles with Jorge to film the video. While they were there, the Nine Trey infighting exploded.

Shotti didn't make the trip but he and Tekashi, as always, were in near-constant contact. So, Shotti's calling on July 16 didn't seem out of the ordinary, at least at first. But Shotti was angry. A Nine Trey member from a rival faction was livestreaming from Smurf Village, Harv's territory. There was a cookout happening, and he was planning to shoot a music video. That was unacceptable. A message needed to be sent to this member, and to Harv. Tekashi had been around the gang long enough that he too was outraged at what was going on.

"How is he doing Instagram Live and no one is doing anything about it?" he asked.

Shotti reassured Tekashi: he would "make it hot"—have someone shoot at the rival. "I got Crippy heading over there right now," he said.

Tekashi, knowing that his whole career depended on Shotti's street cred, agreed. He hopped on the phone with Crippy. Crippy was waiting for "equipment," he euphemistically explained.

Jorge panicked. As a government informant, it would look awful for him to know about a potential shooting and not do anything. So, he managed to sneak a quick call to his handler to inform him about the impending shooting. Because of his actions, the violence ended up being minimal compared to what might have happened.

There was one injury, though. A woman got shot in the foot. The shooting sent her to physical therapy for months, and it also, she says, cost her the chance to attend the police academy.

Causing this mayhem didn't seem to take a toll on Tekashi. He filmed the video without a problem, even showing up on set early. "Fefe" marked a major turning point in Tekashi's career. He had done songs with some big artists, but Nicki Minaj was on a different level. She was a superstar. Working with her benefitted both of them: Tekashi got some legitimacy by association, and exposure to a different, more mainstream audience. And Nicki got the appearance of being connected with someone young, controversial, and above all, current.

After the filming, Tekashi and Jorge came back to New York. The release date was set for July 22. The song was finished. All that remained was to complete editing the video. But even with the deadline looming, Tekashi was never one to turn down a quick payday. The evening before the deadline, he was offered around $40,000 to appear at a party for a pro football player. Jorge prepared to drive him. But on the way, Jorge noticed one of the cars was being loaded up with guns. Jorge called his handler and told him the deal. As a result, the event was shut down.

Instead, Jorge drove Tekashi to a strip club where they met up with some members of the gang. At the end of most nights, everyone would pile into Jorge's Chevy Tahoe, and they would all head back to Tekashi's place. But this night, everyone went their separate ways. Jorge and Tekashi headed home alone, arriving at around three in the morning.

Jorge stuck around, aware that he might be on call at any time. Sara Molina and Saraiyah were there. Tekashi, as usual, took off his jewelry and the nightly ritual began. Jorge wrapped it in a paper towel, and placed it in a diaper bag that had been repurposed as a place to store the expensive pieces—about $365,000 worth, all told.

Tekashi sat down to finish editing the video. Even with this high-budget production involving one of the most famous rappers in the world, he was determined to remain hands-on in his image-making. But there was just one problem. He'd learned all about editing from his friend Drew, but he'd never learned how to do titles. The simplest thing, but they'd never gotten around to talking about it. And now the clock was ticking—it was just hours until the video was due.

Tekashi called Drew. No answer. So the only thing left to do was to go to his house. He turned to Jorge.

"Before you leave, this has to get done. This is the last stop, I promise."

"All right, fine," Jorge responded. It was already four AM, still dark, and raining to boot. "I'm going to get the car ready."

There was a big issue. Because of rising Nine Trey tensions, in particular a fear of Harv, Drew had recently moved. Tekashi knew the neighborhood for sure: Park Slope, Brooklyn. He didn't know the exact address, though. But at this point, he was desperate. So his plan was to have Jorge drive to the general area, calling Drew along the way.

Tekashi grabbed his laptop and hard drive and threw them in a bookbag. They were driving down Atlantic Avenue, approaching a major intersection at Bedford. They went through it, drove down a block, and turned around.

Jorge had driven through there a million times, and knew all the little tricks. At that corner, there was a sewer. A tiny bit of rain is all it takes to fill up the road with a ton of water. So, in order to avoid hydroplaning, Jorge liked to take that intersection nice and slow. Just after they slowed down, and before reaching the intersection, the car got hit from behind. Jorge stopped. He wasn't worried at first. It was late, and it was probably just a drunk guy coming back from the strip club, like they had been not long before.

"Stay here," Jorge told Tekashi in Spanish. "Don't get out. I'm going to let him leave." It was driver etiquette 101: handle the situation quickly and quietly, and never expose the client to any risk. Jorge was perfectly prepared to let the whole thing go. He had been hit from behind, so it wasn't his fault. And he knew that the big metal bar on his bumper almost certainly meant the car was undamaged. He got out of the car while Tekashi stayed inside, still frantically calling Drew.

Jorge walked toward the car that hit him, a Nissan Altima. In it, though Jorge didn't realize it at the time, was Harv, along with a friend, Sha. It was a rental that Harv was borrowing from a lifelong friend, Tiesha. They'd been close for twenty-five years, and Harv was her son's godfather. So, Tiesha hadn't objected when Harv approached her the day before to ask about borrowing the car.

Jorge walked up to the driver's side door. Harv, who was driving, opened his window, and Jorge noticed that there was another person inside. He didn't recognize Harv, though. Harv had been on the outs with Tekashi since before Jorge started driving.

"Are you alright?" Jorge asked. But the answer was strange. Instead of answering directly, or asking about insurance, or apologizing, Harv had one thing on his mind.

"How's my car?" he asked repeatedly.

"Forget about your car," Jorge responded. "Are *you* alright?"

They went back and forth like this for a little while. Then Sha got out. *Okay,* thought Jorge. *He's probably going to look at the damage to the front of the car. That's fine.*

But Sha kept going. *Oh no,* Jorge thought. *He's headed towards Danny. This is trouble.*

Then Harv got out of the car and, Jorge remembers, pointed a gun at his head. Harv forced Jorge back to the Tahoe, near where Danny was sitting.

Shit, Jorge thought. *It's a robbery. This might be the end.*

Meanwhile, back in the car, Tekashi was getting nervous. Then he saw Sha, wearing a black hoodie, running up to his door, gun out. Tekashi froze, not attempting to lock the door until it was too late.

Damn, they caught me slipping, he thought.

All his tough talk and invitations to "test my gangsta" had finally backfired. He was in trouble, and Shotti wasn't around to help him out.

Sha pulled open the door. "Run it. Give me everything, nigga."

"Chill, chill," Tekashi replied, trying to calm Sha down and at least buy himself some time. He recognized Sha as Harv's friend.

Sha ordered Tekashi out of his car and into the Altima. Harv, in a red hoodie, showed up then, wondering about Shotti.

"Where your man at?" he asked Tekashi. And then on to more pressing things: "Where your money at?"

"I'll give you everything. I promise you, Harv," Tekashi responded.

Harv was not mollified. He had one goal for Tekashi.

"Get in the car," he said. "We gonna shoot you."

"Get the fuck in," Sha insisted.

Tekashi, desperate, started pleading with Harv. Hadn't he put money in Harv's pocket? Wasn't this really about Shotti and not him? "I *wanted* to talk to you," Tekashi insisted. "I tried to call you, bro."

"So, why I ain't got your number?" Harv asked angrily in response.

"They told me you changed your number," Tekashi countered. "I put that on my daughter's life."

"You buggin', son. Why you do *me* like that, bro?" Harv

asked. To him, almost everything had been a constant insult. He had protected Tekashi—gotten in brawls, fought people. And for his trouble he'd been pushed out by Mel, stranded in Texas by Tekashi, and now relegated to a rival Nine Trey lineup that was warring with Tekashi and Shotti. He was owed something—money, respect, something. Tekashi, meanwhile, was still trying to gain Harv's sympathy.

"I'm scared, bro," he said. "Everyone is saying extortion this, extortion that."

Sha came back, insisting that Tekashi get in the Altima. "We gonna talk to him," Harv reassured Jorge. Harv climbed back in and grabbed Tekashi's bookbag with the laptop and the hard drive. "We just wanna talk to him. That's it, man," he told Jorge.

The Altima went off with Harv driving, Sha in the passenger seat, and their prisoner in the back. Jorge started following them. He wanted to get as much information as he could—the license plate, where they were going—so he could tell the cops. The Altima pulled in front of Jorge and moved to the left lane, signaling a turn onto Bedford. While it was stopped at the light, a busker, coffee cup in hand, strolled up, with no idea that one of the biggest stars in America was in the backseat, the victim of a kidnapping.

Harv turned left on Bedford and sped down the street, taking a right at the next corner. Jorge followed behind, speeding frantically and running red lights to keep up. Meanwhile, he called Onstar to report what happened. After a few more turns, he finally caught up to the Altima, which was parked on a lonely side street. Harv noticed that Jorge was there. He jumped out of the Altima and ran towards Jorge, gun drawn. Jorge backed up, turned, and sped away. He headed toward the only place he could think of: a Nine Trey member's nearby apartment. There were always people there, no matter the time. They'd know what to do.

Meanwhile, Harv got back in the Altima and they started driving again. A few minutes later, they stopped and Harv and Sha got out to talk privately. When they got back in, Tekashi started begging.

"Bro, I'm scared," he told Harv. "I got a three-year-old daughter at home."

They continued driving for a little while, and then stopped again. This time, Harv had a plan. Sha pulled Tekashi out of the car while Harv pulled his phone out to capture everything. Sha threw Tekashi to the ground and pinned his head down. He started hitting Tekashi in the back of the head.

Harv, meanwhile, wanted to make sure Tekashi said something on tape. He was livid that this rainbow-haired pretender had ripped him off, stolen his livelihood. And on top of that, he was running around claiming he was Nine Trey. Harv knew how to deal with that, how to prove to everyone that Tekashi 6ix9ine was a phony. It was the exact same dynamic as Nuke robbing Ro, or Tekashi robbing Rap-A-Lot. The robbery was a bonus. Public embarrassment was the goal.

"Say you not Billy," Harv demanded.

"I'm not Billy," Tekashi responded. It was embarrassing, but what choice did he have?

"Say you not Billy," Harv said again.

Tekashi again gave in. The cycle repeated one more time.

Goal accomplished, Sha grabbed Tekashi and ordered, "Get back in the fucking car."

Sha had a dark, murderous vision of how to end the kidnapping. "We should do this nigga right here," he told Harv.

"You're right," said Harv. "Ain't nobody gonna know." They could burn the car afterwards, Harv suggested.

But then Harv got another idea. "What do you have for me?" he asked Tekashi. If they were going to go through the trouble of robbing a rap star, they should at least get paid for it.

"Yo, don't kill me," Tekashi said. "I could stay with you until the bank opens. I'll give you a hundred grand."

There was only one issue: it was a Sunday. Banks would be closed all day.

"What you got right now?" Harv asked.

"All I got is my jewelry," Tekashi said.

They came to an agreement. If Tekashi gave them his jewelry, they would let him go. Tekashi called Sara Molina as they drove toward his house. She was just about to get in the shower.

"Sara, where's the baby?" he asked.

"What do you mean? She's sleeping. You were just here."

"Don't say nothing. Just do everything I tell you to do. You need to bring down all the jewelry," he said.

"For what?"

"Stop asking questions. Just do everything I tell you to do."

Sara, numbed by years of Tekashi's beatings, cheating, and misbehavior, didn't suspect foul play. In a towel, she grabbed the jewelry and headed downstairs.

She called back: "Where are you?"

"I'm pulling up right now."

A car pulled up that wasn't Jorge's, which puzzled Sara. Sha got out of the car and went toward the house. Sara was hesitant to hand over all of Tekashi's jewelry to someone she didn't recognize, so she paused for a second.

The Altima window rolled down just enough for Tekashi

to yell to Sara that yes, she should give over the bag. Sha grabbed it and ran back to the car, and it screeched away, headed toward Smurf Village. Sara, confused and a little worried, started calling around. Tekashi wasn't picking up. Jorge wasn't picking up. Eventually, she got in touch with Tekashi's brother, who came to the house.

She briefly reached Tekashi on FaceTime. She could see that he was in a car. His eye was bloody, and he said that the other people in the car wanted to kill him. She realized then that he really was in trouble.

After a few minutes, Harv and Sha stopped the car just behind Smurf Village.

"Get out the car," Harv demanded.

Tekashi was wary. If he got out, he worried, they'd just shoot him in the back.

"I'm not gonna shoot you," Harv responded. "Yo Bix, get the fuck out the car."

"If you *don't* get out the car, I'm gonna shoot you," Sha added.

Tekashi got out of the car slowly, making sure to keep his eyes on his kidnappers. When he got one foot out of the car, Harv said menacingly, "Come here and let me tell you something real quick."

No chance of that. Tekashi took off, running. He made the first left he could make, ran down the street, and then made another left. Then he came to an Uber sitting at a stop sign, and decided to take a chance. Anything was better than being left out on the street, on foot, with two angry kidnappers nearby. He jumped in the backseat of the car.

"What the fuck, man? Get out of my car!" The driver was, reasonably, surprised by his new passenger.

"Shut the fuck up," said a frantic Tekashi. "If you don't shut up, I'm gonna die. They're gonna kill me."

"Who's gonna kill you?"

Tekashi was reluctant to say. Even after all Harv had done, there were still rules. *You didn't tell on gang. You didn't snitch.*

"You need to relax. Just drive."

The car made a few turns and then ended up exactly where Tekashi had been running from. Right behind the Altima.

"That's the car, right there," he told the driver. "Pull right behind it. Do not turn your blinkers on." Whichever way Harv was going, Tekashi wanted his new friend to go the other direction. Harv went straight, so Tekashi's car went right. The driver, at this point resigned to his fate, agreed to drop Tekashi off at the nearby 79th police precinct.

Officer Moses Lebron was processing an arrest when he saw Tekashi stumble in the door. His swollen face had blood, cuts, and bruises all over it. He seemed dazed.

"I need help" was all he could manage.

Lebron didn't know who Tekashi was, so he treated him like any other person who staggers in, injured, to a police station at five AM. He gave the victim some water, had him sit down, and called an ambulance.

Lebron's partner asked some questions. Tekashi gave the rough outlines of what happened. He'd been kidnapped and beaten up. He'd been taken to his house and robbed.

While they were waiting for the ambulance, Sara FaceTimed.

"Danny, where are you?" she asked. He was fine, he said. He was with the police. Did she know where Jorge was? Tekashi asked again and again.

While on his way to the Nine Trey hangout, Jorge saw a police officer. He pulled up to the cop.

"They just kidnapped 6ix9ine. Tekashi 6ix9ine. They just kidnapped him from my car."

Even for the cop, a veteran officer with more than twenty-five years on the job, this was unusual. This black SUV comes speeding down the street at 4:30 in the morning and pulls up to him. Then the driver starts yelling about a kidnapping.

The officer didn't recognize the name, and he wanted to make sure he had everything straight. It sounded crazy.

"Hold on a sec. Did *what*?"

"Tekashi 6ix9ine? The rapper? The singer?"

"Uh-huh," he responded.

"Yeah, they just kidnap him." Jorge was excited, frantic. Normally his English was great, but he started to lose it a little bit. "We get pulled over, right, by two guys with guns, and they just take him out from the car."

"Take him?" The officer wanted to be sure he had it right.

"Yes."

"Where'd this happen?"

"Yeah, right here. Around the corner." Jorge explained that he wasn't able to get the license plate, despite his best efforts. And then he explained how he'd ended up barrelling toward this cop in the first place.

"The guy come over and tried to shoot me, so I back it up and I came this way."

"Okay, show me where it happened," the cop said. "Turn around. Be careful."

Jorge was anything but. He turned around and sped the wrong way down a one-way street. He and the officer made it back to where Jorge had last seen the Altima. It was gone.

Jorge, frantic and frightened, told the cop a little more about what had happened. Then he said he wanted to go to Tekashi's mom's place. A little while after they arrived, the cop got a call saying that Tekashi just entered the precinct. He headed over.

By the time he got there, just a few minutes later, the ambulance arrived and EMTs were treating Tekashi. Officer Lebron climbed in the ambulance with Tekashi, and they headed to Kings County Hospital.

On the ride over, Tekashi kept saying "I thought I was going to die" and "I thought I was never going to see my daughter again."

They arrived at the Trauma Center ER at 5:40 AM. Tekashi was still groggy, and talking slow. Shotti barrelled in. He wanted no part of this hospital. It was too public.

"These are just a bunch of fuckin' fans in here," he muttered. He demanded that Tekashi be discharged. Shotti wanted to get his star someplace quieter, and someplace not in Brooklyn. It was okay by the doctors—they couldn't force Tekashi to stay. So, Tekashi threw a sheet over his head and walked out.

They went about thirty miles away to a hospital in Nassau County. The Long Island location was far from prying fans. It was there that Tekashi and Shotti tried to regain control of the narrative. Shotti took a picture of Tekashi in the hospital bed, and texted it from Tekashi's phone to a reporter at TMZ. At 10:41 AM Eastern, the photo was up, attached to a story headlined, 'TEKASHI69 PISTOL WHIPPED, KIDNAPPED, ROBBED AND HOSPITALIZED.'

The story had most of what had actually happened—the kidnapping, the beating, the robbery. It also contained the souped-up, exaggerated version of Tekashi's escape that he would soon repeat in interviews. Most importantly, it didn't talk at all about *who* had done the kidnapping.

At the new hospital, the doctor gave Tekashi a quick physical exam and a CAT scan. The scan showed a bit of swelling on his forehead and cheek, but nothing broken. Tekashi just got some Tylenol for his headache.

In the immediate aftermath, everyone decided to play it safe. Jorge took the rest of Tekashi's family, and his own family, to a house in upstate New York, where they stayed for the next four days. Tekashi went to New Jersey, to stay with one of Shotti's friends for a few hours. But by that night, he was back at home, Jorge again by his side.

He sat down with Shotti, Mel, and Crippy to talk about what happened and plan their revenge. Shotti had his assault rifle ready to go. He and Mel were determined to go out and "spin the block"—to look for Harv and respond violently if they found him. Tekashi told Shotti that he'd give $50,000 to anyone who "got" Harv.

Meanwhile, Harv was laughing it up. He was texting a friend, trading memes about the kidnapping he'd just conducted. They featured the then-popular photo of a young, attitudinal Cardi B, juxtaposed with the picture Shotti had taken of Tekashi in the hospital.

"My momma said she think Treyway set you up," read one caption. "Momma said Treyway wanna talk to you outside," said another, which added to the two images a third photo of dozens of people wearing red bandanas and throwing up gang signs. "Big homie said you not treyway," read a third.

While Harv was yukking it up, Shotti was looking for Harv. And he had a suspicion his target could be found at Maddy. Two days after the kidnapping, Shotti drove there a little before 9:30 PM and waited outside. Ms. Tr3yway saw his car through her surveillance camera. She texted Harv, so he would know to stay away.

The day after the kidnapping, Pvnch had an idea. As a media-savvy guy, he knew that Tekashi had to set his own narrative to counter the idea that he'd been caught slipping. He needed to tell the story his way. And the best way to do that would be to have Pvnch interview him. It would show that Tekashi was unbowed and unbroken.

Everyone met up at Tekashi's house to strategize. They debated filming there. Pvnch and his cameraman tried out different angles and checked the lighting while Shotti's sons hung around, bored, with their dad watching them; and Tekashi, wearing a red cap and a white t-shirt, walked around with his phone attached to his right hand. "Fefe" had just come out, and he was obsessed with how it was doing on the charts.

"Billboard updates every Tuesday at 3 PM," he told Pvnch. It was Monday, so they'd have to wait until tomorrow to find out the results. Tekashi continued his analysis.

"I released Sunday," he said. "It only has two days." He meant that the song would have just a few days of sales and streams to count towards the Billboard Hot 100, as opposed to a full week.

"I release all my shit on Sunday, so it goes onto the *next* Tuesday, not this Tuesday," he explained. He drilled down further—the song was now number 2 on Apple Music, and he was delighted.

"It passed Drake's whole shit," he said, smiling. He predicted that despite only being out for two days, "Fefe" would make it onto the next Billboard chart.

"It's gonna hit," Pvnch agreed. "But it's gonna *peak* next week."

"I think it's gonna go top 10," Tekashi predicted.

"I think it's gonna go top 7," Pvnch countered. "As long as Obama don't go, 'Keke...'" he joked, imagining the former President singing the beginning of Drake's then-popular "In My Feelings."

They were both right. "Fefe" entered the charts the week of July 28 at number 4, and moved up to number 3 the following week. It was Tekashi's highest-charting single ever up to that point.

Ultimately, everyone decided it would be best to film the interview on Locust Street, in front of Tekashi's childhood home. To outsiders, it would look like a normal Brooklyn street background. But to insiders—and more importantly, to Harv—it would be a signal that Tekashi and Shotti were still outside, still around, still in their usual places. They weren't scared.

Shotti wore a black Death Row Records sweatshirt and smoked a blunt while the camera crew set up. Tekashi continued to check his phone. And then the interview began.

Pvnch emphasized that Tekashi survived what happened to him. The DJ began with his favorite word.

"We outside," he said. "Good, strong, healthy."

Pvnch made an oblique reference to Tekashi having run away from his attackers. "Fastest man in the world," he said, gesturing toward the star. Tekashi was wearing a gold link chain and an expensive watch, some of the few pieces of jewelry in his orbit that *hadn't* been stolen.

Pvnch talked about the attention the kidnapping had gotten, rather than the incident itself.

"Yesterday, you just raised the temperature up," he said.

"I break the internet," Tekashi agreed. "That's what I do. That's what I'm known for."

They bantered about his recent European tour, with Tekashi giving a special shoutout to his day one fans in Slovakia. But they quickly moved to why they were actually there.

"No matter how much fame I got," Tekashi began, "everybody know me for being in the heart of Brooklyn, staying in the heart of Brooklyn."

And then, a modified mea culpa: "I lost touch with reality. I'm eight for eight on the Billboard. When the incident happened, I was seven for seven on the Billboard." Even when explaining why he slipped and allowed himself to be kidnapped, he still had to mention "Fefe"'s chart position.

He continued. "I just lost touch. I'm like, yo, I'm a superstar. I'm in the hood, walking around like I'm just regular. I'm just numb. I don't even feel famous, because I'm so used to being down to earth."

Tekashi went on for a little while longer, but that was the crux of his argument. He "slipped up" because of his insistence on feeling like a regular person. He hadn't realized what a giant star he was. It was the best possible way of spinning what happened—he looked humble, and at the same time successful.

And the attack? Well, Tekashi said, just "charge it to the streets." Things like this happen to people every day.

After that, it was time to get vulnerable. He talked about how during the kidnapping, he begged the kidnappers (who he didn't name) to spare his life because he had a young daughter. He mentioned how he'd thought of XXXTentacion's recent murder.

He even got a little existential.

"If I die today, do I die happy? Do I die knowing I was a good father to Saraiyah? Do I die knowing I was a good nigga to Sara?"

On that last part, the answer was a definitive no. Tekashi's abuse of Sara was so frequent and so public that people in his orbit saw it happen. He was also, according to people close to him, sleeping with more than his share of "startenders."

As the interview continued, it was apparent that, despite the failure of his stunt, Tekashi was not done talking about Summer Jam. "How you not gonna have the hottest artist in New York City at New York City's own concert?" he asked rhetorically.

And just like that, they were past the kidnapping and back to normal—Tekashi bragging about how he was "the hottest artist in the city" and praising the incarcerated Brooklyn rapper Bobby Shmurda, one of Pvnch's longtime friends. The only acknowledgement in the video that things were different now was the man standing in the background with a T-shirt that read "Shadow Group."

Shamir "Shadow" Bolivar's security business had been hired to protect Tekashi, pushing out the ad-hoc security by Nine Trey members. Shadow was taking control of the business side of things, too. He was trying to set the manager-less ship right. And he was making some enemies along the way. Jorge, for example, had gotten used to ever-increasing responsibilities. Beyond driving, he had moved up to dealing with payments for shows. And Shadow, he felt, was trying to push him out.

Back on Locust, Pvnch and Tekashi continued to banter. Even Shotti ended up with a rare extended interview.

"You created the phrase of the year," Pvnch said to Shotti, cementing the idea that "Treyway" was his creation, and not Ms. Tr3yway's. "How does it feel to be the hottest manager of the hottest..."

Before he could get the word "artist" out, Shotti interjected.

He was determined to set himself up as a CEO, as a boss. He didn't want his career to be tied solely to the mercurial Tekashi. So he tried to thread the needle.

"I'm the CEO of Tr3yway Entertainment," he corrected. "I am the hottest *CEO* in the game. Nobody can't manage 6ix9ine. It just won't happen, you dig? He's like a wild animal. You just gotta let him be. He roams free."

Shotti also tried to downplay the fact that about $365,000 in jewelry had been stolen from his prize artist—a fact that was reflecting badly on him. "Shoutout to y'all for borrowing his jewelry," he joked. "He needed a new look anyway." Shotti also took a subtle shot at J. Prince by calling Tr3yway Entertainment "the new Rap-A-Lot."

After the interview, they walked up Locust and headed to a nearby barbershop, where Tekashi got a haircut and Pvnch continued their interview. They could have done either of those things anywhere, but it made sense to stay local. Tekashi got an ego boost, as he was stopped on the street by friends and fans. And it continued the optics: he was outside, in Brooklyn, walking the streets. At the barbershop, before the interview, Tekashi and Pvnch bantered about basketball and TV. Pvnch threw out the possibility of Tekashi appearing on *Power*, the television drama 50 Cent was producing.

"That'd go viral, you heard?" Tekashi answered, ever attuned to the prospect of something getting attention. Once the interview started, Tekashi admitted that even though he'd been trying to "cool down," to stay out of the spotlight, he was unable to do it.

"I been trying to, like, stay off headlines, but I just can't," he said.

After the barbershop, the crew went to Dave and Buster's. As they walked in, Eminem's "Without Me" was playing.

Now this looks like a job for me
So everybody, just follow me
'Cause we need a little controversy
'Cause it feels so empty without me

If it struck anyone in the crew as appropriate, their faces didn't show it.

CHAPTER 9

'YOU COULD GET US TOUCHED'

A fter the kidnapping, Harv tried to sell off some of Tekashi's jewelry. But no matter how much of it he tried to sell, he couldn't stop his nemesis's rise. Somehow the incident, instead of embarrassing Tekashi out of existence, had only made him bigger.

On July 27, Tekashi sat down with Angie Martinez for an interview that found him recounting a mostly accurate but slightly fantastical version of the kidnapping. He included a made-up detail about jumping out of a moving car into oncoming traffic, and a significant exaggeration of how much the stolen jewelry was worth. It was typical rapper stuff. But later on, those lies would come back to haunt him.

While Tekashi was blowing up the charts with "Fefe" and doing interviews with New York radio legends, there was a darker underside. The day before the Angie interview, Tekashi, Shotti, Crippy, a security guy, and Jorge were all in Jorge's car when Shotti decided to get some things straight. He unloaded on Tekashi with a nineteen-minute nonstop monologue—one that Jorge's ever-recording phone captured and promptly sent to the government.

Shotti's speech was meant to keep his charge off-balance. He yelled at Tekashi one minute, and insisted the young rapper was the *real* boss the next. The main reason for Shotti's ire was Tekashi's insistence on remaining in Bushwick despite his stardom. Shotti thought that Tekashi should be acting like a celebrity—living the high life, going to fancy restaurants. Instead, he was in the hood every day, moving from Bushwick to Bed Stuy. This tendency got him kidnapped and robbed. And that reflected badly on Shotti.

"You can't put us in situations where we gon' be at risk, nigga," Shotti said. He reminded Tekashi that Harv still had his jewelry, and that was most definitely not okay. That was, Shotti explained, the same as taking his own jewelry. And it was all due to Tekashi's insistence on acting like he was still normal. Being in the hood meant that Tekashi remained a target to rival Nine Trey factions.

"You could get touched, bro," Shotti continued. "They could come up right now and just start drumming at us...[I]t's gonna be a shoot-out, bro, and we gotta kill somebody."

They would get revenge, Shotti insisted. But the crew would have to be smart about it. Because one thing Shotti was not doing was going to jail.

"That shit ain't good for my system," he explained.

He had plans for Harv, though.

"These niggas can't stop bullets, bro," he said. "I ride around with a fucking semi-automatic assault rifle, bro. Harv, nigga, I taught him that."

It was time, Shotti insisted, for Tekashi to grow up and get a bulletproof truck. It was a necessity. This wasn't just music beef for Instagram. This was real.

"Don't make this like some internet shit when it's not," he said, desperately trying to make Tekashi realize the difference. "Internet shit we could carry all day long. Chief Keef, the rappin' niggas, we could do that shit all day long. Them niggas pussy, bro."

Then Shotti cut to the chase. It was time for violence.

"Niggas robbed you. Now it's time to clip somebody."

And Shotti was down to do it. He reminded Tekashi of the Nine Trey gangsters he had around him, people like Mel and Ro. Those were people, Shotti admitted, he was *using*.

"This shit is chess, nigga," he explained.

If Tekashi was surprised or put off by Shotti admitting to using people he'd fought and bled with for a decade-plus, he didn't say anything.

Shotti insisted that Tekashi should act like the rich rapper he was. No more cheap Dominican food at Mi Sabor, the rapper's beloved local spot, a five minute walk from Locust Street. Instead, he should be eating high-priced Chinese food in Manhattan.

"You supposed to go to Jue Lan's right now and act like the rich nigga you are," Shotti said, referencing a pricey place on West 20th Street. "That's not 6ix9ine changing, bro. That's 6ix9ine *maturing*."

But far more important than restaurants was the general principle. They had to be careful.

"You can't be king of New York because you dead," Shotti warned. But they also needed revenge. Harv had been trying to intimidate Tekashi from day one, Shotti reminded him.

"Now what the fuck you gonna do about it? All gloves is off... We gon' rock this nigga."

After all, Shotti was not shy about violence. He reminded Tekashi about an incident he'd mentioned before, where he'd shot five people in one night as revenge for an attack on Mel Murda.

"Five niggas, one night," he reminded Tekashi. "I did that on my lonesome." And that was just for "love," for friendship. Now that both love *and* his financial future were on the line, what did Tekashi think was gonna happen?

"We don't give a fuck about women, children, kids, none of that shit," he said.

In the meantime, Tekashi's job was to keep making money for the gang. That would keep him alive and safe. "You a top earner, they can't touch you. Nobody touches a top earner in the mob."

Meanwhile, Tekashi should rest assured that Harv and anyone associated with him would be dealt with. But, again, they had to be careful, Shotti reminded Tekashi.

"Niggas know they got a federal investigation against us right now."

Jorge didn't say a word.

During the end of summer in 2018, Tekashi continued to blow up. His popularity grew and grew. He was performing big shows in the U.S., including one just a few days after his kidnapping, in Tampa. But Europe was an even bigger deal. He played huge festivals overseas, including the Weekend Festival in Helsinki, Finland. It was a massive outdoor event, and Tekashi's set on August 18, 2018 was received rapturously.

Wearing a pink and white Puma sweatsuit, Tekashi came onstage after Pvnch warmed up the crowd by playing hits from Drake and ASAP Ferg and even, in a wink to the fans who knew all about Tekashi's beefs, Chief Keef and Trippie Redd.

Tekashi had developed into a commanding onstage presence. He didn't really rap that much—he let the backing track and Pvnch's hypeman yells handle most of the vocal work. He rapped, at best, about half of the actual lyrics.

To the crowd, it hardly mattered. What was important was seeing Tekashi run around, shouting out "Treyway!" at every opportunity and throwing up Nine Trey signs in front of the 50,000 or so attendees. He was a ball of energy, running around from side to side, and throwing water.

But while he was soaking in adulation from fans, Tekashi continued to beef with everyone and anyone. His back and forth with YG, a Blood-affiliated L.A. rapper who started taking shots at Tekashi back in March, began to intensify. On August 8, Tekashi hopped on Instagram and let off a long series of complaints. It was a quintessential Tekashi trolling video. He pushed the limits, knowing full well two things: that it would get headlines, and that, if push came to shove, Shotti had his back.

"I don't know how more disrespectful can I get," he began. "YG, suck my fuckin' dick, stupid."

Insult out of the way, he moved on to his favorite stomping ground: chart performance. It was the one area he felt most confident. Other rappers needed co-signs or features with big stars to have hits. He didn't need any of that. Everyone was against him, and he still managed to hit the chart with every song he put out. Why *not* revel in it a little bit?

Tekashi teased YG that his last single "Big Bank" featured three giant stars: 2 Chainz, Big Sean, and Tekashi's pal Nicki Minaj.

"How my record doing better than your shit?" he asked, mockingly. "You a whole bum out here."

Tekashi took exception to YG dissing him. He positioned it as an irrelevant rapper bringing up his name for clout.

"Stop going on radio stations trying to promote your

album, mentioning my name. You a big-ass dummy. I see right through you."

He wasn't going to play by the rules and he certainly wasn't going to respect YG.

"Do something about it," he dared. He mockingly danced and rapped along to YG's 2010 hit "Toot It and Boot It."

"This your last hit," he said. "This was in 2004, I think." The year was off, but his point was made. YG was old and irrelevant, and Tekashi was here now, ready to conquer the charts without any help.

Just as all that was happening, the biggest star of all jumped in on Tekashi's side. Kanye West was being interviewed by his longtime friend DJ Pharris at the end of August. He was coming off the June release of his divisive album *Ye*. At the very end of the hour-plus conversation, Pharris asked Kanye whch new rappers he was enjoying. "I love 6ix9ine," he said.

"You like 6ix9ine?" Pharris asked incredulously. After all, Tekashi had been attacking a ton of rappers from Kanye's home city of Chicago.

"I love his energy, his spirit."

Pharris was still startled.

"Have you seen the controversy that he has created?"

"Don't talk to me about controversy." Kanye was dismissive. To him, Tekashi was "family." Sure, he could be a little outrageous. But we all had that cousin who was locked up, Kanye continued. He was still family. Plus, a rapper who wore a MAGA hat in public knew a little something about pissing people off.

"I'm *past* 6ix9ine on troll level," he boasted.

The interview set off shockwaves. And DJ Relentt was there to capitalize.

Relentt had first met Tekashi during a session at Penthouse Recording Studios. He grew close to Shotti and became, as he describes it, "the go-to white dude to get in touch with 6ix9ine."

Around the time of the Pharris interview, a friend of Relentt's reached out.

"Yo, you gotta come meet this guy Joe. He owns a store downtown. He really wants to meet you."

"Joe" was Joe Einhorn, the founder and CEO of the e-commerce site Fancy.com, which had a store on Bond Street in downtown Manhattan.

At the meeting, Joe was straightforward.

"Listen, man. Kanye is my good friend and he really wants to meet 6ix9ine but he doesn't know how to approach the situation," Relentt recalls Einhorn saying. "He doesn't want to just hit him on Twitter. He just wants somebody to make the introduction, but I don't know how to do it."

Relentt had an idea. They'd use Einhorn's store to have a pop-up shop for Tr3yway. Shotti and 6ix9ine could sell merch.

"Yeah, bro. If you can make it happen, let's do it." Einhorn was in.

Relentt brokered a meeting between Tekashi's camp and Einhorn, and plans were made to have a pop-up store with "Tr3yway"-branded merch on September 3. Kanye showed his support by designing the flyer for the event.

"I love my brother Joe and his new store. Invitation by Donda," Kanye tweeted.

The invitation looked like an iPhone home screen, with what appeared to be five apps. But they all, taken together, gave information about the event. It was for Tr3yway, put on by Fancy, on September 3 at 8 PM at the store on Bond Street. West also gifted Tekashi an unreleased version of his Yeezy

Boost 700 sneakers. The relationship grew from there. Joe put Kanye and Tekashi on a group chat, and the duo quickly began Facetiming. By the second week of September, they'd be together in a recording studio in Colombia.

In late September, Tekashi and his crew went to Dubai, where he'd been invited to perform a few shows.

The Dubai trip was the beginning of the end for Tekashi 6ix9ine. But it was also the scene of the beating that would finally bring Tekashi's years-long history of domestic abuse to light. Tekashi had become convinced that Shotti was sleeping with Sara Molina. He claims that he saw flirty texts between the two of them on Shotti's phone, which confirmed his growing suspicions. Shotti and Sara both deny it.

With these worries swirling in his head, Tekashi insisted Sara fly out and meet him in Dubai. Once she was there, Sara remembers, Tekashi begged that she confess to him. As a twisted way of winning her trust, Sara recalls Tekashi confessing to sleeping with more than seventy other women since making it big, with results including more than one pregnancy and him ending up with several STDs.

And then, by Sara's account, he went on to beat and rape her after she denied sleeping with Shotti. Tekashi confirmed some parts of this in a 2020 interview with the Shade Room's Angelica Nwandu.

"I went into a rage. I blacked out," he'd said. "I beat the shit out of Sara."

Months after the Dubai trip, Sara would tell the *Daily Beast* about her experience there, as well as other incidents, including a time when she alleges Tekashi beat her in front of their daughter.

The incident with Sara was the most horrific part of Tekashi's Dubai trip, but it was far from the only notable thing.

While Tekashi was away, Jorge had been put in charge of over-seeing a move from Tekashi's house in Brooklyn to a place on Long Island. Jorge noticed during the move that there were some secrets hiding in one of the closets in the house. Just sitting there was Scumlord D!zzy's backpack from the This Is 50 robbery, and an assault weapon of Shotti's.

Jorge told his handlers. They had to act quickly, because the move was imminent. So on Friday, September 28, with Tekashi in Dubai, federal agents and the NYPD raided the house. They found the assault rifle—the same one Shotti had been waving around in the aftermath of the Ro Murda robbery. And they found the backpack. It was conclusive proof that Tekashi had been involved in the This Is 50 robbery.

As the raid happened, Jorge called Shotti's lawyer. Surely he'd know what to do. The lawyer's response, Jorge remembers, was to call TMZ.

Back in Dubai, the raid put Tekashi seriously off balance. Pvnch, who was on the trip, remembers Tekashi swinging wildly between extremes; one minute convinced he was going to jail, the next minute certain that everything would be fine. He ended up staying in Dubai for several weeks, hanging with rich kids and shooting a video for his song "Stoopid."

(It should be noted that Tekashi has, in a 2020 interview, told a longer, confusing account of how he spent this period, involving some traveling around Europe).

Meanwhile, Nine Trey was continuing to splinter. There was the "Murda Line," the crew officially led by a now-some-what-reclusive Mel Murda. There was the "Smurf Line," named after Harv's territory of Smurf Village. There was the "Madison Line," for the people attached to Maddy. And, finally, the "Wavy Line," which was the territory of the Nine Trey drug dealer Aljermiah "Nuke" Mack.

From Tekashi's point of view, the main conflict was between his Murda Line and the Smurf Line. His success was the thing that had super-charged the conflict between Harv and Shotti. It was a conflict that had turned Smurf Village into a war zone. The shooting at the cookout in July was the beginning. But it was about to get a lot worse.

The factions of Nine Trey were fully at war. Shotti was determined to get an advantage. He was put in charge of Smurf Village by gang higher-ups. So, it was time to take control of his territory. He talked to Tekashi and told him the deal. Shotti was determined, he said, to "make it hot" out there.

On the night of October 24, Shotti demonstrated what that meant. He sent two Nine Trey members to Smurf Village, lending them his black Mercedes Benz for the mission. The mission was to shoot Harv. But Harv wasn't around. So instead, one of the guys shot and paralyzed a friend of Harv's named David.

That happened a little before 9 PM. Harv had planned to spend the night at a hotel with his girlfriend. She'd booked a $240/night place and was looking forward to it. It took pets, so she could bring her dog. She sent Harv the info.

"ITS SOME WHITE PEOPLES SHIT," she texted.

At 9:07, Harv got a text: "DAVE JUST GOT SHOT."

The same message two minutes later.

Then someone else: "HEY GOT SHOT IN THE BACK."

Another person hit him a few minutes later: "MY CITIZEN APP SENT ME A ALERT THAT SOMETHING HAPPENED IN SMURF. I GOT NERVOUS."

Within a few minutes, more and more people were telling Harv what happened. "DAVID GOT SHOT BUT I DNT KNO

WHERE," wrote one. "IT HAPPENED BY IN SMURF JUS NOW."

Harv's longtime friend who'd loaned him the rental car he'd used for the kidnapping messaged him too. "IS DAVID OKAY?"

Harv told his girlfriend that there was a change of plans. His friend got shot, and he had to attend to it. She should take a cab from the Bronx, where she was, and meet him in Brooklyn, near Smurf Village. The girlfriend was worried.

"IS HE ALIVE," she texted.

Harv was in midtown Manhattan, but immediately started driving to Smurf Village. By the time his girlfriend arrived, he was there.

He met her while surrounded by a bunch of people his girlfriend had never seen. He was completely frantic. The group started walking, but then Harv said he needed to leave and peeled off in a different direction. The girlfriend and her dog holed up at Harv's aunt's house for hours, and waited for him to finish his business.

That business was revenge. Harv couldn't find the guy who shot his friend. So instead, he found Mark. Mark was a young-looking guy, stocky, with short dreads and a thin mustache. He'd been close with the shooter, who had managed Mark's music career. It wasn't the guy who shot David, but it was close enough.

Harv slashed Mark, deep. The wound went from up near his left ear all the way to his chin, and it left him covered in blood and with a long permanent scar. An NYPD detective who had been chasing the shootings in the area all night came across Mark in the aftermath. The detective was holding a rag to Mark's face, to try and stop the bleeding. Mark couldn't talk —blood kept coming out of his mouth—and his face was covered in blood. The detective called for an ambulance, and Mark was taken to Kings County Hospital.

After slashing Mark, Harv saw the two Nine Trey members in Shotti's car. That was all he needed. He shot at the car. The two guys got out, and Harv started chasing after them. In the confusion, he dropped his gun. The gang member who shot Harv's friend grabbed it, and he was arrested with it when the cops showed up.

Hours later, when Harv and his girlfriend were finally ensconced in a hotel in Manhattan, he filled her in on what happened. He said he got back at the guy who shot his friend. He'd stabbed a guy in the face.

Just two days later, Tekashi faced an entirely different kind of reckoning. He was finally going to be sentenced for the 2015 incident involving the 13-year-old girl. It was time for a judge to decide whether Tekashi had been living up to the terms of his plea deal. If he had, he'd just get probation. If he hadn't, he could get one-to-three years in prison.

The whole thing was open to interpretation. The plea deal said that Tekashi had to stay out of trouble for two years, and then he'd be sentenced. But his fast-paced rap star lifestyle had caused a year of delays. And in that year, he had been in legal trouble several times. So he'd violated the spirit of the agreement, but maybe not the letter. The judge had to decide which of these was more important.

The Assistant District Attorney on the case had a two-pronged argument. First, she explained that Tekashi had been arrested twice between the time of the plea deal and that day. Once was for allegedly choking a sixteen-year-old kid in a Houston mall. The other was for driving without a license. So, he'd violated his agreement, and it was time to send him to prison.

Secondly, she brought up Tekashi's behavior. His trolling and beefs, and his endless advocacy of Nine Trey. All of that was certainly against his post-plea promise to stay out of trouble until he was sentenced for the heinous crime he'd committed. That was the deal—don't get arrested, and we'll let you slide. But he'd gotten arrested, twice. And he was endlessly promoting a violent street gang on top of it.

Tekashi's lawyer Lance Lazzaro argued the opposite. He said that all of the gang stuff was just for show. It was to promote Tekashi's music. Plus, Tekashi wasn't a bad guy at all. In fact, he cared deeply about other people. He gave away money to those in need, and he visited sick fans. Most of these good deeds had been conspicuously performed on camera in the months leading up to the hearing. But the judge seemed not to understand that. She praised Tekashi for his generosity.

Lazzaro also had a different spin on the arrests than the ADA. He admitted they happened. But he emphasized they'd happened *after* the two-year deadline. Never mind that Tekashi himself was the one who pushed the sentencing deadline back—two years was two years. The arrests shouldn't count as violating the agreement.

To the ADA, this was absurd. The plea agreement said two years, she admitted. But that was with the understanding that the sentencing should happen by then. Since it hadn't, and Tekashi had gotten arrested—twice!—for other stuff before he had been sentenced for this crime, it was time to lock him up.

In the end, the judge sided with Lazzaro's take. She sentenced Tekashi to probation, and he walked out of the courtroom, seemingly invincible.

In the courtroom that day was Elliot Grainge, the head of Tekashi's label. He and Shotti were finally in the same place at the same time, and met face to face. Their interactions had been minimal up to that point. That was in large part because Shotti's whole plan was to move Tekashi away from Grainge, and into a more lucrative record deal that he could have more control over, and get more money from. But Tekashi's relationship with Grainge pre-dated his one with Shotti, and Tekashi treasured the creative freedom Grainge gave him. But Shotti knew that killing the deal with Grainge and signing with a bigger label could provide an instant up-front payment of millions, and major execs were already reaching out to him about that possibility. That was money Shotti couldn't afford to turn down just because Tekashi liked some English guy.

It was time for Shotti to put the pressure on. So when he got wind that, after court, Tekashi and Grainge were going to have a dinner meeting at a fancy restaurant in Manhattan, he needed to be there. He grabbed Crippy and a boxer friend for muscle.

Elliot had known that Shotti was likely to do something like this. He'd made sure he was surrounded by two private security guards. Shotti followed Tekashi to the restaurant, Philippe Chow, where Grainge was sitting inside, ordering. He'd set up his security guards outside the door, expecting trouble. And sure enough, trouble showed up. Tekashi smartly stayed away.

Shotti and his crew tried to get inside the restaurant, but Grainge's guards weren't having it. An argument broke out. Shotti's crew began throwing chairs and flashing guns. Finally, someone in Shotti's crew threw a chair at one of the guards that hit him in the head and left a gash big enough that it required some stitches to close. That was enough. The guard pulled out his gun and fired, hitting Crippy in the chest.

Crippy was arrested, and then taken to the hospital. He'd end up with a colostomy bag due to his injuries, which would make his already-bad prison experience horrifically worse. All three men who'd tried to enter the restaurant were arrested, and the incident made the news. It contributed to the impression that violence followed Tekashi everywhere, even to Manhattan's tony Upper East Side. And if the judge watched the news that night, she couldn't have helped but rethink her decision earlier that day to believe that Tekashi's violent demeanor was all a showbiz trick.

Violence continued to follow Tekashi clear across the country. In early November, he was out in Los Angeles to film a video with Kanye West and Nicki Minaj. Eight shots were fired towards the set, one of which went through a bedroom window.

Tekashi needed to get out. The continuous violence, his obsession with the idea that Shotti was sleeping with Sara, his growing worries that Shotti was stealing money from him—it all merged into a toxic stew. There was only one way to escape. A dramatic break with everything and everyone.

It happened on Instagram.

A week to the day after the shooting in L.A., Tekashi got on IG to announce that he was firing everyone around him. By extension, though he didn't say it directly, he was also announcing his escape from Nine Trey.

"I'm letting everybody know that I cancelled my whole tour," he said. "I fired everybody on my team. I don't got no manager, I don't got no booking agent, no PR, I don't got no publisher. I don't got nobody on my team. It's just me." He made accusations about people around him stealing money. "I don't give a fuck who you used to see me with, they no longer around."

The next day, he went back on the *Breakfast Club*. He was ostensibly there to talk about his upcoming album *Dummy*

Boy, but all anyone wanted to know was why he fired everyone.

Tekashi went into a rambling explanation, complete with spreadsheets, about how people around him had been stealing his gig money. And he made sure to send shots at Nine Trey, calling the members "dirty Bloods" and taking sole credit for the gang's increased public profile. "Treyway is nothing without me," he said.

The interview set off a firestorm. A day later, Mel Murda got on the phone with Shotti.

"Your man is crazy," Mel told his friend. "The nigga got to be on drugs. He said, 'Fuck Treyway, them is some bum-ass niggas, dirty niggas, niggas thieves. Like, ain't no more Treyway.' This kid is crazy, homie."

Shotti, always one to deliver a threat in the least amount of words, said, "He's gonna get what's coming."

Mel said he was "depressed" by the interview. Shotti, ever-confident no matter the circumstance, laid out his plan. He was going to see what Tekashi had to say, "and then I'mma start firing on everything." He already made plans to go on TMZ on Monday, he told Mel. "Everybody—me, you, Crippy, the homies, everybody on camera."

But Mel was still pissed. While he was on the phone with Shotti, he started conducting an imaginary one-sided conversation with Tekashi.

"We created you," he said. "You was a mutt. We found you and we put a muzzle on you and showed you how to be a dog, nigga. We made you who you was, so you could help us in our situation, nigga."

Shotti, who knew better than anyone exactly how true that was, chimed in. "That's a fact."

"Don't try to act like it wasn't an even exchange," Mel

continued, drawing deep into his hypothetical talk with his betrayer. "We gave you life and you introduced us to the bag. But you ain't make Treyway, scrap. We made you."

Shotti laughed as he mentioned his plan for revenge. "I'mma feed him, though." That was, the federal government would soon after contend, barely-hidden code for shooting.

At another point on that same day, Mel was still processing what had happened. He got on the phone with one of his closest friends, Jim Jones. By now, Mel had a theory: Tekashi had fired everyone to convince the cops that he was separating himself from the gang, and from Shotti specifically.

"That's cool," Jim said. Jim, though, knew the rules. He knew you couldn't just claim Blood one day and run away from it the second there were some problems. There had to be consequences. "But now he got to get violated."

"Yeah, super-violated," Mel agreed. "Super, super duper. Ain't too much he can really do unless he gonna run around with a hundred security all day."

Jim, long accustomed to the rap star lifestyle, knew something important about the security guards Tekashi was likely to hire if he felt like he was in trouble: they don't want to protect high-risk targets. Jim knew Shotti was ready to take violent revenge. And if he aimed at Tekashi's security first, his real target would soon be isolated.

"Once one security get injured, them niggas like, 'Nah, he's too much of a liability. I'm not gonna protect nobody that I know is causing harm to myself.'"

On this call, Mel continued his imaginary dialogue with Tekashi. "We wasn't friends, nigga. You ain't never put no work in to be a part of this entity of ours, nigga. Niggas made that little nigga, and niggas can break that little nigga."

At one point in the conversation, Jim started laying out a PR plan for Shotti's upcoming TMZ appearance.

"He need to be very, very, very articulate about...why he made people think that nigga was a gang member. He needs to let niggas know that he was never a gang member. He was always a money ploy for the gang members." Jim continued, thinking out loud. "He got to figure it out. But they gonna have to violate shorty, 'cause shorty on some bullshit."

There was one problem with all this planning and tough talk. The two Joneses weren't the only ones listening. The feds were, too. Mel's phone was tapped, a consequence of the investigation into Nine Trey that was kick-started six months before. Law enforcement ran to Tekashi, knowing he was in danger. A dead rap star, especially one with firsthand knowledge of a street gang, wasn't good for anybody. The government found Tekashi shopping, engaging in a bit of retail therapy at a sneaker store.

They took him to the Homeland Security Investigations office in Manhattan. It was a big gathering, with representatives from Homeland Security, the FBI, and the NYPD. They didn't let Tekashi know about the phone calls. But, they asked, was there anyone who would want to hurt him? Did he think he was in danger? They could offer him protection, and put him up in an apartment or a hotel.

Ever image conscious, Tekashi turned them down. He was ready to tell on the gang. He didn't need to hear any wiretapped phone calls to know that Nine Trey members were ready to kill him. "But I can't be seen with no feds," he explained. "I've got an album coming out." However, at that first meeting, he gave them some information about the structure of the gang, and helped them identify some members.

The next day, after a meeting with a booking agent to try

and figure out his chaotic finances, Tekashi was ready to get out of town. He decided to go to Foxwoods Resort Casino in Connecticut. The singer Anuel AA, with whom he'd recently collaborated, was performing there.

Law enforcement, who were shadowing him, quickly discovered his plans. They had to act. They knew the Bloods were out to get the guy who had publicly embarrassed them. They couldn't take the chance of a shooting in a giant casino. They had planned on waiting a little while longer and continuing the investigation before making arrests. But now there was no choice.

They rounded everyone up.

PART 2
THE FEDS

CHAPTER 10
THE AFTERMATH

TMZ broke the story just after 10 PM Eastern time on November 19, 2018. *TEKASHI69 BUSTED BY FEDS FOR RACKETEERING ...FACING LIFE IN PRISON* read the giant headline.

ATF agents took Tekashi into custody, along with five other people including Shotti, Mel Murda, and Crippy. Crippy wasn't arrested, exactly—he was already in jail, having been busted the month before for his role in the restaurant brawl.

All of them were in a very stark position. They weren't just charged with their individual crimes. It was a racketeering case. That meant the government believed all of the crimes were done to further the aims of Nine Trey. And it meant that individual members, whether or not they committed particular crimes, were held responsible for the actions of the gang. It was an approach to law enforcement that had begun in 1970, as a way to fight the mob. But in recent years, it was being applied more and more frequently to street gangs.

The defendants were almost certainly facing long prison sentences. The federal government has an often-talked-about conviction rate of well above 90%, because they don't bring cases until they have a mountain of evidence. Even though they'd been a little rushed by Tekashi's would-be casino trip, they were still more than ready. The only way to avoid prison, besides the remote possibility of winning at trial, would be to cooperate.

For everyone but Tekashi, cooperation was unthinkable. Snitching was prohibited by Nine Trey's 31 rules. The punishment was to be put on the "worldwide menu" of people who should be killed at the earliest possible opportunity. (Feeding as a metaphor for violence was not original with Shotti).

There were myriad reasons for the prohibition on snitching. It appeared to protect all the members of a criminal enterprise. But according to gang experts, it most frequently serves to protect members in the upper ranks, while leaving the foot soldiers out to dry. And violations of the rule happen more frequently than you might expect.

Edwin Santana is the president of the New Jersey chapter of the East Coast Gang Investigators Association. He explains that while the prohibition on snitching in gangs is heavily emphasized and maintained through fear, "I've yet to bump into a gang member that follows that code."

"The same people that push it are the same people that will basically ask to speak to the D.A., the prosecutors, the detective, and give up information," he says. "The same individuals saying [no snitching] are the same individuals that are working a deal and working for less time."

Shotti was an exception. His often-stated motto for the gang was, "We don't fold, we don't bend, we don't break." The prospect of jail time was not about to make him abandon his principles.

Tekashi, on the other hand, was primed to cooperate. He

was facing a minimum sentence of almost five decades, and was surrounded by people whom he believed had betrayed him and stolen from him. Plus, he was already telling law enforcement about the gang.

At the indictment the next day, Tekashi was brought out in front of a judge separately from all the other defendants. His solo status was likely a nod to the fact that just a few days before, his co-defendants had been caught on tape saying they wanted him dead.

At Tekashi's indictment, the government laid out all of the crimes they knew he'd been involved with—a whole slew of robberies and shootings. But they weren't charging him with all of it, at least not yet. There were eight counts against the crew in total, six of which included Tekashi. A close reading of the indictment reveals something that was unknown to the arrestees at the time: the hand of the Nine Trey drug dealer, Kristian Cruz, who turned undercover informant months before.

"Members and associates of Nine Trey sold heroin, fentanyl, furanyl fentanyl, MDMA, dibutylone, and marijuana in and around Manhattan, Brooklyn, and the Bronx, New York," it read, a perfect translation of Cruz's confessions into legalese.

Here's what Tekashi was charged with at first: one count was for being in a gang; one was for generally having guns; three were for the This Is 50 robbery; one, which would later be dropped, was for the shooting at the cookout. (Although Tekashi wasn't present at that event, he and Shotti had been the ones to order it.)

After hearing the charges, it was time for Tekashi's high-powered lawyers to do their thing. During this initial court date, his primary attorney Lance Lazzaro knew full well that his famous client was on the verge of cooperating. But before everything was official, before there were any guarantees, he had to put on a show, to give something resembling a defense. He laid out an alternative scenario to the scary picture the feds had painted of his client. Tekashi hadn't been part of a gang. He hadn't used them to rob, beat up, and shoot at his rivals. He'd just met some people and hired them as management and security.

"There's nothing wrong with that, judge," Lazzaro said. "That doesn't mean you're guilty of a crime by hiring these people."

Besides, Lazzaro argued, most of the crimes the feds were bringing up were months old. If Tekashi really had something to do with them, the lawyer said, he would be behind bars already.

Lazzaro tried for bail, offering up a million and a half dollars and the rapper's passport. But despite his best efforts, Tekashi was denied. A meeting was set with the government for the next morning.

The hearing made big news. In particular, *Page Six* honed in on the lead prosecutor's mention of the "superviolate" conversation between Mel Murda and Jim Jones. At this point, though, Jim Jones's name was kept out of it. He was referred to only as "Individual-1."

At Tekashi's meeting with the government the day after the indictment, he told them about a few Nine Trey crimes, including the Chief Keef shooting. He also talked about his kidnapping. Harv was already sitting in jail for that. He'd been indicted on Halloween and arrested a few days later. But he wasn't a part of this case, because the crime hadn't yet been linked to Nine Trey. That would change soon enough.

On Monday, November 26, Tekashi and Shotti got their

first chance to meet the judge who would eventually hold both of their fates in his hands. Paul Engelmayer was fifty-seven. He'd followed a pretty standard playbook to get behind the bench of Room 1305 at the Thurgood Marshall Courthouse. He'd attended Harvard for undergrad, worked briefly at the *Wall Street Journal*, and then gone back to Harvard for law school. He'd landed a few choice clerkships, including one with Thurgood Marshall himself, just a few years before the legendary Justice's retirement.

"I think about him almost every single day," Engelmayer said at a panel on "Remembering Thurgood Marshall." "I've got his picture up in my chambers. I walk in there every day and it reminds me that we are in the justice business."

Engelmayer had been nominated by Barack Obama to the federal bench in February 2011, and was confirmed a few months later. In this role, he'd overseen no shortage of gang cases. So when he directed the Nine Trey proceedings for the first time, he was clear and confident.

At that initial hearing, Engelmayer had his first encounter with all the lawyers on the case. Unsurprisingly, Tekashi and Shotti had the most prominent of the bunch. Shotti's lawyer was Scott Leemon, known as a go-to attorney for rappers. *XXL* once named him one of the rap game's best lawyers.

The day before the hearing, Leemon had visited his client in the Manhattan Correctional Center, the infamous federal jail located just near the courthouse. Shotti had sworn up and down that Leemon would get his retainer fee in just a few days. In reality, Shotti had no plans to pay—he was ready to pull, as Nine Trey members might call it, a "Shotti move" and welsh out. The conflict over Leemon's fee would eventually lead to one of the most dramatic moments of the whole case.

At the hearing, the government revealed that Ro Murda

was arrested a few days before, and was now a part of the case. The feds' lead prosecutor was Assistant U.S. Attorney Michael Longyear. He explained that the investigation into Nine Trey had been going on since February.

Also at this hearing, the government revealed that, even in a case with multiple cooperators, the vast majority of the evidence had come from defendants effectively snitching on *themselves*.

"We have several social media search warrants that were executed on various accounts for Instagram and Snapchat," Longyear said.

These included Tekashi and Crippy's Instagram accounts. They also had the iCloud accounts of most of the defendants. It was a lot of material. Tekashi's social media alone, Longyear said understatedly, was "quite voluminous."

"Because it is so large, we are having difficulty loading it onto a platform to actually review the return," he admitted.

The information came from many different sources. Tekashi's phone was seized and copied in March 2018, when he was crossing an international border. Crippy's was recovered from a crime scene after he was shot. The government got two phones from Shotti when he was arrested in New Jersey in the spring. In total, they had 20 phones.

And then, Longyear dropped another hint.

"We have other audio records of certain of the defendants, your Honor," he said.

"These are consensual audio recordings?" the judge asked. Engelmayer had been around long enough to know that gang members generally don't consent to have talk about their crimes recorded. "Can you elaborate?"

"Consensual audio recordings from a confidential informant, your Honor."

None of the media in that packed courtroom knew it yet, but Longyear had just acknowledged the existence of a third cooperator. Not the drug dealer who gave the case life. Not Tekashi. It was the first subtle reveal of Jorge Rivera's true role.

After that subliminal nod to Rivera, the conference continued. Issues were laid out, and a trial date was set for September 4, 2019. It was a long time away, and the judge was a little worried. Setting it that late would mean that everyone would have been locked up for nearly a year by the time the trial started. But the defense attorneys, knowing how much evidence the feds had, and how incredibly difficult it would be for their clients to review it all while behind bars, were adamant that the extra time was needed.

At the end of the conference, as the judge was heading back into his chambers, Shotti turned to the audience. He was determined to demonstrate that, despite the fact he was in handcuffs, he was still on top.

"We don't fold, we don't bend, we don't break," he said as the courtroom was emptying out. "It's Treyway."

That wasn't the only bit of theater going on. Outside the courthouse, Lazzaro talked to *Fox 5*'s Lisa Evers. Evers was a veteran journalist whose program 'Street Stories' frequently covered hip-hop-related topics. Lance knew full well that his client was guilty, was already informing, and was just weeks away from finalizing a guilty plea. But he couldn't say any of that just yet. He had to stick to the script: Tekashi 6ix9ine was a good kid who made the unfortunate mistake of trying to help some bad people.

"It's a far-reaching indictment that Mr. Hernandez has very little involvement with, other than basically using his social media to promote his music," Lazzaro said. "As far as being part of this Treyway Blood gang, completely false."

It was a lie. But it was a necessary one. Tekashi's team couldn't tip their hand until everything was in order.

But when that happened, the blowback would be massive.

Behind the scenes, Shotti's pal Mel Murda tried a Hail Mary. Mel's attorney wrote a letter to the judge, offering a $100,000 bond co-signed by three of Mel's aunts. The next day, the government unloaded in response. And in doing so, they gave their deepest public look yet into what they'd uncovered about the Nine Trey Gangsta Bloods.

No way should Mel be allowed back on the street, they said. Mel was a Godfather, the highest rank in the gang. They made reference to something else, too: a phone call Mel had made to an incarcerated Nine Trey member a few months before.

"Ro flipped his clip?" Mel had asked.

"At the bookout?" was the response.

"Based on its investigation, the Government understands that, during this call, the defendant was reporting that a co-defendant, Roland Martin, emptied a magazine of bullets at the July 16 cookout," the letter read. (Replacing "c"'s at the beginning of words with "b"'s was a common Blood practice, meant to show disrespect to their historic rivals, the Crips. Hence the reference to a "bookout.") The feds knew all about the Tekashi- and Shotti-ordered shooting at the cookout, including about the woman who was shot in the foot.

Another big strike against Mel Murda happened just one day later, when the government laid out the new indictment that folded Ro Murda into the case. Down at the end of the document were two charges showing that Mel was under some very heavy pressure. There was a narcotics trafficking charge against him for dealing between 2015-2018. And then, at the end, there was a parting gift from Cruz, the Nine Trey drug dealer who was cooperating.

"On or about November 15, 2018, in the Southern District of New York, JAMEL JONES, a/k/a 'Mel Murda,' the defendant, intentionally and knowingly did distribute and possess with intent to distribute a controlled substance," it read. "The controlled substance involved in the offense was one kilogram and more of mixtures and substances containing a detectable amount of heroin."

Of all the brazen crimes Nine Trey committed, this was in its own way the most head-slapping. At the direction of the cooperating drug dealer and law enforcement, Mel sold two kilos of heroin, on tape, directly to an undercover cop. He made $10,000. When he was arrested four days later, he had $9,000 of that money still on him.

CHAPTER 11

LAWYERS, GUNS, AND MONEY

With the racketeering case now up to seven defendants, some of whom were caught on tape threatening others, it was only a matter of time until the lawyers found themselves at cross purposes. Especially in such a high-profile case, with defendants who had in some cases known each other nearly their whole lives, the tensions ran as high as the stakes.

The first indication things weren't going well came just a few days before Christmas, 2018. Scott Leemon finally realized that there was no way Shotti was going to pay him. Leemon wrote a letter to the judge in which his indignation boiled just below the formal wording. The only reason Leemon bothered showing up at the status conference on November 26, he explained, was because he'd met with Shotti in jail the day before "and I was assured by Mr. Jordan and his family that I would receive my initial retainer fee early that week." He added bluntly, "That never happened. It has now been several weeks since that appearance and I still have not received payment."

It seemed, he implied, like Shotti was trying to get a freebie.

"I was told by a family member of Mr. Jordan's that the family is still trying to put funds together...and, once they do that, they are going to pursue new counsel at that time."

"I respectfully request," he ended his letter, "that I be relieved of counsel... I thank you in advance for your consideration of this request."

But Leemon had a backup plan. At the beginning of the month, Mel Murda's family reached out, seeing if he'd be available to rep Mel. He hadn't been then because he'd still been tied to Shotti.

Within weeks, Leemon would officially flip clients.

Shotti wasn't the only one weighing his legal options. Tekashi was, too. And they both had their eyes on the same person. On many lists of high-profile defense attorneys, Jeffrey Lichtman would be right at the top. He had represented rappers like Fat Joe and The Game. But he'd also repped drug dealers, cops, and mobsters, including John Gotti. So it wasn't a surprise that Shotti and Tekashi were both vying for his services.

On January 2, 2019—after Shotti already reached out to him—Lichtman got a phone call. Tekashi's new girlfriend, with whom he'd gotten together just before his arrest, called him on three-way and connected him with the rapper. Lichtman knew that Tekashi already *had* a lawyer. Not a big deal, Tekashi insisted. Lance Lazzaro knew about this call, and was down with the idea of adding Lichtman to the team.

Lichtman told him that someone else in this case was trying to hire him. Tekashi guessed that it was Shotti, and Lichtman told him that he was right. Tekashi was dismissive. No way Shotti will be able to afford you, he'd said.

Two days later, Tekashi's girlfriend texted Lichtman back. The deal was off. They weren't going to add him, or anyone else, to the team. No one said that Lichtman's dalliance with Shotti was a deal-breaker. But they didn't have to.

So, Lichtman took on Shotti as his client. And, although he wasn't aware of it just yet, he set himself on a crash course against Lance Lazzaro. It was one that would reveal a hidden history.

It was supposed to be run-of-the-mill. On January 22, 2019, the attorneys all got together with the judge to talk over this change in lawyering. There was a noon hearing set to make sure that Leemon could move from Shotti to Mel Murda; and a 2:30 one to make sure that Lichtman could rep Shotti. No one anticipated any problems. This type of thing happened all the time. Despite their clients' sometimes-murderous differences, all of the lawyers were colleagues and all knew the rules.

The noon hearing went along swimmingly. The stakes were so low that Mel's current lawyer wasn't even there, sending someone else in her place. Everyone—all the lawyers, Mel and Shotti, the judge—was just fine with what was going on.

And then, at the very end, as everyone was preparing for the afternoon conference to follow, Shotti's temporary, in-between, lawyer Jeffrey Einhorn dropped an absolute bombshell.

"Judge, just one more thing before we break," he said. "I was only recently informed of this, but there actually is another *Curcio* issue that's not been explored as yet," he said, using the legal name for conflict-of-interest concerns. "And that is...Mr. Lazzaro...previously represented my client, actually at trial once and I believe in two other cases as well. I wanted to get that before the Court."

Engelmayer was incredulous. *Lance Lazzaro, Tekashi's lawyer, represented Shotti not just once, but at least three times? And at trial? And hadn't bothered to say anything?*

The usually-reserved judge seemed pissed.

"When did you become aware of this?"

Einhorn said he'd learned about it the previous Thursday —it was now Tuesday.

"Is there some reason why I'm learning of this now, as opposed to later on Thursday?" the judge wondered. *This was a huge deal.*

"Your Honor," Einhorn stammered, "I left the state after I met with Mr. Jordan."

That wasn't going to cut it. "The internet didn't leave you," Engelmayer fired back. "For heaven's sake, that's five days ago."

Engelmayer wanted all the details. But Einhorn only knew some of them. Lazzaro told him about some trial where Shotti was acquitted. But there were two other cases, and Lazzaro couldn't remember all the details.

As if Lance Lazzaro weren't in the doghouse enough already, Shotti had another tidbit that he knew would discredit Lazzaro further. Lazzaro had also represented *another* defendant in this case, Crippy. Shotti knew all about it, because it was for the restaurant brawl incident.

Engelmayer, meanwhile, seemed like he was steaming. "I'm less than satisfied with the speed by which the government and I are being told of this." He took a pointed dig at Einhorn. "You're sitting on this information. I'm glad you got to go out of state, but meanwhile you've messed up this 2:30 conference." Had Einhorn even talked to Lazzaro about this, the judge wondered.

"I have not yet," he admitted.

Engelmayer was just getting warmed up. "So in other words, except for talking to your client and then going away for the long weekend, you've done nothing."

At the afternoon hearing, Lazzaro was promptly removed from Tekashi's team until everything could be resolved. The hostility between Shotti and Tekashi was now playing out in the courtroom. Lazzaro was caught in this proxy battle.

Lichtman and Shotti did their best to keep Lazzaro out of Tekashi's case, arguing that the lawyer's long history with Shotti meant that "he gained intimate knowledge of Mr. Jordan's affairs"—knowledge they were determined to keep out of the courtroom.

This gambit ultimately didn't work, but it set a tone. And it reminded Tekashi, in case he forgot for a second, that Nine Trey was still out to get him. But he wasn't the only defendant with problems. Everyone in the case was about to get seriously damaged by one thing they could never have foreseen: right as all of this legal wrangling was going on, the federal government was about to turn the lights off.

On December 22, 2018, the federal government began its longest shutdown in history. It would last for a shocking thirty-five days. And among the places on which it had an especially horrific effect were federal prisons and jails.

Even in the best of times, being in the federal jail in Manhattan or Brooklyn can make it difficult for inmates to find time and resources to plan their defense. Now, the shutdown made it even worse. Defendants in the case were locked down, kept in their cells for days at a time. While some of them had CDs with evidence on them that they were in theory allowed to look through, that was a hollow promise since they were unable to leave their cells to get to a computer. But the shutdown wouldn't be the last time that government neglect put these men at risk. It wouldn't even be the last time that winter.

The federal jail in Brooklyn, the Metropolitan Detention Center or MDC, was without heat for days on end that winter due to a blackout. The head of the corrections officer's union said that the conditions, which included indoor temperatures hovering around freezing, were "unbearable." According to a *New York Times* investigation, there was almost no hot water, and certainly no hot food.

Crippy was there, and he suffered mightily. After being shot during the restaurant brawl, he was using a colostomy bag. Because of the blackout and power outage, he couldn't change it, sitting in the freezing dark for days with, as his lawyer explained, "feces all over his body."

Meanwhile, Lance Lazzaro being kicked off Tekashi's defense team couldn't have happened at a worse time. While Lazzaro was busy digging up fifteen year-old legal records for cases with Shotti, his current client was about to take a huge step into the unknown.

One day after the hearing that had landed Lazzaro in hot water, Tekashi sat down in front of Judge Engelmayer, ready to accept responsibility. He finally, formally agreed to become a cooperating witness and tell everything he knew. He began a series of briefings with the government. And now, to keep everything going, he had to plead guilty.

Tekashi wasn't going to confess to his crimes because of a sudden change of heart. It was because he got the best deal that he could. The charges he pled to had a potential term of forty-seven years to life behind bars. There was no way he wanted to do that kind of time. And since he was willing to cooperate, he might not have to.

Agreeing to cooperate was a gamble. While things often work out well for cooperators, there are no guarantees. In federal cases, suspects agree to help the prosecution for the *potential* of a better result, not a surety.

Someone agrees to cooperate. They meet with the government many times—in Tekashi's case, it was over two dozen. During those sessions, they tell everything that they know, and plan their testimony in a trial, should there be one. In return for all this, the defendant receives one thing: a letter. However, it's a very important one.

The so-called "5K1 letter" is named after the section of the United States Sentencing Guidelines that spells out its function—Section 5K1.1. If the government is happy with how a cooperating witness has done his or her job (technically, if the defendant "has provided substantial assistance in the investigation or prosecution of another person who has committed an offense,") then the feds spell it all out in the 5K1 letter. The judge is then *allowed*, but not *required*, to sentence the defendant below the minimum required by law. How far below? Well, that's completely up to the judge. It can be as low as time served, meaning that the defendant would be free on the day of the sentencing.

This was the scenario that Tekashi's lawyers were hoping for. They had one more big hope as well. Once Tekashi's guilty plea and cooperation became public—which was set to happen just days after he pled out—his lawyers assumed that the other defendants would all see that their number was up. If Tekashi was turning on them, then the government knew everything. There was no possible defense. They may as well plead guilty and take the best deal they could get. And if everyone pled out, then there would be no need for a trial. So, Tekashi's cooperation would remain forever in the realm of legal documents and news stories, but would never happen in person. He wouldn't have to get up in front of Judge Engelmayer, a packed courtroom, and the whole world to tell his story. At least, that was the hope.

At 12:35 PM on January 22, 2019, Tekashi came into the courtroom and sat down next to his one remaining attorney, Dawn Florio.

What they were doing had to remain secret. The world-famous Tekashi 6ix9ine pleading guilty, and the fact that the plea might tip people off to his cooperation, created a very dangerous situation for him and for his family, the government argued. Also, the government was about to add more people to the case, and a few of them didn't know it yet. They didn't want to make arresting people any harder than it had to be.

Engelmayer went through his normal spiel, which he would use nearly verbatim at future pleas in the same case. When someone was pleading guilty, you had to make sure they meant it. He asked Tekashi a series of questions.

How old are you?

Twenty-two.

How far did you go in school?

"I believe about the tenth grade."

A few questions in, the handful of people in that secret room got a glimpse of the traumatic past that turned shy, quiet, respectful Danny Hernandez into the outrageous, trolling, and ultimately criminal Tekashi 6ix9ine. Engelmayer asked another boilerplate question.

"Have you ever been treated or hospitalized for any mental illness?"

"Yes, sir," came the reply.

The judge had to make sure this hadn't happened recently, since that might put the plea at risk.

"When was that?" he asked.

"I believe in 2011. 2011/2012, around that time," Tekashi said. "It was depression and post-traumatic stress for the murder of my father." He paused for a second. "Stepfather."

CHAPTER 12

THE BIG DAY

Some eagle-eyed observers, including people at the *New York Post*, noticed several weird things about Tekashi's treatment in the months since he'd been arrested—indicators that made it seem he was about to snitch. He was initially put in the Metropolitan Detention Center in Brooklyn when arrested, but quickly taken out. Initial reports said it was due to threats on his life. But he wasn't transferred to a different federal facility. Instead, he was taken out of the Bureau of Prisons custody entirely. The *Post* found that interesting.

"Being removed from federal custody is unusual—even when prisoners are the targets of threats," they wrote on November 22, 2018. "Past prisoners who have been removed from Bureau of Prisons custody include Reza Zarrab, who was abruptly 'released' from Manhattan federal prison and placed in FBI custody after agreeing to cooperate with the feds in a high-profile money laundering case."

The implication was clear—Tekashi was ready to snitch—but not many people picked up on it at the time. It wasn't until early in 2019 that everything became apparent. There was a hint before the explosion. On January 31, an updated indictment in the case was made public. It listed all of the defendants in the case, including the relatively new ones like Kooda, who had orchestrated Chief Keef's shooting; and Harv, whose existing case for kidnapping Tekashi had just been made part of this overarching one against Nine Trey. But Tekashi's name was nowhere to be found. That was strange.

The next day, there was an explosion. The record of Tekashi's January 23 guilty plea became public. And with it, proof in black and white that Tekashi 6ix9ine, the big bad Blood, was a snitch. The news ricocheted around the world. And while it was picked up in national papers like the *New York Times*, it was in the hip-hop world that the news had the most impact. What did it mean that one of the hottest rappers of 2018 was violating one of the deepest-held codes of the rap world?

There are few places outside of actual street gangs where the prohibition against snitching is as strong as it is in hip-hop. The longstanding ties between rappers and gangsters plays no small part in this. To take just one notable example, it was Nine Trey affiliate Jim Jones's crew the Diplomats who sold "STOP SNITCHIN" t-shirts, and Dipset leader Cam'ron gave a famous interview on CBS News in which he took the idea of never-snitching to a near-comic extreme.

"Is there *any* situation where you think it's okay to talk to the police?" interviewer Anderson Cooper asked.

"Yeah definitely," Cam answered. "Say hello, how you feel, everything alright. Period."

Cooper pressed. "If there's a serial killer living next door to you, though, and you know that person is killing people, would you be a snitch if you called police and told them?"

The rapper didn't back down. "I wouldn't call or tell anybody on him. I'd probably move, but I wouldn't call and be like, 'The serial killer's in [apartment] 4E.'"

The sentiment was over-the-top, but it wasn't uncommon among rappers. There are few insults worse in the rapper play-book than "snitch." It means someone who cooperates with the police, at the expense of their friends. And there are no more consistent enemies in hip-hop songs than the police.

From NWA's "Fuck tha Police" in 1988 to YG's "FTP" thirty-two years later, rappers have firmly set themselves against the police. And the police, in turn, have a long history of surveilling, harassing, and arresting high-profile (and not-so-high-profile) rappers. So, the idea of one of their own teaming up with the cops in order to avoid prison time is anathema to many in the rap world.

It makes sense that rappers would publicly be on the front lines of the fight against police abuses, and often against the police as an institution. As an art form largely created by and reflecting the viewpoints of young Black men and women, rappers are in large part reflecting the concerns of the communities they come from. People in those communities have been the victims of police racism and corruption for decades. The art created by people from these communities would naturally reflect those concerns. Rappers, as the people with among the most public voices, are a small but visible part of a much wider fight.

Tekashi appeared to have chosen the enemy in that fight. Rather than "snitch" being an accusation or a slur, it was a fact. Right there in black and white.

Rappers jumped in front of each other to be the first to condemn him. Lil Boosie went on Instagram in mid-February not only to blast Tekashi as a rat, but also to suggest a likely outcome. "IDK ABOUT NEW YORK BUT N LOUISIANA U WILL BE MURDERED LESS THAN A MONTH AFTER YOUR RELEASE," he wrote. "YOU PUT ALL YOUR FAMILY N GRAVE DANGER FOR LIFE CAUSE OF THIS BS, DID U THINK BOUT THEY SAFETY?"

Boosie mentioned that even though at one point in his life he was facing lethal injection, he had never thought for a second about snitching. It was a common sentiment. 50 Cent, 21 Savage, Meek Mill, Fat Joe, Snoop Dogg, and more all joined in the condemnation.

As February turned into March, tempers among lawyers and defendants in the case began to cool. Lichtman and Shotti even saw that despite their best efforts, Lance Lazzaro was going to be allowed to rejoin Tekashi's legal team, and they dropped their objections.

Then, the biggest domino of all. On the morning of March 28, a few minutes after 10 AM, Shotti and Jeffrey Lichtman sat down in front of Judge Engelmayer. The time had come for Shotti to pay the piper. He was about to plead guilty to charges that would lock him up for at least the next fifteen years, until he was in his 50s.

It was a decision that, as bleak as it was, made sense. He pled to involvement in the This Is 50 robbery and the time he fired on Tekashi's hecklers in downtown Brooklyn.

By pleading, Shotti got out of responsibility for the Chief Keef shooting and for the shooting at the cookout. He wouldn't serve any time for those.

His guilty plea was very formal and staged. Most are. There's a rhythm to them: the judge talks, the lawyers talk, the defendant says what he did and maybe how sorry he is, and everyone goes their separate ways. But this guilty hearing had a hiccup that inadvertently revealed a deep truth about

Tekashi's rap career, and his relationship with Shotti and Nine Trey.

While pleading, Shotti had to explain that the two crimes he was pleading to weren't just crimes. They were crimes done for a specific reason—to further the aims of Nine Trey. This was the whole point of the feds' case, and the entire rationale behind racketeering cases in the first place. But when Shotti admitted to the downtown Brooklyn shooting, he skipped that part.

The judge needed to hear it.

"When you shot the gun at this other car, what did that have to do with racketeering?" Engelmayer asked. "Why don't you take a moment and consult with your lawyers."

It was an order, not a request. Engelmayer needed this verbiage—that the shooting was done in furtherance of a criminal organization—to make the plea stick. Otherwise, everyone's time would be wasted.

Shotti talked with his lawyer for a second, and then he was ready.

"Both of these actions were in furtherance of the crime of a racketeering organization, your Honor."

Shotti was almost home-free. All the key words were there. All he needed to do was name Nine Trey.

Engelmayer prompted him: "What organization?"

"Treyway Entertainment."

Engelmayer was puzzled. "I think the racketeering organization that's been indicted and charged here is the Nine Trey Gangsta Bloods."

What did Treyway Entertainment *have to do with anything?*

Lichtman tried to smooth things over: "He is part of both those organizations. So, I think, in his mind, that's related."

Engelmayer let it slide, and Shotti went on with the plea.

But it was the first public indication of what everyone knew in private: that "Treyway" was the same thing as Nine Trey. It was a polite, publicly acceptable way to talk about the gang, especially if you happened to have tens of millions of followers on social media. (Shotti, for his part, has never admitted publicly to this interpretation. In a 2021 court filing appealing his sentence, he described his original answer—that he'd committed his crimes on behalf of Treyway Entertainment—as "truthful," and said that he'd "never admitted to being a member of the Nine Trey Gangsta Bloods.")

Shotti's answer made clear that Nine Trey was the internal name, the one for initiates only. "Treyway" was a way to get their name and message out in the world—to show their power to their enemies, to gain new recruits, and to gain fame, and by extension money, to help in their efforts.

Tekashi eventually copped to this directly. He was asked under oath what Treyway was.

"Treyway, from my understanding, it was a more sophisticated way to name the gang, something that we could market."

Once the big homie Shotti pled guilty, a lot of defendants sensed that their chances were slim. Within a week, Crippy, Mel, and one more defendant all pled out. As the guilty pleas piled up, a sense grew among Tekashi's lawyers that maybe he wouldn't have to testify at all. If everyone pled, there would be no one left to go to trial. And the colorful rap star could be spared from telling on gang members in person, in front of the whole world. It would be so much easier, and the idea of Tekashi snitching would be a lot less visceral, if all the telling happened behind the scenes. One of Tekashi's attorneys went as far as to tell TMZ in April that she was hoping for exactly that.

It seemed likely. Guilty pleas kept coming in: One in mid-

April, another in early May, two more in early June. And there were strong hints that Ro Murda was on the way. But then, on June 6, things changed. A new Nine Trey member was added to the case: Aljermiah "Nuke" Mack, the Nine Trey member who had drunkenly robbed Ro Murda of his car and watch. Nuke's addition would make things very complicated.

When Nuke got arrested on June 6, the calculus changed. Now there was a new, unknown element in the case. Someone who wasn't a part of the big, flashy crimes done to protect the famous rap star Tekashi 6ix9ine. He wasn't on tape committing armed robberies in the middle of midtown Manhattan, or shooting at people in downtown Brooklyn or at arenas. The feds brought up the Ro Murda robbery. But other than that, it had been drugs: "conspiring to distribute heroin, fentanyl, and MDMA," as Longyear had put it to Engelmayer at a hearing on June 10.

At that hearing, the government showed its hand. There were now just three defendants remaining: Nuke, Harv, and Ro. And one of them—they didn't say the name, but it turned out to be Ro—would almost certainly be pleading guilty before June was out (he ended up doing it on June 27, barely beating the deadline).

That left Harv and Nuke. The pairing was somewhat ironic. Nuke once said that, in Nine Trey, you could either "play with the shit"—he meant engage in violence—or "be the nigga that's grinding," by which he meant dealing drugs. Now, all that remained of the case was one man on either side of the dyad.

Harv's prospects looked bleak. The evidence was stacked against him. He was charged with kidnapping Tekashi, and with slashing Mark. For the kidnapping especially, it seemed like the government had him dead to rights. The victim and his driver were both cooperating witnesses, ready and willing to tell what had happened that night. Plus, the government found the policeman Jorge talked to, the one Tekashi saw when he stumbled into the police station, the doctor Tekashi saw at the hospital, and the medical records showing his bruises. They also had Harv's then-girlfriend, who heard him brag about it. They had the joking meme texts sent afterwards. And more texts too—ones Harv had sent just before the kidnapping, showing him trying to buy a gun from a friend; and ones in the aftermath, showing him trying to sell Tekashi's jewelry. Add to that Shotti's post-kidnapping rant, and it seemed like a slam dunk.

But Harv and his lawyers were determined not to give in. His lead attorney was Deveraux Cannick, a dapper, smooth-talking attorney with a penchant for getting his message in the media. At a hearing on July 9, 2019, after everyone but Harv and Nuke had pled guilty, Cannick made things clear. Judge Engelmayer was trying to read the tea leaves to see if there was going to be a trial, or if these two defendants were going to plead out as well.

"Mr. Cannick, without saying anything that you're uncomfortable saying, am I safe to assume at this point that your client is going to trial?" the judge asked.

"I think that's a safe statement, your honor," Cannick responded.

Talking to reporters after the hearing, Cannick gave a preview of what his defense was going to be. He couldn't deny that the kidnapping happened. It was on video. Instead, he was going to use Tekashi's image as a master troller against him. This kidnapping? It was just another troll. Another stunt. A way to promote "Fefe" and ensure its chart success.

At this point, that sounded plausible to a whole lot of

people. In the hallway just outside of the courtroom, Cannick laid it out.

"Tekashi has mastered the art of marketing, trolling, and, for lack of a better word, fabricating," he said. After another hearing the following month, he made his position even more explicit: The whole thing was faked.

"No robbery or kidnapping or assault happened," Cannick said. "It didn't happen. He had an event that made it look like a robbery or kidnapping. He was about to drop an album. He trolls every time he's about to drop another album. Gotta get your buzz up. That's how you make money."

And what about Tekashi's offer of $50,000 to "get" Harv? Well, Cannick said, Tekashi certainly had the money. If he really wanted it done, and was really offering that kind of money, why didn't it happen?

"You have to wonder whether or not it was real," he said.

As summer 2019 came to an end and the September start date of the trial loomed ever-closer, the possibility that Tekashi would have to rat out his former friends became a certainty. Harv and Nuke were determined to fight until the end.

That left a big problem for the government, and especially for Tekashi—his own past. There were two aspects of his life that were so horrific that they were likely to make any juror who heard about them dismiss him outright. One was the 2015 incident with the thirteen-year-old girl. And the second was his years of domestic abuse. When it showed up in legal paperwork, that horrific past sounded cold and clinical: "incidents of domestic violence from approximately 2011 through in or about November 2018."

So, of course the government wanted to make sure no jurors heard anything about either of those things. And Harv and Nuke, and their lawyers, wanted nothing more than to tell everybody in earshot about them.

All sides tried to negotiate. But nobody involved was budging. In the end, Judge Engelmayer decided that Tekashi's domestic violence would not be mentioned at trial. And what about his 2015 case? The one that was so horrific that the defense was chomping at the bit to mention it to jurors? That was mostly shielded from view as well. The *existence* of a prior conviction could be brought up. But the details were off limits. It was a win for Tekashi. His credibility as a witness wouldn't be damaged by his own prior misdeeds—at least the non-gang-related ones.

What was Engelmayer's reasoning?

For the 2015 case, it was that what Tekashi did was so bad that it would effectively write him off in the minds of any jury. The judge said that if the defense brought it up, it "would transparently be an attempt not to impeach the witness's credibility"—that much would be okay—"but to lead the jury to discount the witness altogether on the separate grounds that he is immoral and loathsome." And that that "would be unfairly prejudicial to the government and to the overall truth-seeking process." It would also be confusing and distracting, since the prior case in question had nothing to do with gangs, racketeering, guns, or drugs—all of the things at issue in this case.

When it came to the history of domestic violence incidents, Engelmayer laid out the cold, hard truth. First off, Tekashi hadn't been convicted for any of them. Also, he said, "it is well settled that incidents of domestic violence do not have any intrinsic bearing on a witness's veracity." If Tekashi's history of domestic violence were revealed, there was a huge risk the jury would disregard everything he said, no matter how true it was.

"There is to be no hint or suggestion of such alleged incidents at this trial," Engelmayer said.

There was one more issue that had to be worked out before the trial could start. The government wanted to play some rap videos at trial. But unlike many cases where this is done, it wasn't in an attempt to prove the rapper's criminality. That part was already well-established. Instead, they wanted to include "Billy," "Gummo," and "Kooda" in order to show that the songs and videos had plenty of information about the people in Nine Trey and how the gang worked. And they were going to have the ultimate decoder—the rapper himself. The plan was to screen the videos, and to have Tekashi break down both the meaning of the lyrics and the people in the videos. He would tell who everyone was, and he would explain how his own songs served to promote Nine Trey. The government also wanted to include Casanova's "Don't Run," which they said was his response to an attempted robbery by Ro Murda.

Engelmayer, despite the strangeness of having to quote lyrics like, "Whole squad full of killers, I'm a killer too," did his best to take each video at its own merits. He was stepping onto a minefield.

A 1996 study by Carrie B. Fried of Indiana University showed that reactions to violent lyrics are stronger when they are presented as rap than when the same lyrics are said to be from country or folk music. "Rap music, which is seen as a predominantly Black form of music, may be judged through the tainted lens of a Black stereotype which includes such traits as violence, hostility, and aggression," it reads. Prosecutors, consciously or not, have used those stereotypes to their advantage in case after case in the past decades. They take rap lyrics written by a defendant and use them to convince a jury of the person's real-world, actual violent behavior.

Sometimes this process can border on the comical, as with the rapper Nuke Bizzle. He was arrested in October 2020 for allegedly stealing peoples' identities to get unemployment benefits from California's Employment Development Department—a scam he bragged about on his song "EDD."

But most instances are far less direct. Prosecutors will use rappers' lyrics and videos to point toward gang membership and criminal activity. There has been a spate of this in Tekashi's native Brooklyn especially, with prosecutors going out of their way to mention rap crews, lyrics, and videos in criminal complaints. This is something that does not happen with any regularity with any other form of music. There is a rising outcry against this practice, but it is still common.

Before rap songs could be blasted in front of unsuspecting jurors, Engelmayer had to watch the videos himself and decide on their merits. He did that, and revealed his conclusions on September 4.

Casanova's "Don't Run" was ruled inadmissible. It was recorded long before Tekashi's crime spree, and was unrelated to the issues at hand. The feds would have to find some other way to talk about Nuke's robbery of Ro. Luckily for them, they had Nuke's own video showing off the proceeds of the robbery and mocking Ro, and plenty of texts from Nuke bragging about it in the aftermath.

So, "Don't Run" was out. But what about Tekashi's songs and videos? There, hip-hop crashed into court decorum. The feds wanted to use the entirety of "Gummo," "Billy," and "Kooda." Nuke's team was against all of it.

The government's argument was that the lyrics "pertain to

certain disputes between [Tekashi] and other rappers." Those disputes led to violent crimes that the feds were trying to prove in order to bring down Nine Trey. The lyrics, Longyear and company argued, were "admissible as co-conspirator statements."

The government said they were striking the right balance between "probative value"—how much actual information the songs and videos contained—and "the danger of unfair prejudice." They also quoted from a 2017 decision that said that people who "have appearances in the Rap Tracks and are seen participating by wearing gang colors, making gang signs, throwing money and singing along to the lyrics in the videos" can be seen as making "adopted statements"—effectively that by being in the video, they can be seen as saying they agree with what's being expressed.

For "Billy," the government made a multifaceted argument. First off, a ton of relevant people were in the video: Kooda, Tekashi, Harv, Shotti, Mel Murda. The name of the song itself was a reference to Nine Trey. And part of the whole point of the trial was to prove that Nine Trey existed, and that Harv was in it.

And then they got to Tekashi's role, referring to him as "CW-2" for "cooperating witness." He was "expected to testify that the lyrics were in response to certain members of Nine Trey (including MACK) as well as other non-Nine Trey gang members (including [Casanova]) who challenged the authenticity of CW-2's gang membership, and the propriety of other Nine Trey members associating with CW-2 and focusing more on the rap industry instead of Nine Trey priorities."

Tekashi was also supposed to break down Shotti's intro on the song, which insisted on the need to "follow the protocol." "'Follow protocol' is an admonition to Nine Trey members to follow the rules of the gang," they wrote somewhat awkwardly, if not inaccurately.

"The entirety of the 'BILLY' rap video, from its title, to its lyrics, to its visual imagery, relates to the Enterprise," they summarized.

When Engelmayer ruled on "Billy," he started out by being on the government's side. Portions of it, he said, were indeed "highly probative."

"The video is strong evidence of the existence of the Nine Trey gang, of the important role in it played by Hernandez and his rap music business, and of Ellison's association with the gang," he said. It made sense to show that Harv was in the video, since that was a demonstration of him "promoting the gang and contributing to its cohesion."

But to Engelmayer's mind, the government had made one big mistake. It ignored that, in the judge's words, "the bulk of the video is filled with rank misogyny." He continued, "These statements could easily alienate a jury and therefore be unfair to Ellison and Mack."

The judge seemed angry that the government hadn't thought about this. Were federal prosecutors really asking a jury to listen to lyrics like, "Dick up in the pussy, bet that shit get gushy gushy/She want the whole gang bussin' all in her pussy"? *Really*?

"Your brief was silent about this striking part of the video," he told prosecutors. Then he let go one of his patented blink-and-you'll-miss-it insults. "You need in the future to examine evidence you are proposing to offer with a great deal more precision."

Japes aside, Engelmayer seemed aware that he was dealing with a heavy issue. Aspects of almost any rap song might well offend a juror with, as he delicately put it, "a more traditionalist bent." But the information in the first half of the video was worth that risk.

"Gummo" was up next. The government's argument with this one was pretty simple. Tekashi was first introduced to Shotti at that video shoot. It was filmed at Maddy, which Tekashi would argue was effectively Nine Trey headquarters. And the lyrics contained an insult against Trippie Redd, whom Tekashi would soon direct Nine Trey members, including Harv, to attack.

The video was probative, Engelmayer ruled. It talked about violence committed by the gang. And the judge ruled that the video *itself*—the ton of gang members, the guns, the lyrics—was a message.

"Once uploaded to YouTube, the video served as a public display of the existence of the gang and the bonds between its members. And it served as a means to tout the gang's power and threaten its rivals," he said.

Engelmayer again split the baby, ruling to exclude "Gummo"'s "misogynistic statements," which he admitted, made up "the majority of the video." He kept only the first seven lines of the song.

After dealing with "Gummo," Engelmayer turned his attention to "Kooda." The government said that some of the lyrics were directed at Casanova. And then, they leaned on one particular argument coming out of Tekashi's mouth: His rap lyrics were real.

"CW-2 is expected to testify that the lyrics refer to the fact that CW-2 and other members of Nine Trey were real gang members, as opposed to rapping about gang activity," the feds said.

They were going to argue that Tekashi's words, "niggas runnin' out they mouth, but they never pop out" "means, in sum and substance, that the rival rapper would talk about committing violence, but would not actually commit such acts; whereas CW-2 and members of Nine Trey actually would commit acts of violence."

It might sound funny to an observer to hear arguments about rap lyrics in an august federal courtroom. But this was unusual. The government was planning to put Tekashi on the stand to confirm that his lyrics were real.

However, all over the country, courts were skipping over the artist, and using lyrics and videos directly to prove rappers' criminal intent. This had been the case for years. In 2001, the No Limit rapper Mac was sentenced to thirty years behind bars for a murder that an entourage member had confessed to. A good chunk of the prosecution's evidence was Mac's own lyrics, sometimes combined from different songs or slightly altered to make them sound more damning. Many believed that it was a case of the prosecution cynically using rap lyrics to pin a crime on an easy, high-profile target—an idea that was bolstered by accounts of witness intimidation unearthed by recent NPR reporting.

Tekashi's case was different. He was arguing that his rap lyrics and videos were reality. They were really talking about the dynamics of a street gang. The lyrics really were advertisements of the gang's strength. But Tekashi, new at that time to the world of gangs, and the world of mainstream hip-hop, was so eager to enter the gates that he'd forgotten something else. Rap lyrics, even his, were also art. There is room for metaphor, fiction, exaggeration, and a playful blurring of the lines between fantasy and reality. By making the choice to out his own lyrics as literal, Tekashi was contributing to a legal atmosphere in which rappers have no choice to do otherwise, when it comes to the justice system.

This dynamic can be seen in depth in Andrea Dennis's and Erik Nielson's 2019 book *Rap on Trial: Race, Lyrics, and Guilt in America*. The book lists case after case in which rap lyrics were used to attempt to show criminality. This is something that largely white forms of music like folk and country have never had to deal with, no matter how many murder ballads or shoot-'em-out epics are recorded. It is an atmosphere rooted in racial prejudice. And it's one, for all their careful line parsing, the government and the judge in this case didn't take enough care to address.

Engelmayer's ruling on "Kooda" followed the same pattern of the other two songs. He let in the first five lines and excluded the rest as "either prejudicial or repetitive." But jurors would still get to hear—and get to hear Tekashi explain—how lyrics like "niggas runnin' out they mouth, but they never pop out" and "all my niggas really gang bang" were meant to demonstrate that, yes, he really was involved in gang activity. The jury would be spared Tekashi's crude, juvenile sexual boasts—*dicky stiffy, uh/bet she give some licky, uh*—for fear that it would shock their delicate sensibilities and possibly prejudice them not just against Tekashi, but against the other two defendants who had their freedom on the line.

With the decision on lyrics made, and the darkest parts of Tekashi's past blocked off, all that was left now was the trial. Two Nine Trey members were prepared to take Shotti's "We don't fold, we don't bend, we don't break" motto as far as it could possibly go. They were putting it all on the line. And that choice was going to force Tekashi to do what his lawyers publicly hoped he wouldn't have to do: tell all, in public.

The two men who were forcing the government to go the distance were opposites in many ways. Aljermiah "Nuke" Mack had some ties to the rap world. But he mostly stayed out of the limelight, and had had minimal interactions with Tekashi.

Anthony "Harv" Ellison was the opposite. He had protected Tekashi. Gotten into fights for him. Got hurt for him. And once Harv was pushed out by Shotti, even went to war with him.

CHAPTER 13

'A JUSSIE SMOLLETT, IF YOU WILL'

On Monday, September 16, 2019, the trial in the case of United States of America v. Aljermiah Mack a/k/a "Nuke," and Anthony Ellison a/k/a "Harv" began. The government's side was led by Michael Longyear, though much of his work would be saved for the closing arguments, and for their showcase witness Tekashi. Jacob Warren and Jonathan Rebold would do the rest of the state's work.

Deveraux Cannick remained as Harv's lead attorney.

Nuke had a small team of lawyers led by Louis Fasulo. Fasulo was late-middle-aged and garrulous—the kind of guy who knew everyone in the courthouse. He was always ready with a quote, or with a friendly shrug if he couldn't get you one just then—it was just business, you know, and you'd see each other tomorrow. The crew would congregate together at a table in the courthouse cafe in the mornings and during lunch breaks, planning their next move.

The first step was to select a jury. The attorneys for both defendants knew that the jurors were going to hear about Harv and Nuke being in jail, and they didn't want those jurors to hold previous incarceration against their clients. Engelmayer worked those issues out with a steady hand.

One hundred potential jurors were brought in, from which twelve jurors and four alternates were selected. The only hint of what was to come showed up when Judge Engelmayer said that one of the witnesses would be "a rapper named Tekashi 6ix9ine." Did anyone have an opinion that would prevent them from being impartial?

No one raised their hand.

In a preview of the trial's most shocking moment, a list of prominent people who might be mentioned was also raised, to give the jury a heads up. In addition to expected names like Casanova and Chief Keef, there was one name that might have been puzzling to bystanders. Jim Jones.

With the jury empaneled, Engelmayer gave them the usual rap. You are here to administer justice, be fair and impartial. You are the judges of the facts, and so on. But buried in that patter was one key sentence that surely rang through jurors' heads from the beginning of the trial to the end.

"Statements, arguments, and questions by the lawyers are not evidence," he said. "Only the answers given by the witnesses are evidence."

It cut to the quick. Harv, especially, had a lawyer with a plausible-sounding theory at the ready: Tekashi 6ix9ine, noted publicity hound and troll, faked his own kidnapping as a public relations stunt. But Deveraux Cannick just saying that in his opening and closing arguments wasn't evidence.

After defining evidence, Engelmayer got to a point that would also be crucial to how the jurors dealt with the case: how to evaluate the credibility of the witnesses. Among the government's key witnesses were admitted drug dealer Kristian Cruz, and Tekashi, whose list of crimes was long, and who frequently exaggerated or outright lied in numerous recorded interviews seen by millions. This was something the defense was sure to hammer on.

So, what was the standard the jury had to keep in mind?

"You are to listen to the witnesses, observe their testimony, and then decide as you would decide such questions in your own life. Did they know what they were talking about? Were they candid, honest, open, and truthful? Did they have a reason to falsify, exaggerate, or distort their testimony?" Engelmayer advised.

This was key. The question wasn't, *were they good people?* Or even *have they ever lied?* Instead, ask: *Did they know what they were talking about?* And *did they have a reason to lie?* For the latter question, the answer was most assuredly no. All three cooperating witnesses (Tekashi, Jorge, and Kristian Cruz) were testifying in order to get their 5K1 letter. If the government thought they had lied—or worse, if they weren't effective as witnesses—there would be no letter.

Jorge was facing seventeen years to life in prison, followed by certain deportation. Tekashi and Cruz would face decades in prison, with the added specter of being a (failed) cooperator hanging over their heads. Being honest was their only way out. That was something that Longyear and company would come back to again and again. Don't believe these people because they're good guys. Believe them because they're selfish. They know that they've backed themselves into a corner where telling the truth is the only way out.

Once the jury was chosen and instructed, it was time for opening arguments. Longyear was saving himself for the high-profile moments like questioning Tekashi. So the opening argument fell to Jonathan Rebold. He didn't waste any time in setting up Nine Trey as a dangerous entity. That was part one of his mission—show that Nine Trey was a threat, and prove that Harv and Nuke were members. After that, he could move to the specific crimes each was charged with perpetuating.

Rebold was blunt.

"Drugs get you money. Violence gets you power."

It was a stark first two sentences.

"For years this has been the mind-set of the Nine Trey Gangsta Bloods, or Nine Trey, a brutal gang whose members flooded the streets with drugs and used the city as their personal battleground, committing violent crimes across New York, a kidnapping at gunpoint, armed robberies, assaults, shootings."

It was an opening that set up the whole case. So many of the gang's crimes, especially the ones done to protect Tekashi's status in the rap world, were shockingly public. The This Is 50 armed robbery in midtown Manhattan. The Chief Keef shooting outside a luxury hotel. The Trippie Redd assault inside another one. A gun going off in the Barclays Center. Shots fired on a Brooklyn street or into the side of a car in downtown Manhattan. Whatever Harv and Nuke's involvement in each individual case, the opening painted a picture of a dangerous, out of control gang, albeit one whose poor aim had miraculously not resulted in any deaths.

Then Rebold got into something sure to appeal to jurors who saw themselves as good, upright citizens—and that would simultaneously set up their case against Nuke.

"The defendants were two of the gang's highest ranking members," Rebold said. "For years these defendants and other members of Nine Trey affected the city through violence and through the sale of drugs. That is why we are here today. That's what this case is about."

Drugs. Heroin. Fentanyl. In a country riven by an oft-publicized "opioid crisis," and with one of the defendants accused of drug dealing, leaning into the narcotics side of Nine Trey made perfect sense. After all, the government had an expert who could break down exactly how the gang had not only sold heroin, but also loaded it with dangerous fentanyl to sell to unsuspecting end users. Kristian Cruz knew how that worked because he did it.

Rebold went on to explain something that was obvious to close observers, but might have been confusing to the jurors just getting introduced to the case. A lot of the Nine Trey violence wasn't against rival gangs. It was against itself. Attacks from within the gang on other members were shockingly common. In fact, both of the crimes Harv was defending himself against—the kidnapping and the slashing—fell in that category.

How could you get that across to people not versed in the finer points of gang warfare?

Well, Rebold promised that by the end, jurors *would* become experts. They'd be versed in Nine Trey's structure and hierarchy. And they'd learn about the drug dealing and the violent crimes. They'd learn how those crimes were often committed to raise a person's stature in the gang. And then, Rebold arrived at his key, counterintuitive point, one the jurors had to grasp for his case to have a prayer of holding up.

"Often that violence was directed at rival gangs, but at times that violence was directed inward. You will learn that Nine Trey was filled with internal conflict, competing groups, each vying for power within the gang."

It was a simple way of explaining a complicated dynamic. But the underlying issue was universal. After all, if there's one thing everybody understands, it's infighting.

Rebold then began to spin his tale. Tekashi's sudden

stardom meant money for the leaders of Nine Trey. For a while, Harv had been partly in control of that money, and he had provided muscle for the rap star. But then Shotti had taken control, and Harv had "responded with violence," by kidnapping and robbing Tekashi.

Rebold addressed the slashing as well, ending with a devastating description. Ellison "settled another gang dispute by slicing someone's face open from his ear to his chin. Why?" He paused. "Because that's how Nine Trey members settle their disputes, through severe acts of violence."

It was a harsh blow, and there was to be still more to come. Rebold knew his team had photos of a bloodied slashing victim to show the jury when the time was right. He was just laying the groundwork.

Rebold made sure to take the jury through all the evidence his side was getting ready to present. This was important. It was likely that neither Harv or Nuke would take the stand in their own defense. That was risky because it exposed them to cross-examination. Without it, the burden was on the government to make its case stick.

When it came to Harv, they had testimony from police officers and doctors. They had photographs. They had surveillance video of him actually kidnapping Tekashi. They had cell site evidence placing Harv at the locations of both the kidnapping and the slashing.

They had recorded phone calls and social media posts showing Nine Trey members discussing their crimes. And he closed with the ace in the hole: they had testimony from several Nine Trey members and associates who were cooperating witnesses, including Tekashi. Then he launched into a peremptory explanation of why they should be believed.

"Let me be clear about these witnesses. They are criminals." Rebold was frank, but he needed to be. "They have committed serious crimes, and they will tell you about those crimes, and they have pleaded guilty to those crimes. They will be testifying during this trial not out of the kindness of their heart, but in the hopes of getting a reduced sentence when they are sentenced."

He had to say this. Defense lawyers were sure to hammer on this over and over—that these guys were criminals themselves, and that they were only testifying to save their own skin. Rebold's answer was, effectively, *so what?*

"With respect to these witnesses the question before you is not whether you approve of what they have done. The question before you is whether they are telling the truth."

How could the jurors determine that? They needed to determine if what the witnesses said fit with all the rest of the evidence. The cell site records, the social media posts, the video, the phone calls, the doctors, the cops. If it made sense in the context of the rest of what had been presented, then it didn't really matter *who* was doing the presenting—it was likely to be true.

Alex Huot was next, representing Nuke. He charged out of the gate determined to try and take down a key piece of the government's puzzle: that Nine Trey was a highly organized criminal enterprise. If he could show that wasn't true, then Nuke being a member couldn't mean he was part of a racketeering conspiracy. Instead, Huot argued, Nuke claiming he was part of Nine Trey was something akin to claiming he'd been in a frat.

"Let's talk about fraternities for a second," he said. "Sure, members may all know some signals, some handshakes, some secret words."

The use of "handshakes" and "signals" here was not accidental. He knew that the government had a photo of Tekashi and Nuke outside a nightclub, doing a Nine Trey hand sign. It was a photo that jurors were likely to see as soon as the next day.

"There may be pictures where members from one chapter are in a photo with members from another chapter," he continued. "Members from different chapters, they may even communicate with one another online."

"But they are each still a part of their own organization. If members from one chapter go off and do something wrong, all of the other members from the other chapters aren't held accountable for those actions."

Comparing a set of the United Blood Nation to a chapter of Kappa Kappa Psi might seem like a bizarre move. But in the context of Nuke's case, it made sense. Nuke wasn't around for a lot of the Tekashi-related crime spree. His defense lawyers were doing their best to make sure that he wasn't held accountable for it by arguing that being in the same gang wasn't *really* being in the same gang. It was more like being in a small subset of a large organization, with very little connecting the subsets besides some rituals.

Huot continued on to a comparison of the lines of Nine Trey with the different US states. "Like the saying goes, 'What happens in Iowa stays in Iowa,'" he said at the end of that section.

He then moved on to attacking Tekashi's credibility. The rapper, he said, was "contractually bound to the government." He "manipulated the public and the media throughout his rise to the top." And as a rap star, he was surrounded by hangers-on. Including, Huot argued, people with stories about his client, Aljermiah Mack.

As for Nuke's voluminous taped phone calls that outlined

Nine Trey's drug business? Well, Huot argued, jail is lonely. You can say all kinds of things just to keep yourself entertained.

"Idle chatter amongst friends, that's the best way to pass the time," he argued.

His mission complete, Huot sat down. This brought up Deveraux Cannick.

Cannick was in a difficult position. The evidence was stacked against his client, and all he had was a theory that said that the video *looked* like a kidnapping; and Jorge thought it was a kidnapping; and Shotti thought it was a kidnapping. But that, despite all appearance to the contrary, the kidnapping had been staged.

"This whole thing about a kidnap is a hoax. It's a Jussie Smollett, if you will."

Bringing up the then-in-the-news story of the early 2019 attack on *Empire* star Smollett, allegedly staged by the actor himself, appeared to be a surefire way to sell this theory. But Cannick didn't acknowledge that an opening argument, no matter how many TV star references it contained, was not, on its own, evidence.

Cannick's evidence for his big claim about the hoax? A trolling Instagram post from Tekashi in February, 2018, many months before the kidnapping. In it, he showed off a new chain, a diamond-encrusted piece modeled after the scary doll from the *Saw* movies. The caption was "SOMEBODY PLEASE SNATCH MY CHAIN SO MY PROJECT COULD SELL MORE. MORE PUBLICITY IS GOOD PULBLICUTY [SIC]. I'LL POST MY LOCATION IN A FEW."

In the end, Cannick never showed the post to the jury. And with good reason. It was posted long before the kidnapping, and in fact was one in a long string of trolly posts by Tekashi daring people to test how tough he was. There were dozens, if not hundreds, of examples of this.

Tekashi, Cannick continued, obviously knew who'd kidnapped him, but he didn't tell the cops. And he lied about the incident in interviews in the aftermath. All of that was true. But it was something that Tekashi would soon deal with head-on in his testimony.

And then, seemingly out of nowhere, Cannick brought up Martin Luther King, Jr.

"You will remember Dr. King told us long ago, no lie can live forever."

Was Harv meant to be the Dr. King in this situation? Cannick also implied that the government needed to produce Mark, the slashing victim, in order to prove Harv had slashed him—despite the fact that *Cannick* was the one angling for Mark to show up as a witness.

CHAPTER 14
A REALLY SCARY SITUATION

D ay two of the trial started with a setback for Deveraux Cannick. When the lawyers assembled at 9 AM to work out small stuff with the judge before the jury arrived, Cannick wasn't among them. Instead, he was caught in traffic.

Engelmayer was not amused. "It's imperative that all counsel be ready at 9:00," he said. When Cannick arrived, he got a short talking-to. "You need to be here at 9:00," the judge said. "I start at 9:00."

It was time for the government's first witness. They called the NYPD detective who was working in Smurf Village the night Mark was slashed.

He laid out what happened that night. And then it was time for the big guns. Gruesome photos of Mark's injuries. One showed Mark in the hospital, bandages over the entire top of his head. He was lying down, and the slash was directly facing the camera. The gash was very wide and went from his ear to his chin.

The next photo, from three days later, was less bloody but

still horrible. It showed all of the stitches, running the entire length of the left side of Mark's face.

The next witness didn't want to be there. That much was clear. She showed up only because she'd been subpoenaed. She was Harv's ex-girlfriend, the one who'd been with him the night of the slashing. Her discomfort was palpable. Right off the bat, she claimed to have trouble seeing, anticipating the expected do-you-recognize-the-defendant-in-the-courtroom-today question. The government eventually got around this by showing her a photo of Harv.

Initial hiccup over, she went on. While they were dating, Harv had told her that he was a Blood. He was a part of Treyway.

"And what did you understand Treyway to mean?" Rebold asked.

"Just a part of the Bloods gang."

This was a key part of the prosecution's strategy. They wanted to demonstrate repeatedly that Treyway, the thing Tekashi was always screaming, wasn't a real business. It was a front, a way to market the gang and to talk about it in public. If that was true, it would set up Nine Trey as an entity interested in its own survival and strengthening. It was almost the very definition of a racketeering enterprise.

The girlfriend went through her whole story of the night of the slashing. How she took a car to Smurf Village. How Harv left her alone for hours. And she talked about what happened when they finally got to their hotel.

"He basically told me that he had gotten back at the guy that shot his friend," she said. "He said that he had stabbed the guy in the face."

When combined with the cop's testimony and the photo of the stabbing victim, it was a powerful admission. She also said something else, something the government had hinted at prior. She said that Harv mentioned to her one day, when the topic of Tekashi came up, that he had kidnapped the rap star and robbed him for his chain. She also remembered another time Tekashi had come up.

"I had told him about the fact that I was seeing him all over social media being accused of the kidnapping and robbing of 6ix9ine," she recalled.

And Harv's response?

"He seemed pretty excited about it. He said he is going to be famous for that."

Toward the end of the cross-examination, Nuke's lawyer jumped in, bringing up the circumstances under which she was testifying.

It was, the ex-girlfriend admitted, "a really scary situation. I don't know what Harvey is capable of doing."

CHAPTER 15

'DO YOU RECOGNIZE ANYONE IN THE COURTROOM?'

After lunch that day, it was the event everybody was here for, the reason anyone was paying attention to the case at all. Daniel "Tekashi 6ix9ine" Hernandez, rap star and master troller, was about to take the witness stand.

It was largely up to Tekashi to set up a story, to provide context for the rest of the prosecutors' evidence. Michael Longyear was ready for this. He started off easy: how old are you, what nicknames do you go by, where were you born —softballs.

Tekashi quickly admitted to snitching.

"At some point did you decide to cooperate with the government?"

"On November 19, the day after we was taken down."

There it was. In his own voice, witnesses heard Tekashi explain that he was ready to bend, fold, and break from the beginning. There was never a thought of holding out, or of not betraying the gang that had ensured his safety and street cred during his rise to the top.

Tekashi was squinting incessantly on the stand, something he kept up for the entire three days he testified.

Was it because he couldn't see? Was it nerves? Fear?

There was certainly no shortage of people in red in the courtroom, the traditional color of the Bloods. And there was a ton of media: *Vulture, The New York Times, The Post, The Daily News*. There were fans and curiosity seekers. And there were a small handful of people who weren't aligned with traditional media outlets, or in some cases with any at all, but who were obsessed with the case and had attended a number of the pre-trial hearings.

Tekashi's numerous prep sessions with the government seem to have helped. The normally subject-wandering, conversation-dominating internet troll was clear and direct, at least at first.

What did Nine Trey do?

"We participated in a lot of, you know, violent crimes, robberies, assaults, drugs, stuff of that nature."

The big will-he-or-won't-he moment was out of the way early.

"Mr. Hernandez, do you recognize anyone in the courtroom who was a member of Nine Trey when you were a member?"

"Yes." He ID'd Harv and Nuke, without hesitation.

Longyear took Tekashi through his early life. Where he grew up. Where he went to school. The long string of jobs he'd had since he was thirteen. He continued through meeting Righteous P and starting to rap. Finding a manager and meeting Seqo Billy. And then, finally, the idea to film a video where he was surrounded by Nine Trey members.

In this telling, there was no Seqo trying to get him in touch with the urban community; no previous attempt to do a video with a sea of Crips in blue. How the "Gummo" video came about was simple and straightforward.

"When I was ready to film the video, I approached Seqo Billy and I asked him if we could get[...]some Nine Trey members to be in the video, because I wanted the aesthetic to be, you know, full with Nine Trey Blood members because I'm in the song," he said.

The government began building its case against Nine Trey, brick by brick. They asked Tekashi to identify Seqo.

"Seqo Billy is a Nine Trey member. He's the first one I ever knew."

Neither Seqo nor his aunt Ms. Tr3yway would ever be charged. But both of them would play a role in the narrative the government was building. Having Tekashi point Seqo out was notable, and perhaps a little sad, to those observing Tekashi's career from the beginning. Seqo was by Tekashi's side at early radio interviews and club appearances. It was a position not without its indignities, like the time when they appeared on New York radio station Hot 97 and Tekashi outright lied, with Seqo sitting right next to him, about their relationship, saying they'd grown up together when in reality they'd only known each other for a few months. But that's what loyalty was. And now, Seqo was just Exhibit 22, a photograph and a nameplate in the service of lessening Tekashi's prison sentence.

Interestingly, for all the talk to come about the "Gummo" video being a way to promote Nine Trey, the ostentatious use of red in the video was, Tekashi freely admitted, all artifice.

"I told Seqo that I would like for them to all be in red," Tekashi explained. "Because red is what a Blood member would wear, so I want the video to be full of red." He remembered that he personally went out to buy bandanas for everyone in advance of the shoot. For "Gummo," he wanted an exaggerated version of life on Maddy: all guns, drugs, and gang signs, with him at the center.

From there, Longyear took Tekashi through the other people he'd met at Maddy that day. Most prominent among these was Shotti himself. He was, Tekashi was told, the "big homie," the shot-caller.

Then it was time for the jurors to get their first taste of "Gummo," or, as the court called it, Exhibit 607. The jurors were given a handful of lines of lyrics, with the word "nigga" starred out to read "n****."

Just what it was they were supposed to make of "You run up and they shooting n****s, we ain't hooping n****" wasn't explained outright, but the mention of "them Billy n****s" was clear enough.

They paused the video to ID Seqo and his aunt. Longyear held on the latter. What was her relationship to Nine Trey, he asked.

That was a complicated question. But Longyear wasn't particularly interested in nuance.

"She went by Ms. Tr3yway," Tekashi said.

It was true. Even after the gang takedown, she'd continued to use the moniker, and created a Tr3yway brand of cosmetics in an attempt to exercise the trademark she registered, and to claim the word and concept she saw as rightfully hers.

The government wasn't interested in Maddy as her family home, but instead as a place for the gang. Tekashi spelled it out.

"Members of Nine Trey would have meetings there."

Tekashi continued pointing out people in the video, and even acknowledged that, yes, the gun a Nine Trey member was holding was real.

Then Longyear acted like the most straightlaced music professor imaginable.

"Mr. Hernandez, I'm going to ask you some questions about the lyrics of 'Gummo.'" This could have been dicey territory. Rapping about guns and gangs is not itself illegal, or an indicator of anything except familiarity with hip-hop tropes. But Longyear was being much more literal. "Gummo" mentioned being around Billys because Tekashi was around Billys. Longyear got the rapper to explain what a "blicky" was, and what a "drum" was—both weaponry-related terms that appeared in the song's lyrics. He didn't make explicit, but didn't have to, that he wasn't interested in it because of an artful turn of phrase. If "Gummo" was an ad for the gang, it was important to show that they were bragging about having guns and ammunition.

There was another aspect of "Gummo" left to talk about—its insult to Trippie Redd. Tekashi explained, somewhat confusingly, what his line about Trippie's bodyguard KB actually meant ("No KB, you a loser nigga, up that Uzi nigga"). Losing the thread, he admitted, "I don't know. I thought it was cool at the time." But, he said, "Gummo" as a whole was aimed at Trippie.

"There was a lot of jealousy involved," Tekashi admitted. It was a great setup. Not long afterwards, Longyear would take Tekashi step by step through the November 2017 assault on Trippie at the Gansevoort Hotel.

Longyear guided Tekashi through "Gummo"'s runaway instant success, and into the follow-up, "Kooda." When talking about how to make sure he remained on top, Tekashi's calculations came into full view.

"After we shot 'Gummo,' I knew I had a formula. I knew the formula was to repeat it."

What was the "*it?*," Longyear asked.

"The gang image, I would say, like promote it. That's what people like. It was just a formula, a blueprint I found that worked."

After hearing all about Tekashi's formula, jurors saw its results in "Kooda." Just like with "Gummo," the government went through the clip, pointing out all the Nine Trey members who appeared in it. Longyear again went through the lyrics. Tekashi admitted the track was addressing his career in real time, responding to the controversy that had followed "Gummo." There were haters, he explained, who "didn't understand how, I guess, a kid with rainbow hair could be affiliated with Nine Trey Bloods."

Next in Longyear's plan was to explain how Tekashi moved from using gang members as props in videos to actually becoming involved in, and often leading, their crimes. The rapper recounted the story of how he got into the gang the same way he accomplished everything else—by incessantly joking, trolling, and harrassing people until he got what he wanted.

Then, with Tekashi established as a gang member, Longyear got to the heart of the matter.

"As a member of Nine Trey, what responsibilities, if any, did you have?" he asked.

"Just keep making hits and be the financial support for the gang."

And what was the money for?

"So they could buy guns and stuff like that."

Here was the rap star admitting that his commercial success was intimately tied to Nine Trey's criminal activities. It was the kind of thing the NYPD was always hunting for in its endless, federally assisted war on rappers. But never was it spelled out this clearly, directly from the source.

The NYPD was constantly surveilling people in the hip-hop world. They had been since the 1990s. They even had a unit dedicated to the practice, and a specialized "binder" with information on almost every major rapper in the city. Often, they would collaborate with the federal government in their investigations, through the federal High Intensity Drug Trafficking Area (HIDTA) program.

"The reason they put HIDTA into it [was] they had better computers and better resources," says Derrick Parker, the former NYPD officer who'd started the department's rap unit.

The NYPD spent a lot of time establishing ties between rappers and street gangs. But in this case, it was all set out in court for the public to see. Nine Trey got money from a rap star.

And what did the rap star get in return?

"I would say my career. Street credibility. The music, the videos, the protection. All of the above."

This was the crux of the relationship. Before Nine Trey, Tekashi had been at best a cult figure, making edgy, punk-influenced videos that garnered him a small audience in Eastern Europe, and basically nowhere else. With Nine Trey on his side, he was a worldwide phenomenon. It's easy to see how that may have been worth a handful of five-figure payments.

Next, Longyear introduced a photo of Nuke and Tekashi together, and let Tekashi share an anecdote of Nuke teaching him how to do a proper Nine Trey hand sign. It was a minor scene, but it was meant to set up Nuke as someone who cared about the gang, enough that he would pull a rising star to the side to make sure he was repping it right.

Then it was time to talk about Harv.

Longyear introduced several videos and photos of Harv throwing up the Nine Trey sign. These were not hard to find.

Longyear's whole mission was to demonstrate that Nine Trey was *organized*—the *o* in RICO stood for "organizations," after all. So, he painstakingly took Tekashi through photo after photo. *Who was pictured? What were their names?*

And then, they addressed the hierarchy. *How was the gang organized? Who was on top? What were the different lineups? What were the ranks? Who had each position?*

This line of questioning seemed to be put there specifically to counter Nuke's lawyers' objections that just because there was a handshake, didn't mean there was a coherent organization. In fact, Longyear was saying, here it is, the organization—from Godfather all the way down. The day's testimony ended there.

CHAPTER 16

'LET'S TALK ABOUT THE TIMES WHEN YOU ACTUALLY PAID CASH'

T he second day of Tekashi's testimony got deeper into Nine Trey's structure, and also introduced Mel Murda.

But Longyear was particularly interested in something else: money.

Tekashi admitted to giving gang members large payments around eight times between December 2017 ("when I first started seeing real money") through August 2018. He'd paid Harv. He'd paid Shotti. And he'd even paid Crippy.

To judge by his line of questioning, Longyear was especially interested in the first two. Crippy, injured and already behind bars, and a secondary character in the tale, wouldn't matter much.

Tekashi enumerated the payments. The money was for "the homies." It was for guns. And Tekashi couldn't resist a dig at some of his former protectors: "I spoke to Harv about some of the homies not having places to stay[...]and making sure they were good."

Tekashi didn't have to publicly name Nine Trey members

as homeless and down on their luck. But he seemed to leap at the opportunity. It wasn't the last time. During his testimony, he would at multiple other points go out of his way to insult people. He called J. Prince's Rap-A-Lot label "a wanna-be mafia kind of thing." And he referred to Jim Jones as a "retired rapper"—twice—even though Jones had just released a new album. Shotti, he said, was "playing this fake management role." Billboard had "cheated" him out of a number 1 album. Even with his freedom on the line, and in a prison jumpsuit, his urge to insult and troll was irrepressible.

Longyear began to get into the material that the people packed into the courtroom were really there to hear about: the rap beefs. He began with Trippie Redd, getting Tekashi to recount in detail the incident that began at Trippie's video shoot and ended with Harv punching Trippie at the Gansevoort Hotel.

After that, Tekashi said, he became very close with Harv, who got moved into the role of "enforcer." When Tekashi ran into a threatening person at a T-Mobile store, he called Harv. When a Nine Trey affiliate named Snow Billy was following Tekashi a little bit too closely and threateningly, he called Harv. The Yams Day brawl? Harv was in the mix, beating a man with a stick. Some people throwing insults at an airport? Harv was the first to punch one of them in the face, kicking off a fight that made it to TMZ.

Painting Harv as the enforcer and the heavy was smart, because it made his move to kidnapper much easier to swallow. Any juror could imagine an enforcer changing sides and turning his muscle and violence on the person he used to protect. Longyear carefully took Tekashi through his split with Harv, which had happened in the middle of the J. Prince dustup. Notably, Tekashi pointed to Harv's "RESPECT MY DICK" text as the breaking point.

The courtroom audience of course knew that Tekashi had a long history of telling innumerable people, foe and friend alike, to do something similar. Saying "suck my dick" is, among certain sectors of the hip-hop world, a sort of unbridgeable chasm—they are the ultimate fight-on-sight words. As a result, it was one of Tekashi's go-to insults for anyone who got on his bad side. The taboo breaking was a large part of the point. So to see someone who broke that particular rule regularly, then view someone *else* breaking it as an alliance-ending move, well, the irony was obvious.

Longyear next took Tekashi through the Yams Day brawl. For those who remembered Tekashi's statement at the time denying responsibility, hearing the actual story put some things into stark relief. For one, Tekashi was now finally being honest. He was telling the real story of exactly how uncontrollably violent his Nine Trey-dominated world had gotten. This admission also underscored just how willing he'd been to publicly play the innocent victim of hurtful, untrue rumors when it had suited his purposes.

Longyear continued working his way through a series of messages in the group text with Shotti, Tekashi, Harv, Seqo, and more. He made sure to have Tekashi read a few of Harv's more boastful and threatening missives, like, "It's not a nigga walking this earth that could ever say he violated me on Blood." Longyear drew out from Tekashi all the tensions between Harv and Shotti; particularly that while Shotti ranked higher in the gang, Harv just thought Shotti was a loudmouth.

And then, the message that was in a lot of ways key to Longyear's whole approach. He had Tekashi read, out loud,

Harv's mission statement, said in the heat of an argument with Shotti and Tekashi about respect, power, and control.

"Growing up all I wanted to be a gangsta the right way. Neva look up to nothing else."

It was ungrammatical, rushed in the heat of a text message war. But it formed the basis of the version of Anthony "Harv" Ellison that the government wanted jurors to see. That the man on trial wasn't a normal person. He was violent. He was aggressive. And he was, above all, devoted to his idea of what Nine Trey was. Out of the tens of thousands of texts at their disposal, the government had picked an effective one to focus attention on.

In this part of his testimony, Tekashi also broke down the meeting between Shotti, Harv, and Mel Murda to determine who would have control over his rap career. It was a surreal moment. Normally these sorts of agreements are whispered about in rumors. And here was the biggest rap star of the moment, openly recounting a gang meeting where a Nine Trey Godfather was deciding which of two gang members would be able to maintain an iron grip on Tekashi's cash flow. And then, text messages from said Godfather, impatiently wondering where the money was.

It was the hidden side of the hip-hop economy, exposed.

Tekashi's second day of testimony was by far the most action-packed. In addition to the text messages, he ran through the assault on Frenchie BSM and the dramatic story of the This Is 50 robbery, including his armed subway ride home with Crippy. When surveillance video of the robbery showed Scumlord D!zzy, Tekashi didn't hesitate to throw yet another former mentor under the bus.

"The individual depicted in the frame here at 41 seconds, who is that, Mr. Hernandez?" Longyear asked.

"Scumlord D!zzy."

"And who is that?"

"He's a Crip member, Flatbush."

There wasn't a narrative need to identify D!zzy as a Crip in federal court. D!zzy wasn't on trial, and the question wasn't directly asked. He was at best a tangential character in the case. And yet there was Tekashi, always ready to get a dig in whenever he could.

When D!zzy later heard what Tekashi had said, he wasn't surprised.

"I just thought, this kid is going to do whatever and try to bring down everybody with him," D!zzy responded. "Because his back is against the corner, and that's what rats do."

Tekashi didn't have that much to say about Nuke. But he did know all about Nuke's robbery of Ro—the one he'd found out about while he was enjoying a Mets game. After that story, it was time for lunch.

Engelmayer expressed concern about aspects of Tekashi's testimony. It was taking a long time, in large part because of Tekashi's propensity to ramble and add details he hadn't been asked about. It made sense—most times he had spoken to the public, it was via Instagram, uncensored. Rambling uninterrupted was part of the art form. But the judge wasn't having it, and asked Longyear to make his star witness reel it in a bit. It shouldn't be the defense's responsibility to object every time Tekashi went off the rails.

"The onus is better put on you," Engelmayer told Longyear, "and I urge you to use it."

"Urge" is not a word a federal judge uses lightly, and Longyear did his best to get Tekashi to straighten up and fly right. The judge had one other side note, to Nuke's lead lawyer —*tell your client to stop smirking.*

The government put Tekashi in the decoder position after lunch, breaking down Nuke's text messages. There were texts about the aftermath of the Ro Murda robbery. There were messages about his relationship with Nine Trey leadership. Tekashi was sometimes *too* anxious to do this, reading off the messages so fast that he was admonished to slow down so the court reporter could keep up.

Once his time as the decoder ring was over, Tekashi continued recounting Nine Trey's crime spree. They walked through both downtown Brooklyn shootings: the afternoon one where Shotti had fired on some people who had the temerity to insult Tekashi to his face; and the evening one at the Barclays Center. As a prelude to the Barclays shooting, they discussed Tekashi's war with Casanova and played the final of his three songs, "Billy." It was the only one where Tekashi took a (very) brief sidebar into talking about his art. What did he mean by the line, "whole squad full of fucking killers, I'm a killer too"?

"Just the craft of the song. The craft, like the artist just expressing."

The matter-of-factness of Tekashi's testimony was surprising, especially after a solid year of denials and trolling.

What happened with Chief Keef?

"I gave orders to my friend Kooda to shoot at him."

There it was. No joking denials, no trolling. Just the facts, plain as day. It was both totally expected and startling to hear things stated that openly.

Tekashi even discussed his own trolling in the same matter-of-fact way.

"The very next morning, after it happened, it was publicized I mocked Chief Keef."

As the day went on, Tekashi did more and more rambling,

intent on explaining all of the ins and outs of exactly how Nine Trey had splintered, or details about the time Harv pulled up on people with a gun.

It was nothing anybody wanted to hear.

Longyear's plan called for a step-by-step reveal of facts, not a running monologue that went wherever Tekashi deemed important in the moment. For all their dozens of rehearsals, Longyear's control of the situation, and of his witness, seemed to be slipping away.

"Mr. Hernandez, listen to the question," the judge said. "Just answer the question. Don't just keep talking."

Things didn't didn't get any better when it came time to describe the kidnapping. Tekashi was recounting, beat by beat, an incident that would be traumatic for anyone. So, the fact that his control began to slip even further made sense.

The judge tried his best, telling Longyear to keep Tekashi's digressions to a minimum. But it was tough. Tekashi got hard to hear, because he kept falling off-mic.

Luckily for the jury, there was a surprise. Video of the actual kidnapping, from inside Jorge's car. It was a shock. The central crime of the whole trial was there, with audio and video. You could hear Tekashi address his kidnapper as "Harv." You could see him being taken out of the car. You could see Jorge speed away frantically in search of help. You could hear Harv and Sha's voices.

It was powerful. But that power was somewhat mitigated by two things: Tekashi's too-quiet testimony and his insistence, despite repeated admonitions, to say what he was *thinking* at various times in the kidnapping, as opposed to what *happened*.

The judge was losing his patience.

"I don't know whether it's the emotion of the incident or something like that, but the last fifteen minutes or so the witness' discipline in both responding to questions as directed and in just the clarity of the speech seems to me is breaking down. I will tell you, I think I've said five times, focus on action."

Paul Engelmayer was not the type to have to say something five times in his courtroom.

Longyear went for sympathy. "The witness is visibly shaken up. This is obviously a traumatic experience for him."

Besides, Longyear was doing his best, sticking to "And then what happened?"-type inquiries that should leave no space for inner monologues.

Ask tighter questions, Engelmayer replied. Don't give him a chance to get off course. As for volume, well, the judge would deal with that himself. He admonished Tekashi to get, and stay, close to the mic.

This intervention seemed to work. Longyear's questions—"what did you see happen?" "Where were you?" and the like—cut down on the rambling.

Finally, Longyear led Tekashi to recount what happened the evening after the kidnapping, when he, Mel, Crippy, Jorge, and Shotti met up at Tekashi's house to plan their next move.

"What, if anything, did Shotti bring to your house?" Longyear asked.

"Big assault rifle."

And there it was. Exhibit 100. The actual assault rifle that Shotti was waving around that night. Longyear made sure all the jurors saw it. If there was ever a reason to believe that Nine Trey was a frightening bunch of guys, this was it. This gun was huge.

At around 4:45, news was delivered to the judge that was serious enough to end the proceedings immediately. Audio of the first few minutes of Tekashi's testimony from the previous day had been illegally recorded, and made its way to the internet. Now, everyone had the opportunity to not just read about Tekashi snitching, and not just see a courtroom sketch. They could actually hear him, for himself, pointing out Harv and Nuke. Ratting, for the world to see. It was his lawyers' worst-case scenario, blown up exponentially.

And there was still one more day of testimony to go.

CHAPTER 17

'YOU KNEW CARDI B WAS A BLOOD, CORRECT?'

Engelmayer began the new day by addressing the leaked audio. Yes, it had indeed been "surreptitiously recorded." So, they were doubling up on security. No phones in the courtroom, even from people who had previously been allowed to have them, except for lawyers directly involved in the case. And now there was a new, second level of screening outside the courtroom.

Longyear was pretty sure that Tekashi's testimony would wind down shortly after lunch that day. There wasn't that much left to go over. Longyear got Tekashi to admit that he lied about details of the kidnapping in some interviews afterward. It was smart to bring it up, as Harv's lawyers would assuredly point to the lies as proof that the whole thing was a scam, and that nothing Tekashi said about the kidnapping was to be trusted.

Tekashi said the lies were a natural outgrowth of his tough guy persona.

"I was bragging a lot on Instagram that I was untouchable,

I'm the king of my city. And [the kidnapping] was just humiliating at the time."

There was another factor, too, as to why he embellished some parts of the story, and never admitted to knowing who robbed him.

"I didn't want to snitch. I was still a part of the Nine Trey lineup, and there was no snitching."

The irony of the answer—recalling his reluctance to snitch, while in the middle of the most public instance of snitching in years—was not publicly acknowledged. But it was there nonetheless.

Longyear demonstrated the chaos the kidnapping caused inside Nine Trey. There was tape of Mel Murda talking to another Nine Trey member. Mel said he expressed his horror over the move directly to Harv—referring to him by his other nickname, "Hollywood."

"I'm telling Hollywood, like, 'why the fuck you did that? Like, what the fuck was that? That was stupid, Blood.'"

Why was it stupid? Well, they might be enemies, but they had been allies before. "Niggas know everything about each other."

Following up on that point, Longyear next played the Shotti monologue from a few days after the kidnapping. The entire courtroom listened quietly to nearly twenty straight minutes of Shotti haranguing Tekashi and threatening Harv.

It was a startling moment. It was one thing to see the Tekashi/Shotti relationship play out in curated videos on social media. But it was entirely different to hear this monologue, secretly recorded in the middle of an intra-gang war.

After that, it was time for Longyear to attempt to really bury Harv.

Longyear showed text messages from Harv the day before

the robbery where he was talking about getting a gun. And some from afterward, where an acquaintance hit Harv about buying a "bitch with the red face"—the red-faced watch he stole from Tekashi. It was devastating stuff.

And Tekashi was on the witness stand, helping it along.

Finally, it was time for the slashing. The jury already knew all about it from earlier in the trial, but now Longyear wanted to bring it back. He got Tekashi to recount being told about the events of the night not long after it happened by a Nine Trey member. The gang member told Tekashi about that horrific night in order to show the rapper that Shotti was still protecting him. Protecting him, in this case, by bringing literally paralyzing violence to Harv's doorstep, inviting bloody revenge from Harv in return.

Tekashi was strangely callous in reporting all of this. He referred to the slashing victim as "a little fat kid. I don't know his name."

As his testimony continued, Tekashi again started wandering off-track, unable to limit his answers to what Longyear wanted to know. He always wanted to talk more, to tell what he saw as the full story.

The judge stepped in.

"Mr. Hernandez, you have to listen to Mr. Longyear's question. He's asking you not about back in some other time. He's asking you about what was said by Shotti in October 2018."

Tekashi admitted, again matter-of-factly, that he offered $50,000 for someone to "rob Harv or shoot at Harv." And he continued to callously refer to the slashing victim as "the fat kid who got cut."

Eventually, though, things began to turn a corner. Longyear guided Tekashi into talking about the end of the line with Nine Trey. There was a brief hiccup when the rap star didn't understand the word "ramifications," but Longyear quickly subbed "consequences" and they soldiered on.

Then they got to Exhibit 320.

It was the now-famous "superviolate" conversation, which had made the news in the days after Tekashi's arrest. But there was one previously unreported element. Initial reports had said that Mel Murda was a part of the conversation, but the name of the other person was not public. But now, at the trial, it was out there. They played the tape of the conversation. The second voice was immediately familiar.

Jim Jones.

It was shocking to hear Jones directly involved in such a ground-level gang conversation, even if it did involve another rap star.

The news became a sensation. Jim's name was everywhere on Twitter. He kept quiet publicly—there was no upside to responding. But his voice on the tape was all anybody wanted to talk about.

It was the last big moment of Tekashi's testimony. Now it was time for cross-examination. It was the defense's job to discredit him. They needed to show the jury that no one should believe this rainbow-haired troll, who would do anything to go viral.

First up was one of Nuke's lawyers, Alex Huot. Huot started out with the obvious move: attempting to discredit Tekashi by pointing out that he was only talking in order to get out of a decades-long prison sentence. Then, Huot listed all the crimes Tekashi had pled guilty to. The lawyer went through them one by one, forcing Tekashi to give a clipped "correct" to every misdeed.

Huot pointed out that his client, Nuke, was part of none of these crimes. His line of questioning was aimed at making

Tekashi out to be a liar and a troll, so he asked the critical question: What does trolling mean to you?

The answer was a mission statement.

"Trolling can mean a lot of things, but to me, it means antagonizing, mocking at points. Just, to me, the answer to your question is me showing off a little bit of my personality."

It was an odd circumstance to get an answer about what motivated Tekashi 6ix9ine, but the response was straightforward and honest. The mocking, the insults, the sarcasm, the needless antagonism, the need to turn every situation up to a hundred, burning friend and foe alike? All of that wasn't something Daniel Hernandez learned from the internet, or did because he thought it was smart or a good career move. Ultimately, it was who he was. And the world, hungry for outrage and spectacle, continued to reward him for it, from message board infamy and Eastern European cult stardom all the way to worldwide fame and riches.

Huot charged on, getting Tekashi to confirm the times he'd talked about trolling in public. And then, perhaps accidentally, he hit a deep vein of feeling. When talking about Nuke's robbery of Ro Murda, Huot's main goal seemed to be to confirm that Tekashi had only been told about it, and that he wasn't actually present.

In doing that, he brought up Shotti, one of the people who told Tekashi about the incident.

"Was it ever your experience that Shotti lied to you?"

"Yeah, Shotti lied to me the whole time of me knowing him."

Tekashi couldn't resist. Despite the fact that it weakened the government's argument by giving the defense an opening to discredit a key player in the drama; despite the fact that this was not exactly what Huot was asking; Tekashi needed to have public revenge on Shotti. The list of alleged wrongs was long —stealing money, sleeping with Sara. But it was more than that. Shotti was supposed to be Tekashi's big homie, his protector. Shotti had become a father figure for a young man whose biological father disappeared and whose stepfather was long-dead. Shotti was someone to teach Tekashi the code of the streets. And now that was all up in smoke.

He re-stated the point a few seconds later.

"From the whole time me knowing Shotti it was a lie. He was a liar."

That sprung from a place of real hurt. The kind of hurt you can't get over just by yelling into a phone.

Almost immediately after the Shotti insults, an afterthought from Huot turned into the day's second big media sensation.

The exchange started from a place nobody could deny.

"You joined the Bloods specifically to advance your music career, correct?"

Tekashi answered in the same way he'd acknowledged his own list of crimes: *correct*. But then it got a little strange. Tekashi denied that he had ever seen anyone pull that move before. Huot, seemingly disbelieving, pointed out another popular rapper with Blood ties—Cardi B.

It wasn't an outrageous example. Cardi had tweeted in response to a fan query back in 2017, "BITCH I BEEN A BIG TIME BLOOD SINCE I WAS 16." Later, she had confirmed her teenage membership to *GQ*. Early songs and videos like "Red Barz" (which opened with an intro proclaiming the song contained "Bloody bars") played up the affiliation. Even her biggest hit to that point, "Bodak Yellow," used the Bloods b-for-hard-c sound slang in its very title (the song's flow was borrowed from the rapper Kodak Black), and contained a pun calling Christian Louboutin shoes, with their red bottoms, "bloody shoes." So it didn't seem strange that Huot would bring her up.

"You knew Cardi B was a Blood, right?"

"Correct."

"You knew Cardi B had made music videos with Bloods members in the background of her, right?"

"Correct."

"You knew that before you started making these songs, right?"

"No, I didn't pay attention."

"You didn't know who Cardi B was before you joined the gang?"

"I mean, I knew—I knew who she was. I didn't pay attention to her at the time."

"You knew she was successful?"

"Correct."

That was it. The entire exchange. Huot raced on to another topic. Inside the courtroom itself, the exchange was largely not perceived as a big deal. It was a sideshow at best, and over in a few seconds.

But as news of what happened trickled outside the courtroom, people went nuts. Tekashi had said outright that Cardi B was a Blood! Never mind that her Blood status was self-admitted and even bragged of, or that he was only answering a question being posed by a defense attorney. The image of Tekashi dragging Cardi B's gang affiliations into a federal court case out of nowhere was too good to resist.

Some misreporting helped, too. Huot mentioned only that Cardi had been involved in the overall Bloods organization. But the *New York Post* reported, incorrectly, that Tekashi testified Cardi was a member of Nine Trey *specifically*. They put that in a headline and tweeted it out, and some other outlets picked up on the mistake from there.

It was a subtle distinction, but it was important. Was Cardi a member of the same Blood set that the feds were taking down? She wasn't, but the *Post*'s mistake made many people think she was.

Cardi cleared it up in a quickly-deleted tweet, saying that she had been part of the Brims set, not Nine Trey. She also shared the Keke Palmer "I don't know who this man is" meme as commentary. It took until the end of the day for *Complex* to obtain a rush transcript and publish the Huot/Tekashi exchange in full before the truth was fully out. But by then the idea of Cardi-as-Nine-Trey had traveled far enough that the star's machine was forced to respond. Atlantic Records gave a terse denial to *Billboard* that Cardi was a part of Nine Trey.

It was one of the oddest things about the trial. In a circumstance where crime after crime, many of them against rappers, was being enumerated in extreme detail, and the inner workings of a street gang was being broken down dollar by dollar, the two biggest stories of Tekashi's testimony involved Jim Jones and Cardi B.

It had to do with their celebrity, sure. But it also had to do with snitching. There was the perception that by cooperating, Tekashi was dragging other people into this case against their will. 'ALL HELL BREAKS LOOSE AFTER TEKASHI 6IX9INE OUTS CARDI B, JIM JONES AS GANG MEMBERS IN COURT' read a typical headline from *The Root*.

The rest of Huot's cross-examination proceeded without incident. Then it was Deveraux Cannick's turn. This was his big moment. It was his only chance to try to prove his theory that the kidnapping was faked.

Cannick attempted to enter as an exhibit Tekashi's

February 2018 Instagram post daring someone to steal his jewelry. But the post was from a third-party website, and there was text around it, which was no good. There was no controlling for what that text said, Longyear protested. The judge agreed. Cannick would have to cut that extra material out before he could submit the post as evidence.

Then, in an attempt to prove that Tekashi was a troller and a fabulist, Cannick attempted to introduce a video of Tekashi's hospital prank, where he'd briefly pretended he was dead. But again, this video was taken in whole from a YouTube channel, and had the channel's name and logo in it. Also, the Tekashi clip was only part of a lengthy video filled with unrelated stories and commentary. Longyear said there was no way this video should be evidence in its current state.

The judge agreed. Cannick needed to get rid of the writing on the video. "How are we going to do that?" Engelmayer asked the lawyer.

"I'll speak to my folks. Your Honor, I can move on," Cannick said.

Engelmayer responded, "Please do."

Cannick moved on. But he left the hospital video up, facing Tekashi. Engelmayer wasn't having it.

"I had asked that the video be taken down, please."

Then there was a long discussion about the legitimacy of Treyway as a business enterprise. Tekashi stuck to his earlier statement—there may have been an LLC or some other kind of entity named "Treyway," but that wasn't the point. The name was just something to "try and get deals off." The real purpose was to promote the gang. It wasn't legitimate.

Tekashi was sarcastic. Sure Shotti and company had tried to go legit with Treyway, but that doesn't mean they actually did it.

"I could *try* to make a shot from a three pointer," he said. "It doesn't mean I'm going to make it."

Cannick's questions were sometimes amusing, including a lengthy aside where he tried to get Tekashi to admit that he had told people to "suck your body parts."

"Correct," Tekashi robotically replied.

"What of your body parts did you tell others to suck?"

"My dick."

It wasn't long before Engelmayer jumped in. "Next question, Mr. Cannick."

There were other issues, too. In an attempt to introduce his "the kidnapping was faked" thesis, Cannick asked about a lyric from Tekashi's song "Kika"—"I do my own stunts, Jackie Chan with it."

"I didn't say that," Tekashi answered. It was true. That was Tory Lanez's part of the song. Tekashi seemed like he couldn't wait to correct Cannick.

"By the way, Mr. Cannick, it was my song, but I did not say that[...]Another artist made the hook and he said it." Tekashi gleefully added that he hadn't even written those words.

Cannick continued to ask long questions, and Longyear repeatedly asked for them to be reigned in and simplified.

The only small issue came when Tekashi was describing being beaten during the kidnapping. He was hit with something "heavy," but "I wouldn't say it was a gun." It was a small opening, enough for doubt to be thrown on one of the minor charges against Harv, that he'd used a gun to commit the robbery.

During a break in the testimony, Cannick told the judge that he anticipated calling some witnesses. It was clear he was referring to the slashing victim, Mark. After all this time, there was still no evidence of Cannick's theory of the kidnapping. He hadn't even directly asked Tekashi whether it was staged.

Cannick moved on to Tekashi's getaway and his dash to a nearby Uber, the most outrageous part of the story. The attorney emphasized the unlikeliness of the tale, but the effort got bogged down in a series of questions about what kind of car it was and whether it smelled new or not.

And then it was time for the testimony that Cannick had hoped would be the piéce de resistance: Tekashi's lies in the aftermath of the kidnapping. Cannick brought up that Tekashi lied, on the radio, to Angie Martinez about the value of the stolen jewelry, and about some of the details of the kidnapping and his escape.

Cannick also brought up the interview with DJ Akademiks that Tekashi did in the immediate aftermath of the kidnapping. But Tekashi said he didn't remember any particulars of it, and Cannick hadn't cleared the transcript with prosecutors beforehand, so he was at an impasse.

Cannick quoted a line from the Angie Martinez interview, and then couldn't find it in the transcript and had to withdraw it. He attempted to bring up a line from Tekashi's earlier *Breakfast Club* interview, but mischaracterized it.

Tekashi *did* remember that one, and jumped in with the correct line.

While Cannick had hinted at the idea that the kidnapping was staged, he hadn't ever stated it explicitly, and he had introduced no evidence to back it up.

Tekashi stepped down and went back to his small private jail in Queens. It was the last time he'd be seen in public until his sentencing. What remained to be seen was if the jury believed him.

After three days of superstar testimony, the rest of the day was a bit of an anti-climax. Prosecutors called the cop who'd seen Tekashi when he stumbled into the precinct post-kidnapping. The cop's memory of a bloody, erratic Tekashi helped put the rapper's account of his kidnapping and beating into perspective.

Next up, to finish off the day, was Jorge Rivera. With his freedom and his immigration status on the line, it was now his job to convince a bunch of strangers he was telling the truth.

CHAPTER 18

'DID THERE COME A TIME WHEN YOU BECAME A CONFIDENTIAL GOVERNMENT INFORMANT?'

R umors of Rivera's cooperation had been swirling for months, even before Tekashi was arrested. But everything was confirmed when he appeared on the witness stand.

Rivera recounted how he'd met Tekashi and started driving for him. He pointed out some of the people in the gang, like Shotti and Ro. Then they asked him for his account of the This Is 50 robbery. Despite the fact that he and Tekashi hadn't spoken in months, their stories matched.

Rivera's testimony picked up again after the weekend break. He continued to talk about the This Is 50 robbery. But there was one question, almost an aside, that revealed a lot about Jorge Rivera and how he'd ended up in that situation.

Why did you keep driving for Tekashi, even after transporting his crew to and from an armed robbery? Longyear asked, in essence.

Rivera's answer was simple.

"Because of the pay."

It was true. But it was also only part of the story. The other part lay in Shotti's fearsome reputation. Nine Trey members knew where Jorge, his wife, and his son lived. Him quitting, while knowing all the details of a major crime they'd committed, wasn't a situation he'd been willing to chance.

Jorge walked the government through the kidnapping, pausing the video several times to explain why he'd followed Harv and Sha's car, or why he was heading in a particular direction. His testimony was clear, thorough, and made sense —it was explaining the behavior of someone who was scared, but also trying to help out a client and friend by gathering as much information as he could before calling the cops.

On his cross-examination, Cannick began by asking Jorge about Tekashi's Angie Martinez interview.

But Engelmayer was confused. *Why talk to someone who happened to be there about what Tekashi said, rather than asking Tekashi directly?*

"What's the purpose of that?" Engelmayer asked.

"Just trying to clean it up," Cannick answered.

"Trying to what?" the judge answered. "I don't know what that means."

The only hope for Harv, unless things turned around quickly, would be the chance to question the slashing victim directly. If they could throw the victim's identification of Harv as the person who slashed him into question, they might have a shot at beating the rap for the crime. This was possible, since the victim had given conflicting answers about recognizing Harv. Cannick was trying to get in touch with the victim, but it was proving difficult.

At the end of questioning Jorge, Cannick briefly mentioned a series of topics: Harv's whereabouts at various times the month after the kidnapping; Jorge requesting that the government check in on his family because "Shotti is acting funny"; the fact that Elliot Grainge didn't want Shotti anywhere around Tekashi. It ended with Cannick asking Jorge, who had been testifying in Spanish, whether he spoke and understood English. (He did, and had spoken it with many clients).

And then, abruptly, Cannick was done. No grand summation, no clarification as to why he asked about particular texts or events.

Just "I have nothing further."

CHAPTER 19

BORDERLINE FRIVOLOUS

The next major witness was Kristian Cruz, the Nine Trey dope dealer who had masterminded the gang's heroin-and-fentanyl scheme. His job was twofold: to convince the jury that Nine Trey had a major drug dealing operation, and to demonstrate that Nuke had been a part of it. He was successful on both counts. He recounted numerous drug deals with Nuke, and decoded a number of phone calls between himself and Nuke, which were recorded because Nuke was in Rikers at the time.

For the Tekashi fans in the audience who had perhaps found their attention flagging, there was a special bonus. Cruz and Nuke both hated Shotti. Cruz said Shotti had once taken 150 grams of heroin from him (about $6,500 worth) without paying—the quintessential "Shotti move."

"That nigga a clown, man," Cruz said of Shotti in one of the calls. "I'mma put that nigga on his head when I see him."

He and Nuke had had a good laugh about that one.

At the end of the day, the government told the judge that they were not going to take the chance of calling the slashing victim as a witness. Cannick said that it was a "strong possibility" that *he* would want the victim on the stand.

That's up to you, Engelmayer said.

On Mark, the victim's end, there was zero possibility that he wanted a part of any of it. (In fact, a year after the trial Mark would swear out an affidavit to a firm named Black Ops Private Investigators Inc., saying that "I highly doubt Mr. Ellison was the person who cut me.")

But Cannick wanted to question Tekashi again, about the Angie Martinez interview. Engelmayer's question, essentially, was, why now? You had your chance. What's so important now that wasn't a few days ago? Cannick said that the interview was over an hour long, and they had just finished editing it down to the relevant parts.

When did you first become aware of the interview? Engelmayer asked.

"A couple of weeks before trial, Judge."

That was not the right answer. Longyear jumped in to help bury his opponent.

"It's a publicly available interview that he gave over a year ago," he said. Besides, Cannick had been notified of its existence ages ago by the government, as part of a long list of materials they'd given to the defense.

Engelmayer unloaded.

"Mr. Cannick, this is borderline frivolous. Your lack of preparation, your failure to load up the tape on a computer so that you could be nimble and isolate the relevant portions is not a reason to re-call a witness on the defense case. That's a new one on me. It also was never disclosed to me."

This latest issue, the judge said, reminded him of the hospital video, where the relevant part was surrounded by all kinds of YouTube channel nonsense.

That had been, he said, "a first cousin of the same problem."

"The point is that the failure to be ready for prime time as to using the exhibit during your long-planned cross-examination is not a reason, it's not close to a reason to justify re-calling [Tekashi]. The answer is no."

It was a rough ending to a rough day of a rough trial.

But there was always tomorrow.

Issues with the slashing victim's possible court appearance dragged on over the next several days. It quickly became clear he had no interest in testifying, and that he would have to be forced to do so. By the time, several days later, that he actually showed up in the courtroom, Deveraux Cannick had decided not to have him testify. The victim's sole moment in the courtroom was when the room was mostly empty for a lunch break. He wouldn't be forced to talk about Nine Trey business publicly after all. He didn't say a thing afterwards, but his relief was palpable to the few stragglers left watching.

While all that played out, the government still had to finish up with Kristian Cruz. He continued taking jurors deep into the Nine Trey drug operation—much of which was done via playing and explaining recordings of intercepted phone calls. The calls revealed the day-to-day realities of gang life: an endless supply of four- and low-five-figure deals, debts, and schemes; interspersed with shit-talking about other crew members and requests for jewelry.

The government played taped phone calls between Cruz and Mel Murda—calls in which Mel was openly talking about how Harv had kidnapped Tekashi. Mel said he heard that Harv was wearing Tekashi's jewelry out in public. It was a reminder to the people in the courtroom that, despite the day's focus on Nuke, Harv was there as well, part of the same gang.

There was one interesting detail. Cruz recalled a conversation he'd had with Nuke about the Ro Murda robbery. Nuke claimed at that point, Cruz recalled, that the robbery wasn't about the Always Paid chain at all. There was a different, more nebulous reason.

"He said he didn't like the way Ro was moving, as far as he didn't like the way Ro was doing things in the streets."

It was clear that Nuke had taken Ro's watch. But the motivation differed depending on who he talked to. Was it because of Ro's reluctance to set up Cruz? To set up Tekashi? Was it to get Cruz's chain that Ro was wearing? Was it to teach Ro a lesson about the right way to move in the streets? The mess of possible motives said a lot about the convoluted and interlaced motivations of Nine Trey. Machismo, money, stardom, bragging rights, and arcane codes of conduct combined to make a deadly stew. Also revealed in these conversations was what amounted to intense jockeying for position and, for a group supposedly based on brotherhood, shockingly little loyalty.

For example, about two weeks after Harv was arrested for kidnapping Tekashi, Mel Murda gave up Harv's spot in the gang to Kristian Cruz. Jurors heard the call. Mel barely seemed to think about it at all.

"You wanna take the high spot?" he'd asked. "So, that's what we gonna do then." The fact that the spot went to Kristian Cruz, who was at that point months into cooperating with the federal government, made the whole thing all the more absurd.

Cruz's testimony was followed by a lunch break.

After lunch, Cannick had his chance to contend with Kristian Cruz. It was a short performance. That made sense—his client had barely been mentioned in Cruz's testimony.

"In the record business," Cannick asked at the end, "do you

know members of gangs that perform? Have you ever heard of Young Jeezy?"

The government objected, and Cannick sat down.

By the next day, it was clear that neither defense team planned on calling any witnesses. This is not as unusual as it might seem. In criminal trials, the burden is on the government to prove its case, as the saying goes, beyond a reasonable doubt. There's often little motivation for defense teams to put the accused up on the stand, where they may have to answer uncomfortable questions.

The case's final expert witness was Reginald Donaldson, a no-nonsense investigative analyst for the US Attorney's Office. A former New York City cop, Donaldson was now a cell phone expert. His job on the stand, which was done with the help of maps and patient explanations of cell towers, was to show that Harv's phone (and, by inference, Harv himself) was in the locations of both Tekashi's kidnapping and the slashing.

For the slashing, he even had a chart at the ready, showing everywhere Harv's phone had been during the four hours after his friend David Cheeks got shot. The chart showed Harv's phone in Midtown minutes before Cheeks' shooting. It showed the phone moving in what was presumably a car headed to Smurf Village, and arriving there about an hour later. There were more records, too, of both Harv and his then-girlfriend's phones all the way up until 3 AM, showing that her memories of their whereabouts that night checked out. For a large chunk of that night, the location of Harv's phone could be pinpointed within a hundred meters.

It was a similar situation for the kidnapping. That night, Harv had made twenty-seven calls, and sent nearly a hundred texts and data transmissions. He, or at least his phone, was right there as it was happening.

The government rested, and the jury went to lunch.

Engelmayer confirmed with both Harv and Nuke that they weren't going to testify.

That was it for the day. Everyone would show up early the next morning for closing arguments. Then, the government would do their best to sum up their lengthy, involved case. And Harv's and Nuke's teams would try to demonstrate the other side's shortcomings as if their clients' lives depended on it.

CHAPTER 20

'IMMA TRY TO HURT A NIGGA CLOSE TO YOU'

The day of closing arguments had arrived. First up, was Jacob Warren for the government. Then Louis Fasulo for Nuke. Then Cannick on behalf of Harv. And finally, the government's lead prosecutor Michael Longyear for a final rebuttal.

Closing arguments are, at their best, stories about what the evidence proves, or what it fails to prove. Warren knew exactly the story he was going to tell. He hit his thesis in the second sentence.

"Nine Trey was about violence and drugs," Warren said.

Harv and Nuke, he argued, were key parts of that.

"They each made the choice, over and over again, to commit crimes in support of Nine Trey," Warren said.

He appeared to know the evidence his team introduced like the back of his hand: Nine Trey's long list of shootings, drug deals, fights, and robberies. He was going to use the gang's own words to bury them.

The first thing he had to do was demonstrate that Nine

Trey actually existed. He showed some of Harv's text messages on monitors in the courtroom.

"THEY DON'T WANT TO WAR WITH BILLYS."

"WE BIG BEHIND THE WALL."

"BILLY, WE WORLDWIDE."

These messages held a key to proving how Nine Trey worked.

"Behind the wall"? That was the prison lineup, about which the jury had heard a ton. The Nine Trey members in prison gave the orders, and the members on the street carried them out. And here was Harv himself talking about "Billys," or Nine Trey members, as a worldwide configuration.

"These words mean exactly what they say. This is literally Ellison admitting that he is in Nine Trey."

Warren brought up example after example of Nine Trey members talking about the gang in their own words, on phone calls and in texts and messages. One member was even caught on tape saying the words, "I'm a Nine Trey gangster."

There were countless photos of defendants in the case, including those who had already pled guilty, wearing red and throwing up the Nine Trey sign.

It was a devastating opening.

After that, Warren moved on to Harv. All the photos of him throwing up the Nine Trey sign were a start. But ultimately, Warren's focus was on words, not pictures. Warren brought back some of Harv's texts:

"GANGSTAS DON'T PICK AND CHOOSE THERE BEEF."

"STOP POPPING SHIT AND PICKING AND CHOOSING WHEN TO BE GANGSTA."

"Ladies and gentlemen, think about this slide when you're

back in the jury room," Warren instructed. It was a dramatic touch. But he was just getting warmed up.

"This is Ellison criticizing someone else for being a poser, a wannabe member of Nine Trey. He's giving instructions. He's saying you can't pick and choose when you're in and when you're out. This message alone, let alone the mountain of other evidence, shows you that Ellison was a member of Nine Trey. He is literally giving instructions on membership."

More examples abounded of Harv swearing fealty to Nine Trey. Harv, after all, had taken being in Nine Trey very seriously. His willingness to broadcast his allegiance, and to argue for *his* version of being a Nine Trey gangsta, left him all but defenseless when his correspondence was brought into the light.

But that wasn't all. There was Cruz's call to Mel Murda, asking for Harv's spot in the gang.

Well, Warren asked, wasn't that proof Harv was *in* the gang?

"Mel doesn't say, 'What are you talking about? Harv doesn't have that spot.' Mel isn't surprised in the least when Cruz asks him for this," Warren said.

After that, Warren moved on to the slashing. He brought up the photo of the bloodied victim in the hospital, and let it hang in front of the jury for a moment.

"Think about the sheer force it took to cause that wound," Warren told the jury. "It is strong evidence of Ellison's intent to permanently disfigure [the victim's] face."

"His face will never look the same," Warren continued. "That is the definition of permanent disfigurement."

Scene set, Warren then recapitulated the evidence: Harv was in Manhattan when he got a text that his friend David Cheeks had been shot. He drove back to Brooklyn. His then-girlfriend arrived in Smurf Village. Jurors had already seen her text to Harv, and the pin she dropped with her location.

"Ladies and gentlemen, there can be no dispute that she is within a few hundred feet of where the slashing occurred right about the time the slashing occurred."

Harv's cell records backed this version of events up as well. But Warren wasn't done yet. He brought up one of Harv's own texts on the monitor.

"IT'S LIKE FIRING ON ME AND IMMA TRY TO HURT A NIGGA CLOSE TO YOU IF I CAN'T GET TO YOU."

"Exactly," Warren said, his point made. "That is exactly what happened here." Cheeks's shooter was close with the slashing victim. "That's enough for Ellison to carve his face open." Having made his point about the slashing, Warren moved on to Harv's kidnapping of Tekashi. He began by addressing Cannick's thesis that the whole thing was staged.

"There is a mountain of evidence that this kidnapping and assault were very real," Warren said.

And then he laid it all out. There were texts from Harv from right before, trying to get a gun; and right afterward, attempting to sell Tekashi's jewelry. There was the video of the kidnapping itself. And there was the aftermath: Rivera frantically calling 911, hailing a cop, driving the wrong way down a one-way street with a policeman behind him.

There was audio of Shotti, four days afterward, ranting at Tekashi about the kidnapping and threatening Harv's life.

"You know the robbery was real because, otherwise, Hernandez would be saying on this recording, 'Shotti, why are you screaming at me and berating me? Don't you remember we staged this whole thing to increase our album sales?'"

Warren was being cute, but he had a point. And, he continued, the whole idea of staging a kidnapping for PR doesn't make any sense.

"Does this seem like the type of thing that would help your image or album sales? Getting beaten, your chain stolen, kidnapped, and humiliated by someone within your own gang? Of course not."

In the absence of compelling evidence Cannick's theory was true, Warren's words hung heavily in the air.

Warren reminded jurors of all the testimony, photos, and records of Tekashi's medical condition after the kidnapping. He pointed out that Tekashi's and Jorge's recollections of the night matched up. And Rivera was also a victim that night, robbed of his cell phone. That was pretty far to take a phony robbery.

After that, Warren moved on to Nuke.

Nuke's own messages showed clearly that not only was he a member of Nine Trey, but that he cared deeply about his status within it. Warren pulled up one of Nuke's IG messages.

"U KNOW HOW LONG I BEEN LOOKING OUT FOR WHITE N DA WHOLE LINE."

"This is a devastating message from Mack," Warren said. Frank White was one of the leaders of Nine Trey in prison. Here was Nuke bragging about how long he'd been "looking out" for him.

"He was doing that because he was a member of Nine Trey. It's as simple as that."

Warren was indeed trying to keep a complicated case as simple as possible for the jury, breaking it down piece by piece and charge by charge.

Nuke's IG messages popped up on the screen one by one, each one reminding jurors just how deep in the world of Nine Trey he'd been. His own words were working against him.

What may have been a reputation-saving message, or even a brag, in the moment became, in this context, proof of his deep ties to a criminal organization.

Warren even brought up Nuke's dichotomy between people who grind and people who play with the shit. And he used it to devastating effect.

"He is talking about two different ways to contribute to the gang. Think about that. When you consider whether Mack participated in Nine Trey with an understanding that the gang was involved in committing certain types of crimes, of course he did. He knew exactly what Nine Trey was about, violence and dealing drugs."

Again and again, Warren used Nuke's own boasts. Boasts about shooting at Mel Murda during their long-running rivalry. Boasts about his successful robbery of Ro Murda.

Warren was insightful about the dynamics of Nine Trey. He pointed out that posting a video to Instagram gloating about a robbery and mentioning the victim by name might seem weird if your purpose is actually to rob someone.

"But if the purpose is to let everyone else in the gang know how tough you are, and how weak the other guy is, then you have to let other people know about it," he explained.

That was exactly right. It was the same reason Tekashi bragged about the Barclays shooting, and filmed the This Is 50 robbery. It was the reason he admitted-without-admitting on TMZ that he was behind the Chief Keef shooting. If your enemies—and your friends—didn't know that you had beaten your enemy, there was no point in the exercise at all. Tekashi did it for his millions of followers, and Nuke did it for a small audience of Nine Trey diehards. But it was the same dynamic at work.

Louis Fasulo was up next. He did his best to paint the case

as one of guilt by association. He leaned on the fact that much of the Tekashi-related mayhem came from the Murderville line of the gang, with which Nuke was not affiliated.

Fasulo also dismissed the photographs of Nuke with other Nine Trey members.

People took pictures with their neighbors all the time, he said. *And they gossip all the time. Does that mean there's some kind of conspiracy?*

The attorney did his best to discredit the government's spin on Nuke's robbery of Ro as well, particularly focusing on the discrepancies in the reasoning that different witnesses had provided.

And then Fasulo did something else. He pointed out that a word used in communications seen in the trial, "jack," had two different meanings. In one context, it means "approve," and in another it means "rob." He used that to attack the entire idea that someone like Tekashi could decode conversations and texts.

"I suggest to you," he said, "it's not credible to rely on this coded-language explanation that the witnesses are giving you, because, in fact, they're giving you different definitions for those words."

It was a reach. Words have different meanings in different contexts, and slang is always elastic. But everyone involved—Tekashi, the witnesses, even the jury—was very clear about what each term meant in the conversation in question at the time. But Fasulo continued, pointing out a few more slang terms that had been used in a few different ways over the course of the trial. He was pulling this move in an attempt to save his client from his own words.

Fasulo ended by reaming Kristian Cruz, whom he called a "fraudster." He outlined the crimes Cruz pled guilty to. And he called on the jury to think about the case carefully. Then he wrapped up.

After a lunch break, Cannick was up. He began by hearkening back to his opening statement, talking about Martin Luther King, Jr.

The "country preacher" was threaded throughout the closing argument, and the explanation for this grew more and more clear as Cannick went on. In his metaphor, the jurors were freedom crusaders, standing up to the government, and telling them that they were wrong. Cannick spent a long time on the fact that Cruz once surreptitiously used an iPhone while in jail, attempting to spin that into a reason to discredit his entire testimony.

Then Cannick made a mistake. He said that a call between Mel Murda and Cruz where they talked about Harv happened in the last six weeks, well after Cruz had become a cooperator.

Longyear didn't let that pass.

"I don't want to interrupt, your Honor. I want to object. 'Within the last six weeks' misstates the evidence."

Cannick was caught in an error in the most crucial time of the entire trial. And yet he continued talking about the call, instead of moving on.

There was yet another point in the closing statement that merited a rebuttal. While attempting to exonerate Harv from the slashing, Cannick talked about a video Harv had sent his then-girlfriend from that night, explaining that you can't see any blood on his hands from the slashing in it. But that had been explained in the testimony. Harv had sent that video at 9:30 PM, while he was *on his way* to Smurf Village. He was not alleged to have slashed anyone until nearly an hour later.

Cannick went on to try to discredit Tekashi and Cruz as cooperators, saying they had a motive to lie in order to gain their freedom. Then he spun out his theory of the kidnapping: Jorge *had* thought it was real at first—that explained his frantic behavior while it was going on. But once he met up with Tekashi again, he realized it was all faked.

Cannick's defense continued. Shotti's nineteen-minute tirade to Tekashi in the aftermath of the kidnapping? Well, *Shotti* too thought the kidnapping was real, even as Tekashi knew it wasn't.

Cannick also tried hard to discredit Tekashi, in part by complimenting him.

"He's a bright young man. He understands marketing real well. But he also understands how to take advantage of people and situations."

Cannick finished up by reiterating his call to fight the power.

"Sometimes, when the government gets invested in a project, they live out that project. And sometimes," he repeated for emphasis. "Sometimes. Sometimes. Sometimes we must bring it to you and say: *tell them they're wrong.*"

They were soaring words. But they didn't address the evidence against Harv.

It didn't help that immediately after Cannick was done, the judge pointed out that the "in the last six weeks" call had actually happened almost eleven months earlier. It was the last thing the jury heard before they took a coffee break.

Michael Longyear didn't waste any time with his rebuttal. Right off the top, he pointed out Cannick's misstatements. To Longyear, everything that Cannick and Fasulo had just said was nonsense, a distraction, a way of moving away from the voluminous evidence that the government's team spent day after day presenting.

He took on Fasulo's guilt-by-association idea. To say that

Nuke being in photos with Nine Trey members was like being in photos with your neighbors was ridiculous.

"These are pictures that were taken with your fellow gang members, phone calls with your coconspirators who you dealt narcotics with," he said, calmly but firmly. "Not guilty by association; guilt by participation."

Harv started coughing during the closing argument. A lot. Enough that Engelmayer had to interrupt and ask someone to get Harv water. If it was inadvertent, the timing was exquisite.

Longyear went into Fasulo's argument that Nuke wasn't in the line of the gang that committed all the crimes. In essence, he argued, so what? He was still part of Nine Trey, and still had to do whatever the prison lineup told him. You could see that in the constant mentions throughout the trial of Frank White and Magoo, two of the top leaders in the prison lineup. Don't get distracted, Longyear pleaded.

Longyear followed this up by jumping right into the center of everything. Many of his opponents' statements, and their entire cross-examination strategies, had been devoted to attempting to discredit the cooperators: Tekashi, Jorge, and Kristian Cruz.

"Now, let's be clear why they are making this argument," Longyear said. "If you believe the cooperators, their clients are guilty. It's done. It's over. So they *have* to argue that the cooperators, all of them, are lying. They have no choice."

Cruz, he allowed, had done horrible things. But it wasn't the government that chose him as a witness.

"Aljermiah Mack chose Kristian Cruz. Nine Trey chose Kristian Cruz."

The same was true with Tekashi. *Nine Trey* chose him, not the government. The gang saw the potential for big bucks when Tekashi's video went viral. And Tekashi loved it. He was, Longyear pointed out, "all in" with the violence and the crime.

Harv was right there in the thick of it too. You could see in his own texts that he was proud to protect the gang, and to protect Tekashi, at least until they'd fallen out. The cooperators, Longyear continued, have a huge motivation to tell the truth. If they lie, they don't get their 5K1 letter.

"In the past, in order to get away with crimes, they may have lied," Longyear explained. "They lied to get what they wanted. Here, the only way that these people get less time, the only possibility for something less than the decades of prison time is to tell the truth. Don't believe the cooperators because they are good people," he said. "Believe them because they are selfish people."

In Tekashi's case in particular, the attorney continued, this staged robbery idea was absurd. Tekashi admitted to a ton of crimes: shootings, drug deals, robberies. Would he admit all of that, only to lie about a fake robbery that would put his entire cooperation deal at risk?

"It's madness, ladies and gentlemen."

He went into the testimony of Harv's ex-girlfriend as well. Cannick's fixation on whether or not Harv was bloody when the two of them met at a hotel after the slashing was inaccurate—that was three hours after the crime.

If the ex had been a government pawn, he reasoned, "don't you think her story would have been a little bit better? Don't you think she would have answered, 'Yeah, I saw blood. He is covered in blood'? She didn't. She was telling you the truth, and her testimony was backed up by the phone records, by the text messages, and by the cell sites."

Longyear followed with an analysis of the kidnapping. The jury could see with their own eyes, on the video, that it wasn't staged. He then reiterated Warren's point: how would getting robbed be good for the tough guy, king of New York image Tekashi was trying to project? After all, Tekashi had filmed people getting robbed just a few months before, in an attempt to humiliate them.

"Anthony Ellison lived and breathed Nine Trey," Longyear said. "This poser, this rainbow-haired, tattooed kid singing songs, it was insulting to him. So he robbed him and he kidnapped him to humiliate him."

How could the kidnapping have been staged, when Shotti was giving twenty-minute rants and waving an assault rifle around in the aftermath? Or when Mel Murda, the gang's Godfather, was saying on a phone call that Harv robbed Tekashi for his jewelry? If it was fake, why was Harv inquiring about Tekashi's whereabouts right before the robbery? Why was Shotti driving up to Maddy just hours afterward, looking for Harv?

In summation, Longyear reminded the jury to look at the evidence carefully.

"And if you do that, ladies and gentlemen, you will reach the only conclusion that is consistent with the evidence and with the law: that the defendants, Aljermiah Mack and Anthony Ellison, are guilty of all counts."

The jury left for a long weekend. Rosh Hashanah was coming up. It was Thursday night, so they had five days off. They'd reconvene on Wednesday morning, ready to make a decision about the futures of Harv and Nuke, of Nine Trey, and of Tekashi himself.

CHAPTER 21

HAS THE JURY REACHED A VERDICT?

When Wednesday, October 2, came, Engelmayer began by reading charging instructions—a long, detailed list of things the jury should keep in mind when deliberating, and what each of the counts meant. It took three hours to get through. In the transcript of the trial, it takes up a hundred pages.

After that, the judge noticed something. A bunch of Harv's supporters were wearing identical shirts. They read "POWER FORWARD," the name of his company, and they had his initials "AE" on them. Engelmayer chastised the lawyers for allowing this to happen.

"That's not appropriate for court," he said. "I think you all know better."

When all of Harv's supporters were back in the courtroom toward the end of the day, the judge read them the riot act too.

"I need to admonish people, if you want to attend the trial, please do not wear clothing that is expressive about the rooting interest you may have in the case. It's not appropriate to have a cheering shirt that basically says, I'm rooting for a particular side. You can imagine how people would react if there were shirts that said, 'GO, GOVERNMENT' here." He demanded that everyone wearing those shirts stay seated when the jury walked in, so that Harv's initials would not be visible.

The judge also sidebarred with Cannick.

"This is a courtroom. It's not a place to wear partisan shirts. I realize they must've acted without your authorization."

"This is the second issue of this nature we've talked about today," Engelmayer continued. "You know what I'm referring to."

He was referring to an article *Complex* had published the previous day. Written by this author, it included a short statement from Harv about the kidnapping:

"Danny didn't care if the stunt could be taken as embarrassing, he thought it was believable. He said it would even make some people feel bad for him, which was good after all the trolling he had done. It worked, even Shotti bought it."

Engelmayer had asked Cannick about it, as publishing a statement from a defendant in the middle of a trial was unusual. Cannick denied any knowledge of the story or its source, and there was nowhere to go from there.

As the hours of deliberation went by, the jury asked to see several exhibits and portions of testimony. They reached the end of the day without a verdict. By five hours into day two, though, they'd made up their minds.

At a few minutes after 2 PM, friends, family, and a slew of reporters all showed up to hear the verdict. It was a verdict on Harv and Nuke. But it was also a verdict on Tekashi—on whether Tekashi 6ix9ine, the outrageous rap star who had trolled his way to the top, was believable in his latest role as Daniel Hernandez, cooperating witness number two.

Except that there wasn't a verdict yet. The jurors had a question. They were at an impasse on one remaining count. Could they still deliver a verdict, or did they have to keep going? But as Judge Engelmayer and the lawyers were in the middle of figuring all that out, another note came from the jury room. They'd resolved their issue. They'd decided.

Moments later, it was time. Engelmayer read out the charges, count by count.

Count one, racketeering against both Harv and Nuke: Guilty

Count two, kidnapping in aid of racketeering, against Harv: Guilty

Those were huge. These were the most serious crimes. It didn't look good for Harv or Nuke.

Count three, assault with a deadly weapon in aid of racketeering, against Harv: Not guilty.

This was Harv's first break. It had to do with all of the questions about whether or not Tekashi had been hit with a gun, or a metal object, or a fist during the kidnapping.

Count four had been tied to count three, so since Harv was not guilty, they just skipped it.

Count five, maiming and assault with a dangerous weapon in aid of racketeering, against Harv. This would reveal whether the jury thought he had committed the slashing. He was found guilty, of both maiming and assault.

Count six, narcotics conspiracy, against Nuke: guilty.

Count seven, firearms use, against Nuke: not guilty. This was by far the weakest of all the charges, with only select mentions through the course of the trial of people seeing Nuke with a gun.

But these were devastating verdicts for both defendants. They were guilty, of all of the most serious charges.

Engelmayer thanked the jury and sent them away.

The verdicts meant that the jury, by and large, had believed Tekashi—at least when his testimony was considered in conjunction with reams of evidence and two other cooperating witnesses.

Cannick asked the judge afterwards for extra time to file a post-trial motion. Normally lawyers had fourteen days. But Cannick said he had a number of other trials coming up, so he needed three months.

"Do you really need three months, Mr. Cannick?" Engelmayer asked. "That seems awfully long."

After some negotiation, he cut it down to two months.

And then it was over.

"Marshals," Engelmayer said, "you may take the defendants out."

Tekashi wasn't there. He was in Queens, in a small private prison. But when he heard the verdict, he must have realized the implication. If the jury believed him, that boded well for his own sentencing a few months later. He was sure to get his 5K1 now. And that meant that maybe, just maybe, he'd waltz out of the jail a free man before Christmas.

Harv and Nuke had no such illusions. They'd both be in prison for a long time. How long? That was, like so many other decisions, up to the judge.

CHAPTER 22

'I DON'T KNOW IF THIS IS A JOKE ANYMORE'

As Harv and Nuke's case dragged on, other Nine Trey members had been sentenced. One gang member involved in the This Is 50 robbery got sixty months, or five years, in prison. Crippy got sixty-two months. Days before Harv and Nuke's trial started, Shotti got fifteen years. Just a few weeks after the trial ended, Mel Murda got a whopping one hundred thirty-five months, or over eleven years. That was far more than his fellow Godfather Ro Murda's sixty-six month sentence, issued just a week earlier. One Nine Trey member who'd shot a rival in the head (the victim miraculously survived) got twenty years since his crime was so violent.

In the sentencing hearings, Engelmayer did his best to parse each defendant's accountability. What exactly had they done? What did their family and friends say about them? In Ro Murda's case, a ton of time was taken off because he'd renounced Nine Trey while in jail and was subsequently viciously attacked.

Nuke got it among the worst out of almost everyone,

ending up with seventeen years. Harv's sentencing suffered a seemingly endless series of delays. But the world at large was interested in only one outcome.

Would Tekashi, after cooperating, get to go free?

On December 4, 2019, the world got its first indication. Engelmayer received a letter from the government. The language was formal. But no one could miss the combination of letters and numbers. 5K1.

"In connection with the sentencing of Daniel Hernandez..., the Government respectfully submits this letter, pursuant to Section 5K1.1 of the United States Sentencing Guidelines...."

He'd gotten the golden ticket. Tekashi had snitched, and it had worked. He did a good enough job that the government was doing everything it could to encourage the judge to sentence Tekashi below the statutory minimum, perhaps all the way down to nothing.

The 5K1 outlined Tekashi's cooperation in detail. How he'd met with law enforcement the day before he was arrested, and started his telling then. How he'd met with the government twenty-six times between his arrest and the trial. How his cooperation was one of the key factors in allowing them to charge Harv, Kooda, and even Nuke. How, once Tekashi's guilty plea became public, a bunch of other co-defendants ran to the government to talk about pleading out. How Tekashi walked the government through his social media by providing context and sharing the meaning of code words. He'd even helped them understand taped phone calls by telling the government who was on the calls, and what they were saying.

The letter itself was strange. It had a capsule biography of Tekashi, including details about Scumgang, and even about his early dalliance with the Crips. It also went through his crimes, incident by incident. The first assault on Trippie. The shooting outside Quad Studios. The This Is 50 robbery. The incident in downtown Brooklyn where Shotti fired on the guys who had insulted Tekashi. The Barclays Center shooting. The Chief Keef shooting. The shooting at the cookout. And the attempted getback at Harv after the kidnapping, all culminating in the slashing. It also had other, heretofore unknown, little details, too, like a time Shotti had ordered Tekashi to pay a fellow Nine Trey member a few hundred dollars to move some guns from Atlanta to New York.

The letter fully outlined all of Tekashi's previous criminal history. It mentioned the 2015 case. It talked about his youthful dealing of weed and, one time, heroin. It mentioned a small heroin deal he'd brokered right before his career took off. There was the fight at LAX. The time Tekashi punched a bouncer at a Times Square club. The arrest in Houston for allegedly choking out a photo-seeking fan. And then a two-paragraph, blacked-out section with the words "DOMESTIC VIOLENCE" at the top.

While Tekashi's testimony was important, the optics of him pleading guilty, the letter revealed, were even more so.

"Unlike in other cases, the fact that Hernandez's cooperation was public well in advance of trial let his co-defendants know for certain that Hernandez would be testifying against them should they decide to proceed to trial. This was incredibly significant from the Government's perspective in reaching pre-trial dispositions with nearly all of Hernandez's co-defendants."

The letter was clear about one other thing. Cooperating was extremely risky for Tekashi. Nine Trey was a big gang, and it was violent. Tekashi's family had to move before his cooperation could become public. While incarcerated, he served time in a small private prison in Queens, in a unit with no gang members. Even going back and forth to court, they'd taken "extra precautions" with him.

"There is no question that the defendant's life will never be the same because of his cooperation in this case," the letter said. "He and his family will have to take extra safety precautions when being in public so as to avoid potential reprisals from others."

All of that was true. Tekashi, if he was smart, needed to lay very low to avoid reprisals. His attorney Lance Lazzaro said in a letter to the judge that Tekashi would need extra security "for decades to come." "He will probably truly never feel safe in public," Lazzaro continued.

Lance Lazzaro could certainly lay it on thick when he needed to, but this was not one of those times. Everyone around—the media, Tekashi's family, other rappers, the court—realized the very real risk of violent retaliation. The best hope for Tekashi, it seemed, was to lay low.

If only.

Tekashi's sentencing was set for December 18. It would be the first time he'd been seen in public since the trial. As the date moved closer, speculation reached a fever pitch. Almost everyone assumed Tekashi would get time served and leave the courtroom a free man. The Probation Department had recommended exactly that. There were even rumors, helped on by 50 Cent in a radio interview, that Tekashi's label spent big money on a video shoot that they were planning the very day of the sentencing, betting on him walking out.

(In reality, high-profile, at risk defendants usually do not just walk out of court on the day of their sentencing. Instead, the judge makes public a period of several days in which they may be set free and lets the lawyers work out the details in private, for safety reasons. This is exactly what happened with Kristian Cruz.)

Before the big day, letters in support of Tekashi came rolling in. There were ones from his mom, his brother, and his new girlfriend, who had remained by his side during his incarceration. There was also one from his security guard.

"Danny is a kid from the streets," it said, "but he is no street kid."

His booking agent sent one, and so did a ton of overseas concert promoters.

"He and his crew were very kind to our team and the venue staff," read one.

"Mr. Hernandez has always been polite, punctual, and very professional," another offered.

Another said that, despite a serious foot injury the day of the show, he "gave a decent performance."

There were long letters testifying to Tekashi's renewed purpose and change of heart. Some of them were recycled from the *last* time he'd tried to impress his change of heart on a judge, his sentencing in the 2015 case.

Tekashi wrote his own letter to Engelmayer. It started out hitting all the right beats of a repentant criminal. He was "overwhelmed with emotions," "grateful" for the chance to "express my remorse to you, your Honor, over this situation." He had been reflecting on "the recklessness and foolishness of my decisions." He was still a role model to kids, but this time he would use it to show the costs of gang affiliation.

But the trolling side of Tekashi, the side that couldn't let any slight, real or imagined, pass unanswered, couldn't help but come out. Tekashi made sure to tell the judge that he "became aware of the fact that the mother of my child was having sexual relations with one of my co-defendants and that they were stealing hundreds of thousands of dollars from me."

The letter ended with what he surely meant as a grand gesture, but it fell a little short. If he got a second chance, he said, "I will dedicate a portion of my life to helping others not to make the same mistakes that I've made."

There were other types of letters. Skyy and her assistant both wrote about the devastating impact that being the victim of the robbery at This Is 50 had on their lives.

Those two letters were sobering, a reminder that Tekashi's crime spree affected more than a handful of rappers and label heads. There were real human costs to his stunts. Although no one had been killed (not for lack of gunshots fired in public places), some people caught in the middle of the feuds had their lives changed forever.

Skyy said that in the aftermath of the robbery, she was haunted by "mental anguish and emotional distress," flash-backs, bad dreams, and lack of sleep. She suffered from what she thought was PTSD.

"I find myself unable to do the simple things an adult should do," she wrote. "I have emotional, mental, and financial problems as this uncomfortable situation has left me displaced without work."

She'd moved out of Texas, to avoid "the watchful eyes of Tekashi69's network." And she couldn't be a publicist anymore. "My entire career and lifelong dreams were destroyed as a result of this horrific event," she wrote. She couldn't be in large crowds anymore, and said she was constantly worried her friends would come across video of the robbery.

Her assistant recounted the event. "My life flashed before my eyes... All I thought was, 'What did I do to deserve this?'

What was moments seemed like an eternity burning in fiery pits as I was frozen and watched my compatriots assaulted and robbed along with me." Afterward, he said, he became a recluse. He tried to bring his case to the police, but they wouldn't take any information about it. There was already an investigation, they claimed.

"I felt I was being silenced and if that was the case, I would live silently," the assistant wrote. "I would not do anything to draw extra attention to myself." Once the raid on Tekashi's house made the news, the assistant found out that he lived just up the street from the man who'd robbed him. He left his place immediately, moving in with a partner "for fear of being by myself at any time."

"Please think about my life when you sentence this person," he pleaded. "Why should this person, who nearly ended my life, be free when I am not free?"

On the morning of December 18, 2019, it was time for Engelmayer to balance everything. He had to balance Tekashi's cooperation, his crimes, the harm he had caused to people like Skyy, and his potential for change; to balance all these factors, and come up with a number.

The vast majority of the hip-hop media acted as if it was certain that Tekashi would get time served. The government wanted it. The parole department wanted it, and his lawyers wanted it. It was all the judge was going to hear.

Except for one thing. The young woman who was hit in the foot with a bullet in the July 2018 cookout shooting was on the scene. She was ready to say her piece. But other than her, it was set to be Tekashi's day.

Once everyone got settled, there was an initial shocker. A woman named Marlayna had written to the judge, saying that she had given birth to a daughter by Tekashi right when he was arrested: November 19, 2018. Engelmayer revealed the contents of the letter: Marlayna said that Tekashi had missed his youngest daughter's first birthday and other milestones. Before he was arrested, he was "distracted by people whose true intentions he was very oblivious of." But he was also "humble" and "charming" and has "thought deeply of his mistakes." It was a narrative that would recur throughout the day.

But there was a counter-narrative, too. The judge also received an anonymous letter, scrawled on a copy of Tekashi's own missive to the judge. It read, "Your Honor, do not fall for this. This person belongs behind bars."

The hearing started with a bunch of technical preliminaries. Then Michael Longyear stepped up. This time it wasn't to question Tekashi, but to praise him. Longyear said that Tekashi's cooperation had been extraordinary. He'd been honest from the beginning. He'd put himself at risk. He'd enabled them to tie a number of crimes back to Nine Trey—ties the government might not have been able to make otherwise. Tekashi had even told the government about crimes they'd been completely unaware of, like the Frenchie BSM shooting. Longyear also leaned into the safety risks. Tekashi would have to look over his shoulder for the rest of his life, the Assistant U.S. Attorney emphasized.

This was true. But it was also meant to signal to the judge that this guy was already suffering, even without more time behind bars. Time to let him out. Longyear couldn't come out and say, unless he was directly asked, that he thought Tekashi should be set free. But he got as close as he possibly could to that line.

"His cooperation was not only substantial," Longyear said as he closed his remarks. "It was extraordinary."

After that, it was LL's turn. LL, her initials, was the woman who'd been hit in the foot with a bullet in the shooting ordered by Tekashi and Shotti in July of 2018 in Smurf Village. The incident was part of the internal Nine Trey war between Shotti's and Harv's factions. Now LL, who'd been literally caught in the crossfire, was ready to tell her story. She spoke softly at first, and was obviously emotional. With her was an attorney—LL would go on to file a civil suit against Tekashi several months later, for a whopping $150 million.

She laid out her injuries: scars on her back, knee, and foot. She talked about how she'd almost died—had she leaned a different way, the bullet would have struck her in the head. She mentioned how the injury scuttled her career plans to join the NYPD. She blamed Tekashi, and she wanted him—and the world—to know it.

"At the end of the day, he was the mastermind," she said. "Why do I have to put my life on hold because of his actions? I just want an apology. I forgive him, but I will never forget."

Tekashi, impulsive as ever, told her, "Whatever medical bills you need, I'm willing to pay for." It was a claim made in the middle of an emotional moment, but there was little chance of any follow through, especially since Lazzaro guessed, correctly, that LL had a civil suit on the way.

Lazzaro gave a stellar performance, laying out a portrait of Tekashi as a changed, remorseful person who "understands how wrong he was." Tekashi wanted a second chance, and if he got it, he'd use it to warn against gangs and to do good for his community. On top of that, Lazzaro also emphasized the danger Tekashi would face as a noted cooperator. He "will never have a life in Brooklyn again." Everyday things like picking up a sandwich and going to the movies would be deadly cat-and-mouse games.

The lawyer then repeated Tekashi's biography, telling the now-familiar story. But, as he got to the details about the vanished Daniel Hernandez Sr., it was like he had conjured a ghost. The elder Daniel Hernandez, unrecognizable to everybody in the courtroom except Tekashi, walked in with a woman by his side. They looked a bit disheveled. They forced their way near the front. Hernandez was muttering, "Danny is my son" by way of explanation to the confused people whose laps he was walking past. The couple settled in a row near the front, so they had a clear eyeline with Tekashi.

Meanwhile, Lazzaro, unaware of this momentous appearance, continued with the sob story of the fourteen-year-old Tekashi working until 11 PM at Stay Fresh. And his mother getting up at 6:30 AM to clean houses, only to come home and pick up cans from the garbage for extra money.

Why did Tekashi join the violent Nine Trey Gangsta Bloods? In Lazzaro's telling, it was due to his naïveté. He didn't have a father figure. He was immature. He wanted some street cred to help his rap career.

Sure, Tekashi joined a gang and did bad things, Lazzaro argued. But he was, in his way, facing a "life sentence" no matter what happened—he'd always be a high-profile target for gang members. He'd also given away lots of money all over the world, including to his oft-mentioned terminally ill fans. This was the same script Lazzaro used at the sentencing for the child sex case—painting Tekashi as caring and charitable. In reality, most of the charity Lazzaro mentioned amounted to giving money away on camera to whomever happened to be around.

After Lazzaro finished, it was Tekashi's turn, finally, to speak for himself. It was the first time since the trial that he'd be heard. He started out reading from a prepared statement that was nearly identical to his letter to the judge from a few days prior. But almost immediately, things started to go off the rails. It was then that he offered, unprompted, to pay for LL's medical bills.

And then he saw his father.

That was when Tekashi 6ix9ine, master troll and arguer, lost control. He started speaking off the cuff.

"Your Honor," he said, "I'm telling you, my life is so crazy, I don't even know where to start." It was true enough, especially at this surreal juncture of his biological father appearing for the first time in about fifteen years.

"You would think I'm a liar if I tell you the last time I seen my biological father was in third grade. I took one glance to the audience and I see my biological father. And I have not seen him in fucking...the last time I seen this man was in third grade."

Tekashi was way out on a limb now, repeating himself, cursing in court. He couldn't help it.

"And one little glance I take a fucking...I'm sorry. I don't even know if this is a joke anymore, like everything that I go through."

It was an apt comment. Having his long-lost father show up for the first time in a decade and a half during his sentencing in a federal courtroom? It was insane. No wonder it felt like a joke. And, it turned out, Daniel Hernandez Sr. had not been hiding on some faraway island for the past fifteen years. He told anyone who asked that he was living a borough away from his son, just over in Queens.

Tekashi pulled himself together and got back to reading his letter. It was, for a situation that had been so outrageous and unprecedented from the beginning, relatively standard stuff.

"I made a lot of bad choices in life, but that does not make me a bad person."

"I was more worried about the fame and the success than my own and others' well-being."

"I know I was wrong."

He emphasized Lazzaro's read of his character, calling his not-that-long-ago self "weak" and "easily influenced." And then he talked up his charity work. He mentioned visiting terminally ill fans, a five-year-old named Franklin and eight-year-old Tati.

Engelmayer, who hadn't seen this show during the 2015 case, didn't seem to realize this was warmed-over material. Tekashi said he represented hope to Franklin and "the millions of kids who follow me and look up to me."

His thesis was simple. He wasn't the "arrogant, disrespect-ful" Tekashi 6ix9ine. He was Daniel Hernandez, a human being. "I got organs, just like everyone in this room," he pleaded. If freed, he would use his platform to "inspire the youth." He would grow and be redeemed.

As he was winding down, Tekashi took time to mention one person by name. "The man who changed my life," Tekashi said, "his name is Elliot Grainge."

It was notable. Grainge had stayed out of the public eye almost entirely since Tekashi first gained fame. As the label head of two beefing, gang-affiliated rappers in Tekashi and Trippie Redd, *and* the son of arguably the most powerful man in the music business, he had little to gain by speaking. But he renegotiated Tekashi's contract as the rapper had become a star, and after the trial, he'd re-signed him to a reported ten million dollar deal.

As Tekashi closed, his father raised his hand. Engelmayer,

thinking that maybe it was a victim of Tekashi's crimes who wanted to speak, asked him who he was.

"Your Honor, I'm Tekashi's father, his biological father."

It was madness. Hernandez Sr. wanted to say his piece in front of the packed courtroom, for reasons known only to him.

It was a losing battle. Of all the things that happen during a criminal case, sentencing hearings are among the most formulaic. The government says something, the defense lawyer says something, the convicted person says how sorry they are and often cries. And then the judge gives a long, summational speech, ending with the sentence. It's tightly scripted. The last thing *any* of the parties wanted was this wild card.

Engelmayer asked both sides if they wanted to let Hernandez Sr. speak. Lazzaro unhesitatingly said no. Longyear agreed. And then the judge let the elder Hernandez have it.

"It's way too late to start and show up and speak on his behalf," Engelmayer said. "You squandered that many, many years ago."

There was a short break. People scrambled out into the hallway, and reporters ran up to the elder Hernandez, who gave out his phone number like candy. He had one question for everyone: could you pass this number on to my son?

"I want to tell him I love him and that I miss him," he said.

Then it was Engelmayer's turn. The judge, already prone to long speeches at sentencings, must have been aware that this was a big moment. Like the trial itself, this sentencing had been moved from his normal small room on the thirteenth floor of the Thurgood Marshall Courthouse in downtown Manhattan to a much larger room ten floors below.

"This is going to take a little while," Engelmayer warned the assembled crowd.

He started with some standard legalese, and then praised Tekashi's cooperation, calling it impressive, game-changing, complete, and brave. It would result, he made sure to say to the assembled room, in a sentence far lower than anyone else in the case so far (Kristian Cruz and Jorge Rivera, who would both receive time served, hadn't yet been sentenced).

But then the judge dropped a bomb.

"I cannot agree with defense counsel that a sentence of time served here is reasonable."

That was huge. Tekashi would not walk out free from the front door of the courtroom. There would be some prison time.

The room was surprised. Almost everyone expected Tekashi to get time served. But it would be many, many minutes of speechifying before the audience got the details. To the judge, Tekashi's conduct was "too violent, too sustained, too destructive, too selfish, and too reckless" for him to spend only the thirteen months he'd been locked up so far behind bars.

And then Engelmayer politely, subtly, called bullshit on Lazzaro. Lazzaro's sentencing letter, Engelmayer said, read as if a bunch of violent older gangsters were bad influences on Tekashi. Tekashi wasn't bad, the letter read, just foolish. But that was exactly what Lazzaro had said about Tekashi in the 2015 case—that he was under the sway of some dangerous older people.

"If ever a life experience should have taught you to resist following older people into crime, that was it," the judge said. "So, that excuse may work once. It doesn't work twice."

Engelmayer went through Tekashi's record. He was "a central figure in a vicious and brutal gang" who had committed crimes "specifically to benefit you and satisfy your desire to get even with your actual or perceived rivals."

However little Engelmayer may have known of the rap game before this case started, he was an expert on gangs. He knew how they operated, having previously presided over a number of large gang cases. So, he knew exactly how dangerous and reckless it was to carry out so many attacks in public. It was only by luck and bad aim that no one had gotten killed.

The judge recounted Tekashi's record, incident by incident. The Trippie Redd assault. The Frenchie BSM shooting. The This Is 50 robbery. Shotti firing on people in downtown Brooklyn. The Barclays shooting. The Chief Keef shooting. The $50,000 bounty on Harv after the kidnapping.

And all of it was done to benefit Tekashi.

This was Engelmayer's most perceptive and original moment in the long speech.

"Until you joined, the members of Nine Trey[...]had no independent interest in settling scores with rap artists or their musical entourages. That was not the gang's business model," he said to Tekashi. "The whole area of the gang's violence in late 2017 and especially 2018 is traceable to you."

It was pointed, and direct, and true.

"You chose to use Nine Trey and its literal fire power as a much more potent means of getting even with your rivals."

Engelmayer had been listening, intently, for the entire case. When Nine Trey attacked rappers and their crews in public places, Tekashi was the instigator. Not Shotti or Mel Murda or Harv. And on top of it, Tekashi hadn't even done the "dirty work of shooting" himself, the judge railed. That was left to others.

The judge took a subliminal shot at Lazzaro's argument as

well, saying, "I reject the portrait of you as a passive participant[...]who was taken advantage of by a gang. It is not accurate to paint you as a naive young man whose mistake was merely to get mixed up with the wrong crowd."

Engelmayer was engaging in a little grandstanding. But it had a point. He had to justify keeping Tekashi in jail, and not rewarding a high-profile cooperator with the biggest, most obvious prize he could, the one almost everyone was expecting him to get. So, the judge re-emphasized his central point. Tekashi was "personally responsible" for much of the violence, because of his "symbiotic" relationship with Nine Trey. It wasn't just an evil gang, brainwashing and exploiting a naive young rapper. It was a *relationship*, one where both sides got something out of the deal.

Engelmayer then imagined an alternate universe, in which Tekashi continued using gang members as extras in videos, but that was it. There was nothing illegal in using a gang to promote one's rap career. That would have been okay.

"Your crimes involved the fateful decisions you made later to join the gang and, in particular, to use it then as your personal hit squad," Engelmayer said.

"Personal hit squad" was a good phrase, one that encapsulated the peculiar and violent dynamic between Tekashi and Nine Trey. In exchange for a steady flow of rap money and a worldwide PR and recruiting campaign, the gang took violent revenge on Tekashi's enemies.

To Engelmayer's mind, it was completely unnecessary. By the time Tekashi had actually become a full-fledged Nine Trey member, "Gummo" was already a hit. He was well on his way to riches and fame. To say he joined the gang to get out of poverty, or to provide for his daughter, was nonsense to the judge, "exploitative in the extreme."

After delivering his summary, Engelmayer started having a little fun with jokes and pop culture references. He pointed out that lots of artists make music about organized crime. "Bruce Springsteen sang about Murder Incorporated," he said, referring to the Boss's song, originally recorded in 1982 but not released until thirteen years later. "You, Mr. Hernandez, essentially *joined* Murder Incorporated."

Engelmayer's known pattern in sentencing speeches was to say all the bad things about the defendant up top, and then pivot into the good things. So he did. He talked again about the importance of Tekashi's cooperation (while pointing out that, had he not turned so early, another gangster would surely soon after have cooperated against *him*). Tekashi had testified credibly, and was believed by the jury. With that in mind, Engelmayer turned his attention to the third party in the case: the public. He explicitly addressed them.

He'd followed the commentary and seen the memes. He was aware that most of the online commentary romanticized the gang and mocked Tekashi for cooperating.

"I took much of what was written to be in good fun and jest," he said. "For the record, the judge in this case found the memes funny, too, whether they were at your expense or mine."

But in the end, that message got things totally wrong. Nine Trey attempted to kill people, robbed people, dealt fentanyl and heroin. They weren't the good guys here, done wrong by a rat. In fact, ratting was the *good* part of Tekashi's career. Nine Trey's violent crime spree was the thing to condemn. Cooperation wasn't bad. In fact, it was "necessary and essential" to keep people safe.

"Without it," the judge said, "there would be more killers and violent actors at large in our world."

Finally, it was time for the judge to give a number. Engelmayer said, before giving specifics, that the sentence would keep Tekashi locked up until "late next year"—the exact date would depend on credit for good time.

Then, the moment of truth.

"Mr. Hernandez, would you please rise."

It wasn't a question. Tekashi stood up.

Engelmayer laid down the law. Twenty-four months' imprisonment, followed by five years' supervised release.

Tekashi had already served thirteen months, so that left eleven months. He'd have to serve 85% of that time, given Bureau of Prisons rules, unless he got in some real trouble in the interim. So it looked like he'd be out sometime in the summer of 2020.

Outside the courtroom, Lazzaro didn't mince any words. He was disappointed. "We were expecting time served," he said. "We thought that he deserved it, with all that he had done."

What Engelmayer couldn't have known—what no one in the courtroom could have known—was that by sentencing Tekashi to spend most of 2020 locked up, the judge was throwing him into the middle of a worldwide emergency. And that Tekashi would as a result pull off one more great escape.

CHAPTER 23

EXTRAORDINARY AND COMPELLING REASONS

The coronavirus pandemic hit New York City with startling force in March 2020. Sixty percent of all the new cases in the country were coming from the five boroughs. In jails and prisons, people were worried that things were going to be horrific.

In the crisis, Lance Lazzaro saw his chance. On March 22, he wrote a pleading letter to Judge Engelmayer asking for Tekashi's release. After all, Tekashi was asthmatic. He had health problems while locked up, including a stint in the hospital for bronchitis and sinusitis. So, Lazzaro argued, Tekashi was at risk of death if he caught the virus because of his "compromised medical condition." Tekashi couldn't wait until the summer to get out of prison. He needed to be set free, into home confinement, right now.

From there, things entered a weird legal limbo. The government was against the request, and argued that it wasn't even up to Engelmayer, anyway. At this point, they said, it was up to the Bureau of Prisons. But, Lazzaro fired back, Tekashi was in a private jail, not technically in Bureau of Prisons custody. While the courts were trying to untangle this Kafkaesque knot, the days ticked away and the pandemic got worse.

Three long days after Lazzaro's initial letter, the judge weighed in. He turned down Tekashi's request over the Bureau of Prisons issue, but let it be known that he was extremely sympathetic. This opened up a way out. Once the Bureau had turned Tekashi down, Lazzaro could appeal to the judge. He was almost home free. He just needed a final answer from the bureaucracy.

But the Bureau of Prisons had up to thirty days to issue an answer—time during which the pandemic could spin even more out of control. Lazzaro just needed them to say no so that the case could be put in Engelmayer's hands. At first, the Bureau denied that they even had the authority to *make* the decision. And then, finally, on April 1, Lance got his answer. The Bureau of Prisons declined the request, so Engelmayer was able to take action.

He sent out a short note announcing that he was now in charge of Tekashi's petition, and that if the government had any objections, they needed to submit them by 5 PM that day. They got back just under the wire, assenting to the compassionate release. Engelmayer then okayed it, but that remained secret until 4 PM the next day.

Tekashi was taken out of a back entrance of the jail about an hour and a half before the order became public. He was now out of prison, but confined to his house except for legal and medical visits. He would stay under those restrictions until his sentence ended. He used the time to record a new album and shoot videos inside his house. He even, after a few weeks, got back on social media.

Most of his co-defendants weren't so lucky. Kooda, while

awaiting sentencing, managed to be released on bond temporarily after pleading susceptibility to coronavirus. However, he almost torpedoed that when a video appeared on social media of Kooda hanging out in a room, surrounded by a bunch of friends, some of whom were smoking weed, with no masks in evidence.

The judge was livid, because it seemed like Kooda had been using the Covid thing as an excuse. But, in the end, the fact that Kooda had been so reckless was actually used as an argument not to send him back to jail. The courts didn't want to do anything that could introduce even *more* prisoners to the virus. Kooda was chastised, but allowed to remain out until his sentencing. All the other Nine Trey defendants who tried to get their long sentences turned to home confinement because of the pandemic were turned down.

Meanwhile, Tekashi was making music and shooting videos at a feverish pace. And, regardless of Covid concerns, he was inviting people into his house to work on them. After a month or so of work, he was ready.

On May 6, Tekashi took to Instagram to make an announcement: "I'm going live Friday."

On May 8, he shared a new video for his song "Gooba." The video showed him in the same room with a number of models, including his girlfriend Rachel "Jade" Wattley and her sister Sarah. But the song and video weren't what attracted the most attention. Millions of viewers tuned in to the Instagram Live to see what Tekashi had to say. It would be the first time he'd spoken publicly since the wild sentencing hearing.

It was time to see who a post-prison Tekashi 6ix9ine was. All traces of the repentance he'd shown during his sentencing hearing had vanished. What was left was the trolly, unapologetic, charismatic person whose whole career, whose whole *life*, depended on getting a reaction.

His new schtick was to lean in to being a cooperator. People called him a rat? Okay, sure, he was a rat. So, he started the Live by dancing to the *Cops* theme song while holding a pair of handcuffs.

Tekashi was wearing a lot of jewelry, including copies of the pieces Harv had stolen. He was sporting four watches, one of which he bragged cost half a million dollars, and a new shark chain (to go along with the artwork and video for "Gooba") which he claimed cost the same amount.

He rapped along to his verse from "Kika," emphasizing lines about how "I don't need fifty niggas to roll with" and "fuck all them niggas I used to run with." It was a far-from-subtle message to Shotti and the rest of Nine Trey—and far from the only one he would give that night.

Tekashi's monologue had one main theme. It was the same tune he'd been singing since the days of yelling at Righteous P and ZillaKami: haters were underestimating him, plotting against him, counting him out. And he was defying them all with his success.

"Y'all could never cooperate with the government and come back," he said. "I'm a living legend."

It's telling that this monologue was delivered to haters, rather than fans. It was the haters that Tekashi 6ix9ine needed in order to exist as a personality. He needed the controversy. Otherwise, what was there? Who was he if he wasn't someone who went viral? Long before he first became famous, he'd put every effort into antagonizing enough people to remain relevant. Why change what had so obviously worked?

He spoke directly to the rappers he imagined were mad at him. It was a great device to paint himself as still controversial, and still in the center of the conversation. He directed jabs at rappers who were upset that a "rat" was outselling them. After five minutes of ranting at haters and speaking about his riches, Tekashi turned serious.

He apologized to his fans because "It wasn't worth it." *What* wasn't worth it? What was he apologizing for? He didn't specify.

Instead, he turned to a new favorite theme: by snitching, he hadn't violated any kind of code of the streets, because the whole idea of a "street code" was nonsense. Witness how Nine Trey had treated him—kidnapped him, robbed him, threatened his life, even slept with the mother of his daughter.

It was the mention of Shotti and Sara—albeit neither of them by name—that showed the depth of Tekashi's obsession with that alleged affair. He'd brought it up in his letter to the judge. He'd brought it up at his sentencing. He talked about it so much that the government was obliged to mention it in court. And here he was, in front of two million people, talking about it again. There was no mention of his years-long history of domestic violence. Or what people around him remember as his countless incidents of cheating on Sara. Or the fact that he had allowed Shotti into his circle in the first place because of his passionate desire for riches, fame, and attention.

Tekashi was testing out new lines of attack, some of which he would share in later interviews. The fans, he said, "understand why I snitched, but y'all don't *want* to understand." There was a direct, albeit nameless, dig at Shotti: "when I met son, he was sleeping on a rug."

Most of all, there was defiance. Tekashi hadn't done anything wrong, and no one was going to get him to say otherwise. At the very end, he gave a list of shoutouts. Except, instead of to fellow rappers or people from the block, the list reflected his new reality. He thanked, by name, Lance Lazzaro, Michael Longyear, and Jacob Warren.

Interestingly, Tekashi seemed to have taken some pointers from Engelmayer's long speech at the sentencing. His huge social media numbers proved, he said, that he hadn't ever really needed the gang at all. "I'm the biggest artist in the fucking world," he said. The speech did what he needed it to do. It got attention he would parlay into more videos, including a collaboration with Nicki Minaj.

Finally, Tekashi's release came. Because the exact date was different, due to a weekend, than the date posted on the Bureau of Prisons' website, he was able to go out into the world before most people released what was happening. Tekashi went all over Brooklyn to film a video. He headed, among other locations, back to his old Bushwick stomping grounds—albeit with a ton of security. The video was filmed and dropped rapidly, and Tekashi hopped on Instagram Live with his old friend DJ Akademiks.

Hundreds of thousands of people watched as word got out that this was happening—that Tekashi was free and actually walking around Brooklyn. Somewhat surprisingly given his supposed concerns about coronavirus, he wasn't wearing a mask and got right up next to people, posing for pictures as fans approached.

That trip outside marked Tekashi's final successful stunt of his release period. Diminishing returns began to set in, as views went down on each successive music video. By the time his full-length album *TattleTales* was released, it only hit number 4 on the Billboard chart.

This was a poor enough performance that he could no longer use Billboard chart position as a metric of success. Instead, it became a marker of how he was discriminated against. Streaming services, Billboard, the media: everyone was conspiring against him, to keep him off the charts. It was a desperation that had never before been a part of the Tekashi 6ix9ine persona, even in his darkest days. Sure, complaining about haters had always been his thing. But this time, it appeared, the haters were finally winning.

Tekashi gave a handful of interviews to go along with the album's release. In them, he hammered on the themes he'd been developing: big players in the music industry were cheating him out of his rightful success; he hadn't been disloyal to Nine Trey because they betrayed him first; and yes, he'd abused Sara, but it was because he suspected she was sleeping with Shotti.

Of all these new themes, the one around snitching was the most notable. Tekashi defined snitching so narrowly that his very public snitching effectively didn't even exist. He hadn't snitched, he insisted. It didn't count because Nine Trey members did *him* wrong first.

This new line didn't stop the deepening criticism. Most people defined snitching as telling on people you committed crimes with, regardless of whether they were nice to you afterwards. Others defined it even more broadly, as giving any information that could be used against somebody in court, regardless of the context.

But Tekashi couldn't let it go. Despite comically embracing the accusation, he still railed against being thought of as a snitch. Not long into his home confinement, he saw that the rapper Meek Mill had posted a clip on Instagram of an old freestyle where he denounced snitching. Though Meek didn't say anyone's name, it was obviously a shot aimed at Tekashi. Meek confirmed this later in the day by posting a series of tweets about Tekashi.

"I hope that rat going live to apologize to the people he told on or the victim," he wrote. "Y'all forgot that fast a 'rat' killed Nipsey [Hussle] he wasn't suppose to be on the streets! That's the only thing ima day [sic] because he's dead... left his baby mom and child like a coward as targets!" Meek eventually realized that he was devoting too much energy to the project. "I'm sorry I lash out sometimes when I see people playing like that lol I been locked up too many times like a animal," he wrote.

Tekashi sent several light shots back, but saved the substance of his response for a month. On June 11, 2020, right before he was about to release his Nicki Minaj collaboration "Trollz," Tekashi went on Instagram Live. He raged about what he viewed as Meek's hypocrisy. Meek had criticized him for being a snitch, Tekashi said. But Meek had also worked closely with Desiree Perez. Perez was the CEO of Jay Z's company Roc Nation, which manages Meek. And Perez had been a cooperating witness for the DEA decades prior, following a 1994 arrest. (Perez would go on to receive a last-minute pardon from President Trump).

"You go saying we don't fuck with rats," Tekashi said. "Your executive is a rat."

Attacking such a prominent person in the music industry was a sure way for Tekashi to make even more enemies. But that didn't seem to matter to him. He was convinced that the music industry was dead set against him. In interviews, he gave questioners his phone and had them scroll through new releases on streaming services, in an effort to prove that *Tattle-Tales* wasn't being featured by any of the major players, unlike new albums by more industry-friendly rappers like Big Sean or Lil Durk.

But his complaining didn't really gain any traction. Something worse than a backlash seemed to be happening. Finally, after all the drama, Tekashi's act was wearing thin. Following his big reveal of walking around New York City, he didn't seem to have any tricks left to pull out of his hat.

This feeling was cemented in early October 2020, when it was revealed that Tekashi was hospitalized after mixing a far-larger-than-recommended dose of diet pills with caffeine, in an incident that called back to his days of compulsively eating salads for breakfast while on tour. Tekashi remains mostly quiet on social media as the finishing touches are being put on this book.

Meanwhile, after months of delays, Harv was finally sentenced in November 2020. Judge Engelmayer gave him twenty-four years. Harv took the occasion to slam his attorney, Deveraux Cannick.

"It was inconsistent counsel," he said. "He did nothing that I told him to do." He promptly dropped Cannick as counsel and filed an appeal. But Harv's objections aside, Cannick had a near-impossible task at trial. He was defending someone caught on tape committing a kidnapping, after all.

About a month later, Kooda, the case's final defendant, was sentenced to fifty-four months in prison.

As a result of the case, almost a dozen men are serving prison sentences ranging from fifty-four months to twenty-four years. They did it for themselves, to be sure. They did it for money, and for status, and to get a leg up in long-running personal antagonisms. But almost all of the crimes these men were convicted of were committed to advance the career of the rainbow-haired rap star who, for a brief time, showed us exactly what we wanted to see.

CONCLUSION
OVER THE RAINBOW

Daniel Hernandez created a persona that was perfectly suited to our social media-centric lives. His antics provided a new hit of dopamine every time we looked at our phones. His churning need to take on the scariest, most intimidating foe gave audiences near-constant shocks. We couldn't *believe* he was saying those things to J. Prince, or YG, or Chief Keef—or, at the very end, to Shotti himself. There couldn't be a rapper with *that* many colors in his hair. With *that* many tattoos. He consistently took things to the extreme in order to get our attention.

The end goal didn't seem to be fame or riches, exactly. If that was the only desired outcome, his crime spree would never have started. After all, the attack on Trippie Redd took place after "Gummo" was released and was starting to gain serious traction. There were better ways to get streams and clicks than to have Harv punch Trippie in the mouth.

The need for attention was Tekashi's preeminent motivation. But there was something else underneath it. Looking closely at the relationship between Tekashi and Shotti tells us what was really at the root of the behavior that rocked the world for a solid year. The longer Tekashi was around the hardened Nine Trey big homie, the more they melded into each other. Shotti followed his artist's lead and got on social media for the first time. And he became great at it, issuing threats and jokes in equal measure. Tekashi took from Shotti as well.

"[Tekashi] had the artist position," Seqo Billy says now when he reflects on the story. "But he also wanted to be feared and loved as a gangster."

Tekashi and Shotti wanted to switch roles, Seqo realized. Each wanted what the other had. Shotti desired the audience of millions and the ability to speak freely, without repercussions. Tekashi wanted the fearsome reputation and respect in the street.

"To me, every decision they made together was terrible," Seqo concluded. "They literally just sabotage themselves."

If there's a reason behind the rapid rise and fall of Tekashi 6ix9ine, it is this. The alchemy of Tekashi and Shotti—the brazen, attention-hungry young man and the fearsome, fearless gangster ready to succeed whatever the cost.

But this story also teaches us something about ourselves. Tekashi 6ix9ine doesn't exist without an audience. He needs lovers and haters both in order to succeed. And for that, he needs our attention. And countless millions of people gave it to him, unquestioningly, for months at a time. Even people involved in the maelstrom felt this way.

"It was at a point for months where every morning I would wake up, use the restroom, and go on my Instagram to see what the hell was going on, what they did last night," says Shotti's entertainment lawyer Navarro Gray. "Because every day it was something new."

But novelty and being at the extremes is only good for a little while. There are extremes beyond which people cannot go. For Tekashi 6ix9ine, using a street gang to enhance and protect his rap stardom was a great idea—until it wasn't. The gang wanted too much, and their crimes were too numerous, for the relationship to last. You can see that even Shotti was aware of this, given his attempts to build a brand outside of his star client.

There are many reasons why Tekashi's post-prison career went downhill so rapidly. He had snitched on his gang in front of the whole world, violating one of hip-hop's foremost tenets in the process, and, as a result, he had a much harder time attracting high-profile collaborators. His creativity in videos became circumscribed since he was largely forced to remain at home.

But there was something else, too. His take-on-the-world bravado was gone, replaced by an angry defensiveness. And that seems directly traceable to the fact that Kifano "Shotti" Jordan is now sitting in a federal prison in Pennsylvania. Shotti was Tekashi's first line of defense. Tekashi could say anything and insult anybody, because he knew that Shotti would be right behind him, ready to handle the situation however it needed to be handled. When that backup disappeared, Tekashi's bravado lost some luster. He no longer had the often-literal firepower needed to back up his reckless threats. Sadly, without that, there was less reason to watch.

And maybe, just maybe, Tekashi's audience learned something in all of the spectacle. Learned that, to paraphrase Barry Goldwater, extremism in the defense of nothing *is* a vice. Learned that the latest hit of dopamine delivered via social media isn't an unalloyed good, and that it can have real-world consequences. Or maybe we learned none of this, and a new extremist will come to capture our attention, using new devices and breaking new rules.

Tekashi 6ix9ine now has fancy cars, expensive jewelry, and the other trappings of stardom. But his drive to become like the big homie he admired ultimately cost him other things besides money. Despite Tekashi's ostentatious public appearances, he lives a protected life, surrounded by security and keeping his location secret. As of this writing, he appears to have no relationship to speak of with Sara Molina, or either of his daughters. And to judge by recent legal documents, he has become erratic and essentially impossible to reach, even for key advisors.

It's not just conjecture to say that he's not doing well. In an April 2021 Instagram caption, he admitted as much. "IN ALL REALITY I'M NOT HAPPY. THE FAME AND THE MONEY DOESN'T MEAN ANYTHING TO ME BECAUSE IT DOESN'T BRING ME JOY... I WILL CONTINUE MY JOURNEY TO FIND HAPPINESS WITHIN MYSELF AND FIND THE JOY I ONCE HAD."

If there's any hope for Daniel Hernandez to find that happiness, it surely lies in acknowledging that he has taken internet virality as far as it can go. Now, it's up to him to find out what is beyond the rainbow.

ACKNOWLEDGMENTS

I had no idea when I first came across Tekashi 6ix9ine standing by my desk in the *Complex* office that his story would come to take up years of my life. Thank you to all of my editorial team co-workers, current and former, at *Complex* for allowing me the time and space to report on his case. You let me learn on the job, and I am forever grateful. And thank you to Justin Killion and the team at *Complex* for their partnership in getting this book out into the world.

Thank you to everyone I interviewed, whether for *Infamous,* this book, or otherwise, for sharing your stories. Special thanks go to Jorge Rivera and DJ Pvnch. Both men were endlessly generous with their time, held nothing back, and gave me the unvarnished truth of their experiences.

Thanks to all the court reporters I encountered in my reporting on the Tekashi case, who took me in as part of their family: Victoria Bekiempis, Colin Moynihan, Stephen Rex Brown, Emily Saul, Matthew Russell Lee, Agustin Iglesias, Jack Frost, and everyone else in the gallery.

Thank you to Vikram Gandhi, for dealing with pandemic craziness graciously and including me in your documentary.

A huge thanks to everyone who was a part of *Infamous: The Tekashi 6ix9ine Story*, the podcast that sparked my even deeper dive into this tale, and for which many of the interviews that appear in this book were done: Angie Martinez, who I still can't believe narrated my words. Our superb and patient editor, the inimitable Catherine Saint Louis. The show's sound king Hannis Brown (may we finally meet in person one day!). Our composer Jordan Granados. Everyone at Spotify, especially Charlie Clark and Dzifa Yador. All the people at *Complex* who helped the show get off the ground, especially Myles O'Connell and Marlon Calbi. The mighty Ann Hepperman, who somehow shaped my barrage of facts and dates into a great show.

And this book wouldn't exist if it wasn't for my *Infamous* partner in crime Shiva Bayat. Every insane step of the way, you were right there in forming Daniel Hernandez's story into eight wonderful episodes. Somehow, we did it. I couldn't ask for a better teammate in making shows that matter. Thank you.

A big thanks to Zakia Henderson-Brown for the thoughtful edits and feedback, and to Mandy Keifetz for the copyediting and fact-checking on an insane schedule.

Thanks to my agent William LoTurco. It was your cold call during the Tekashi trial that started this whole process in motion, and your Herculean efforts that kept it going.

Thank you to my publisher Marvis Johnson for believing in a first-time author. See you for the next one!

A grateful nod to Dan Charnas and Joe Schloss. Thank you for the advice, and thank you even more for the group text, which always lifted my spirits.

Thanks to my pre-publication reader Adam Mansbach for going above and beyond with your invaluable notes.

To Louisa and Miller: thank you for making me a part of your family. And thanks for providing an unexpected writing retreat for the last stages of this project.

To my dearest friend Ruby: thank you for your constant support, and for always being proud of me.

To my parents: thank you for instilling in me the love of reading, writing, and music.

Last in the thank-yous but first in my heart is my wife, Nicole a.k.a the person on the planet most tired of hearing about Daniel Hernandez. You were by my side the whole time, and somehow still married me even though our wedding took place right in the middle of the trial this book describes. Thank you for your patience, your love, and for putting up with that weekend where I got those crazy phone calls from you-know-who. I love you now, and forever.

KINGSTON IMPERIAL

Marvis Johnson — Publisher
Kathy Iandoli — Editorial Director
Joshua Wirth — Designer
Kristin Clifford — Publicist, Finn Partners
Emilie Moran — Publicist, Finn Partners

Contact:
Kingston Imperial
144 North 7th Street #255
Brooklyn, NY 11249
Email: Info@kingstonimperial.com
www.kingstonimperial.com

INDEX

A

Adidas Originals, 27
"All Night," 19
"Always Paid" (AP), 89
Angels NYC, 50
Apes, 34, 63
ASAP collective, 66
ASAP Ferg, 66
ASAP Rocky, 66
ASAP Yams, 66, 67
Atlantic Records, 228

B

Barclays Center
   fight at, 91–92, 93, 94, 95–96
   shooting at, 192, 248, 261, 273
Bed Stuy, 39, 130
"Behind the wall," 244
Biddle, Nuke, arrest of, 182
"Big Bank," 133
Big Sean, 133, 284
Billboard Hot 100 chart, 58, 96
Billboard, ranking of *TattleTales*, 282–283
Billboard 200 album chart, 3
"Billy," 216
   playing of, in racketeering trial, 181, 182, 183, 184
   release of, 91
"Billy Dat," 44, 50
Björk, 25
Black Ops Private Investigators Inc., 238
Bloods, 31, 54
   Cardi B as a, 227–228
   Crips and, 48
   Tekashi as member of, 57, 226
Blue Diamond, 106–107, 108, 109
"Bodak Yellow," 226
Bolivar, Shamir "Shadow," security business of, 126
Bolt, Usain, 90
A Boogie Wit da Hoodie, 58, 59
Bourne, Pi'erre, 23, 28
Boxing, relationship between rap and, 91
Braxton, James "Frank White," 32
The Breakfast Club, 80
   Tekashi appearance on, 143

B-Right, 41
Broner, Adrien, 91–92, 93
Brooklyn Crip, 106
Bushwick, 13
Byrd Gang, 35

C

Cambridge, Fitroy, 35
Cambridge, Wally-Emmanuel, 36
Cam'ron, 35
   interview of, on idea of never-snitching 172
Cannick, Deveraux, as attorney for Harv in racketeering case, 178–179, 189, 190, 197–198, 199, 228–232, 234–235, 238–241, 243, 246, 247, 250–251, 256, 258, 285
Cardi B, 226–228
Casanova, 34, 190
   affiliation with Apes, 63
   Barclays Center fight and, 93–94, 95
   "Don't Run" as song of, 181, 182
   Harv's dislike of, 64
   at racketeering trial, 185
   release of "Set Trippin," 64
   Tekashi's issues with, 91, 216
Cheeks, David, shooting of, 138–139, 244, 245–246
Chief Keef, 97, 98–101, 130, 287
   beef between Tekashi and, 100–101
   shooting of, 100, 103, 154, 172, 174, 190, 192, 216–217, 248, 261, 273
Clark, Aareon "Slim Danger," 101
Club Freq, 63
Cohen, Az, 19, 21
Cohen, Lyor, 19–20
Consensual audio recordings, 156–157
Cooper, Anderson, 172–173
Coronavirus pandemic, 277, 279
Create Music, 26
Crippy, 81, 82, 84–85, 110
   as defendant in racketeering case, 141–142, 151, 164, 211, 214
   efforts to keep Tekashi safe, 84

guilty plea of, 176
Instagram account of, 156
kidnapping of Tekashi and, 122
Lazzaro, Lance, as attorney for, 164
in Metropolitan Detention Center, 166
recovery of phone, 156
sentence for racketeering case, 259
Shotti's monologue on robbery, 129–130
wounding of, 141

Crips
Bloods and, 48
Scumlord D!zzy ties with, 17, 18

Cruz, Kristian, 252
arrest with drugs, 104–105
as cooperating witness in racketeering case, 33, 105, 159, 190, 191, 193, 237–240, 245, 249–251, 252
sentencing of, 272
taped phone calls between Mel Murda and, 239–240
as undercover informant, 153

Cuban Doll, 96–97, 98
offering of Shotti's protective services to, 97
Tadoe beating up of, 98

Curcio as issue in racketeering case, 163

D
Day69, 67, 68
on Billboard album chart, 96
release of, 68

Dennis, Andrea, 187

Diplomats, 34–35
Jones, Jim, as "capo" of Harlem's, 34–35
sale of "STOP SNITCHIN" t-shirts by, 172

DJ Akademiks, 57, 86, 106, 282
interview of Tekashi, 85–86, 231

DJ Pharris's interview of West, Kanye, 134, 135

DJ Pvnch, 48, 49, 50, 51
closeness to Casanova, 63
idea on Tekashi kidnapping attempt, 123–124
release of "Set Trippin" and, 64

DJ Relentt, capitalization by, 134–135

DJ Thoro, 80

Dollhouse Cosmetics, 39

Donaldson, Reginald, testimony of, in racketeering case, 241

"Don't Run," 63, 95
playing of, in racketeering trial, 181, 182

Drake, 50, 71–72, 123, 124

Drew, 43
Danny and, 24, 29–30
direction of Tekashi 69 videos, 18
editing of videos and, 112
involvement with videos and song writing, 50–51
King, Chris, and, 29–30
recordings of, 43, 67

Dubai, Tekashi's visit to, 136–137

Dummy Boy, 3, 143–144

"DWB," 21

E
East Coast-West Coast rap wars, 79

"EDD," 182

Ehigiator, Chris, 29–30, 73
Drew and, 29–30
firing of, 76–77
as manager, 44, 45, 46, 53
as publicity shy, 56
push out of, 67–68

Einhorn, Jeffrey, as attorney for Shotti in racketeering case, 163, 164

Einhorn, Joe, as founder and CEO of Fancy.com, 135

Elliot Grainge Entertainment, 26

Ellison, Anthony "Harv." See Harv

Engelmayer, Paul, 164–165
on illegal recording of Tekashi's testimony, 221
as judge in racketeering case, 155, 164–165, 166, 168–169, 174–177, 180–181, 182, 184–185, 187, 190–191, 199, 211, 215, 229, 234, 238, 242, 255–258
Lazzaro's letter to, on Tekashi's sentence, 277
sentencing of defendants in racketeering case, 259, 260

sentencing of Tekashi and, 265–266, 270, 271–276, 282

Epic Records, 47
  negotiations with, 24

Evers, Lisa, interview of Lazzaro, 157

F

Fancy.com, 135

Fasulo, Louis, as attorney for Nuke in racketeering case, 189, 243, 248–250, 251–252

Fat Joe, 162
  on snitching, 174

"Fck Them," 12
  You Tube page of, 45

Federal government, shutdown of, 165–166

"Fefe," 124, 129
  chart position of, 129
  filming of video for, 110–111
  promotion of, 178

Fetty Wrap, 58, 59

50 Cent, 127, 261
  on snitching, 174

Five-Nine Brims, 34

Five Stairsteps' "O-o-h Child," 4

5K1 letter in racketeering case, 167, 191, 253, 260

5-Trey Gangsters, 40–41

Florio, Dawn, racketeering case and, 168

Follow protocol, as admonition to Nine Trey members, 183–184

"For a Scammer," 45

Foster, Chad, as style guy, 10

Foxwoods Resort Casino, 147

Franklin, at sentencing of Tekashi, 270

Frenchie BSM, 266
  assault on, 78, 79, 214
  shooting of, 273

Fried, Carrie B., study on rap lyrics, 181–182

Future, 50

G

The Game, 162

Gansevoort Hotel, assault on Trippie Redd at, 54–55, 192, 207, 212, 260–261, 273

G-Eazy, 78

Goldwater, Billy, 289

"Gooba," 279, 280

Gotti, John, 162

Grainge, Elliot, 25–26, 46, 234–235
  court appearance of, 141–142
  family tree of, 26
  at sentencing of Tekashi, 270

Grainge, Lucian, 25

Grandmaison, Adam, 19–21, 96

Gray, Navarro, 288

Greenhorn, Jeffery, as attorney in racketeering case, 163, 164

Greenpoint Youth Courts, 7–8

Guiterrez, Pedro "Magoo," 32

"Gummo," 46, 51, 58, 63, 97, 274
  chart position of, 59
  filming at Maddy, 185
  as gold, 96
  lyrics of, 207
  mention of, in racketeering case, 205
  misogynistic statements in, 185
  playing of, in racketeering trial, 181, 182, 185
  release of, 46, 287
  runaway success of, 207, 208
  Tekashi's performance of, 63
  video for, 43–44, 48, 50, 56, 59, 205–206

"G-Wall," 32

H

Handshakes as gang symbol, 195–196

Harv, 39–40, 54, 73–75, 254
  attempted getback at after kidnapping, 261
  Cannick, Deveraux, as attorney for in racketeering case, 178–179, 189, 190, 197–198, 199, 228–232, 234–235, 238–241, 243, 246, 247, 250–251, 256, 258, 285
  in car chase, 54
  charges against, 260
  conflict between Shotti and, 138
  as defendant in racketeering case, 179–180

189, 190, 192, 194, 201, 211, 213, 214, 234, 242, 243, 245, 251, 252, 253, 255, 256, 258, 260
dislike of Casanova, 64
enforcer role of, for Nine Trey, 212
gang dispute settlement and, 194
kidnapping of Tekashi and, 129, 139, 172, 177, 178, 193, 194, 197, 201
as member of Nine Trey, 184, 244, 254
possession of Tekashi's jewelry, 130
protection of Tekashi and, 188
"RESPECT MY DICK" text of, 212
selling of Tekashi's jewelry and, 129, 178
sentence for racketeering care, 259–260, 285
"Shotti" and, 73–74, 103–104, 188
as Tekashi's bodyguard, 56
wearing of Tekashi's jewelry, 239
Harv's ex-girlfriend as witness in racketeering case, 200–201
Haus, 50
Hernandez, Daniel, 22, 24, 25, 46, 269. *See also* Tekashi
antics of, 287
arrest for racketeering, xv, 151, 153
arrest of, in 2015, 24
backstory of, 30
bail for, 16
birth and early childhood of, 5–6
birth of Saraiyah, 17
change in direction for, 43
charisma of, on camera, 24
Christian Ehigiator as manager of, 44, 45, 46, 53
collaboration with Schlosser and, 19–22
connection with Tripple Redd, 22
Cruz, Kristian, as cooperating witness in case against, 33
desire for number 1 album, 3
Drew and, 24, 29–30
drug dealing and, 33
duets of, with ZillaKami, 18
early accomplishments of, 28
efforts to start music career, 17
employment of, 7–8
family of, 5

as father, 16
father's abandonment of, 5–6
as flop, 3
formation of plan with Yaksha, 12
gang affiliation and success as a rapper, 18
guilty plea of, in racketeering case, 168
homemade clothes with slogans of, 11, 18, 20, 24
hyperactive energy of, 26
on interim probation, 16–17
involvement with Nine Trey, 33
involvement with street gang, 4
love of music, 9
manager for, 43
Mexican heritage of, 44
need for GED, 16
nicknames of, 8–9
as physically abusive to Molina, Sara, 7, 126, 136
plans for video shoot, 17–18
pleading out, to sexual abuse charge, 16
post-prison, 279–280
poverty of family, 6–7
production of viral videos with Christopher Schlosser, 18–19
rap career of, 13
recording of "Gummo" and, 43
record label of, 43
release of videos by, 18
rise to stardom, 4
Scumlord D!zzy and, 17
sentence of, for racketeering case, 260–261
sentencing to Rikers, 16–17
sex videos made by, 14
on Snapchat, 27
star power of, 9
stealing of money from ZillaKami, 25
street people and, 17
success with hip-hop, 17
Tay Milly and, 13–14
as Tekashi 6ix9ine, 46

"Tekashi 69" as rap name for, 10
tension with ZillaKami, 27
transformation into star, 8
use of Instagram by, 12
videos of, 10–11, 12, 18
video taping of "Gummo" and, 44
villain status of, 8–9
violence and, 33–34
viral fame of, 18, 41
voice of, 8, 9
"Wallah Dan" as rap name for, 10
Yaksha and, 12, 25
Hernandez, Daniel Sr. (father)
abandonment of family, 5–6
drug use by, 5
sentencing of son and, 268, 269, 270–271
Hernandez, Oscar (brother), 5, 7
High Intensity Drug Trafficking Area (HIDTA)
program, 209
High Snobiety, 99
High 020, 32
Hip-hop
Danny and, 17
prohibition against snitching in, 172
"Hollywood." See Harv
Hot 97, 205
Houston incident, 71–86
Huot, Alex, as attorney in racketeering case,
195–197, 224–228

I
iCloud accounts, 156
"I Don't Like," 98
"I Kill People," 98
"I Love Party Productions," 12
"I Think I Can Beat Mike Tyson," 91

J
Jakkboyzz, 90
Jay-Z, 105, 284
Jewelry
Clark's wearing of Tekashi's, 101
Harv's attempt to sell Tekashi's, 246

Harv's possession of Tekashi's, 130
Harv's selling of, 129, 178
Harv's wearing of Tekaski's, 239
kidnapping of Tekashi and, 117, 127, 129,
130, 231, 254
non-stolen, 124
Tekashi's nightly ritual with, 111
Tekashi's wearing of, 280, 290
Jones, Jamel, 35. *See also* Mel Murda
dislike for Mack, Alijermiah "Nuke," 34
rapping and, 35
Jones, Jim, 70, 145, 146, 224, 228
as "capo" on Harlem's Diplomats rap
crew, 34–35
in court case, 190
Diplomats and, 172
as retired rapper, 212
superviolate conversation between Mel
Murda and, 154
Jones, Jim DVD, 77
Jonez, Fluff, 78
Jordan Kifano "Shotti." *See* Shotti
Jordan, Sasha, 35, 36
Jordan, Suzette, 35
Jorge, 68–69, 81, 84, 112–113
arrest of, 104–105
Barclays Center fight and, 94
as confidential informant, 105
as cooperating witness in racketeering
case, 191, 197, 235, 252
as driver for Tekashi, 69
efforts to calm Shotti down, 84–85
as government informant, 110
kidnapping of Tekashi and, 112–128
at Mets game, 88
overseeing of move from Tekashi's hous
to Long Island, 137
paranoia and, 84
pre-fight publicity and, 92–93
role as cooperator, 157
sentencing of, 272
Shotti's monologue on robbery, 129–130
testimony of, in racketeering case, 233–234

246, 247
This Is 50 robbery and, 88
Jue Lan's, 130
Juice WRLD, 109
Junya Boy, 80, 81, 82

K

Kappa Kappa Psi, comparison of United Blood
Nations to chapter of, 196
Kareem Harvey, 37. *See* Shotti
Kasheem, 37, 38
KB, as bodyguard for Trippie Redd, 207
KD, 80
"Keke," 59
    video for, 58, 60
Kevo, Flee, 66
"Kika," 230, 280
King, Chris, 22, 23, 27–28, 107
    calling Tekashi names, 55
King, Martin Luther, Jr., 250
    mention of, in racketeering case, 198
Kodak Black, 226–227
Kooda
    charges against, 260
    as defendant in racketeering case, 172, 260
    sentencing of, 278–279, 285
"Kooda," 47–48, 58, 99, 100, 207, 208
    chart position of, 59
    as gold recording, 96
    playing of, in racketeering trial, 181, 182, 187
    release of, 56, 57, 79
    shooting and, 100
    video for, 50, 56

L

Lanez, Tory, 230
Latin Kings, as force in Rikers Island jail, 31, 32
Lazzaro, Lance
    allowing of father to speak at Tekashi's
        sentencing, 271
    Engelmayer on argument of, 273–274
    Evers, Lisa's, interview of, 157
    letter to Engelmayer, on Tekashi's sentence, 277,

278
    as member of Tekashi's legal team, 141,
        153–154, 164, 165, 174
    sentencing of Tekashi and, 262, 267–269,
        276, 277–278
    Tekashi's thanking of, 282
Lebron, Moses, kidnapping of Tekashi and,
    119, 121
Leemon, Scott
    as attorney for Mel Murda, 163
    as attorney for Shotti, 155, 161–162
    flipping of clients by, 162
Lichtman, Jeffrey
    as attorney for Shotti, 163
    as defense attorney in racketeering case,
        162–163
    efforts to keep Lazzaro, Lance, from
        Tekashi's case, 165–166
    as public defense attorney, 162
    in racketeering case, 175
Lil Boosie, 173–174
Lil Durk, 284
Lil Uzi Vert, 50
Lil Yachty, 97
LL, letter in support of Tekashi and, 267
Locust Street, 5, 124, 130
Longyear, Michael
    allowing of father to speak at Tekashi's
        sentencing, 271
    as Assistant U.S. Attorney, 156, 157
    as government attorney in racketeering
        case, 18, 177, 189, 203, 204–210, 211–232,
        243, 250, 251, 252–254
    sentencing of Tekashi and, 266
    Tekashi's thanking of, 282
"Love Scars," 47
Lovick, Fuguan "Fubanger," Barclays Center
fight and, 91, 93, 95, 96
Low 020, 32

M

Mack, Aljermiah "Nuke." See Nuke
Maddy (brownstone on Madison Street),

40, 41, 43–44, 47, 48, 122, 137, 206
    Nine Trey meeting at, 206
    ownership of, 43
    shooting of videos at, 43, 185
    Shotti at, 53–54
    Tekashi at, 47, 53–54
"Madison Line," 137
Magoo, trial of, 252
Mark, as slashing victim, 139–140, 198, 199, 230–231, 245
Marlayna, letter in support of Tekashi, 265–266
Martinez, Angie, 4
    interview of Tekashi, 128, 129, 231, 238
Martin, Roland. See also Ro Murda
McKenzie, Leonard "Deadeye." formation of United Blood Nations and, 31–32
Meek Mill, 283–284
    on snitching, 174
Mel Murda, 137. See also Jones, Jamel
    attempt at Hail Mary, 158
    as defendant in racketeering case, 151, 162, 163, 222–223, 224, 245, 254
    drug sales by, 159
    evidence against, 158
    getting revenge on, 132
    guilty plea of, 176
    as highest ranking member of Nine Trey, 61–62
    Leemon, Scott, as attorney for, 163
    narcotics trafficking charges against, 158–159
    phone call with Shotti, 144–145
    search for lawyer by, 162
    sentence for, 259
    superviolate conversation between Jones, Jim, and, 154
    taped calls between Cruz and, 239–240
Migos and Young Thug collaborations, 19–20
Milwaukee Brewers, 88
Minaj, Nicki, 109, 111, 133, 284
    Tekashi's filming of video with, 143
Mi Sabor, 130
"Mob Ties," 72
Molina, Sara, 290
    Dubai trip with Tekashi, 136–137

kidnapping of Tekashi and, 111, 117–119
    pregnancy of, 16
    Shotti's sleeping with, 143, 226, 281
    Tekashi's abusive treatment of, 7, 126, 136
    Tekashi's cheating on, 281
Mo Murda, Nuke's robbery of, 225
Moses, Joe, 79
Mr. Jordan, racketeering case and, 161, 162, 164
Mr. Met, photo of Tekashi and Shotti posing with, 87
Ms. Tr3yway, 40, 45, 55, 90, 122–123
    lack of charges against, 205
    mention of, in racketeering case, 206
    trademark of Tr3yway by, 65
Murda. See Mel Murda; Ro Murda
"Murda Line," 137, 138

N
Nazario, Luis
    murder of, 6–7
    as stepfather, 6, 7
Neja, 37, 38
"New wave," 11
New York City, gang dynamics in, 48
Nielson, Erik, 187
Nine Trey, 4
    Brooklyn faction of, 34
    chance for revenge against Prince, J., 81–82
    chaos caused by kidnapping in, 222–223
    crimes committed by, 159, 175, 208, 216
    Danny's involvement with, 33
    demand for loyalty, 51
    discussion of crimes by members of, 194–195
    drug dealing and, 33, 70, 153, 192–193, 237, 243–244, 248
    efforts to further aims of, 151
    Ellison, Anthony, and, 254
    end of line of, 223–224
    Federal investigation into, 104–105, 132, 156

formation of, 31
formulas for videos, 207–208
"Gummo" video in promoting, 205–206
hand signals for, 51, 133, 196, 209, 244
Harv as member of, 192, 212
hierarchy in, 210
internal rift in, 55
leaders of, 32
Longyear's mission in demonstrating Nine Trey
   as organized, 210
meetings of, at Maddy, 206
Mel Murda as highest ranking member of, 61–62
mission to shoot, 138
Nuke as member of, 192
as out to get Tekashi, 165
purpose of, in Rikers, 31–32
as racketeering organization, 175–176
rank structure of, 32–33
role as Tekashi's defenders, 66
Seqo Billy as member of, 34, 205
settlement of disputes in, 194
splintering of, 137, 216–217
spread of, on East Coast, 32
structure and hierarchy in, 193–194, 211
symbiotic relationship with Tekashi, 274
31 rules of, 152
This Is 50 robbery and, 88
treatment of Tekashi by, 281
violence and, 33–34, 243–244, 248, 261
White, Frank, as prison leader of, 247
No Jumper, 19, 26
No Limit rapper Mac, sentencing of, 186
Notorious B.I.G., 91, 105
NPR reporting, 186
Nuke, 137, 252, 254
   arrest of, 177
   as defendant in racketeering case, 189, 192, 194,
      196–197, 219, 224–225, 237, 242, 243, 247–248, 256
   dislike between Jones, Jamel "Mel Murda" and,
      34
   dragging of case and, 259
   guilty plea of, 177
   Huot, Alex, as attorney for, 196

robbery of Ro Murda, 88, 89–90, 116, 177,
   182, 215, 225, 240, 249
sentence for racketeering care, 259
ties to the rap world, 187–188
Nwandu, Angelica, interview of Tekashi,
   136
NYPD
   Nine Trey's criminal activities and,
      208–209
   raid on Tekashi's Brooklyn house, 137
   survey of people in the hip-hop world,
      209

O

Obama, 124
"O Block," 100, 101
OG Deadeye, 32
OG Mack, 32
"Oh What a Night," 20
Onfroy, Jahseh, 107–108
"On the Regulars," 58
"Oowee/Thots," 22

P

PACkmaN, 68
Page Six, 154
Palmer, Keke, 228
"Pedigree Vine," 18–19
Perez, Desiree, 284
Perez-Hernandez, Natividad (mother)
   involvement with Nazario, Luis, 6
   move to U.S., 5
   poverty of family, 6–7
"Personal hit squad," 55
Pirus, 78
"Poles1469" video, 22, 25, 26, 29
Police abuse, rappers fight against, 173–174
Polo Grounds label, 24
Pop Out Boyz, 45
Portee, Omar "O.G." Mack"
   formation of United Blood Nations and,
      31–32
Power, 127

Power 105.1 (radio station), 80
Prince, J., 71–72, 81–82, 127, 287
    need for retaliation against, 77
    Nine Trey's chance for revenge against, 81–82
    Rap-A-Lot label of, 212
Prince, J. Junior, 75–76, 77, 86
    birthday party of, 72
    posting of video on Instagram by, 72
"Prison Lineup," 32, 34

Q
Quad Studios, 79
    shooting outside of, 261

R
Racketeering case/trial
    Cannick, Deveraux, as attorney for Harv in,
        178–179, 189, 190, 197–198, 199, 228–232, 234–235,
        238–241, 243, 246, 247, 250–251, 256, 258, 285
    charging instructions in, 255–258
    closing arguments in, 242, 243–254
    Crippy as defendant in, 141–142, 151, 164, 211, 214
    Cruz, Kristian, as cooperating witness in, 33, 105,
        159, 190, 191, 193, 237–240, 245, 249–251, 252
    Curcio as issue in racketeering case, 163
    discussion of media in, 204
    Donaldson, Reginald's testimony in, 241
    Einhorn, Jeffrey as attorney for Shotti in, 163, 164
    Engelmayer, Paul, as judge in, 164–165, 166,
        168–169, 174–177, 180–181, 182, 184–185, 187,
        190–191, 199, 211, 215, 229, 234, 238, 242, 255–258
    Fasulo, Louis, as attorney in, 243, 248–250, 251–252
    5K1 letter in, 167, 191, 253, 260
    guilty pleas in, 168, 172, 174–177
    Harv as defendant in, 80, 179–1, 201, 211, 213, 214, 234,
        242, 243, 245, 251, 252, 253, 255, 256, 258
    Harv's ex-girlfriend as witness in, 200–201
    Huot, Alex, as attorney in, 195–197, 224–228
    Jorge as cooperating witness in, 191, 197, 235, 252
    jury deliberations in, 256
    jury selection in, 189–190
    Kooda as defendant in, 172
    Lazzaro, Jeffrey, as Tekashi's lawyer in, 164, 165

Leemon, Scott, as lawyer for Shotti in,
    161–162
Lichtman, Jeffery, as high-profile defense
    attorney and, 162–163
Longyear, Michael, as government attorney
    in, 177, 189, 203, 204–210, 211–232, 243, 250,
    251, 252–254
    meaning of "jack" in, 249
Mel Murda as defendant in, 162, 163,
    222–223, 224, 245, 254
Mr. Jordan and, 161, 162, 164
    need for rebuttal in, 250
Nuke as defendant in, 196–197, 224–225, 237,
    242, 243. 219, 247–248, 256
number of dependents in, 161
opening arguments in, 191–195
playing of rap videos in trial, 181–182,
    184–185, 186, 187–188
Rebold, Jonathan, as attorney in, 189,
    191–195
Rivera's testimony in, 233–234, 246, 247
Shotti as defendant in, 161–162, 163, 164, 183,
    197, 211, 216, 233–234, 246
start of, 189
status conference in, 161
"superviolate" conversation in, 224
Tekashi as cooperating witness in, 166–169,
    183–184, 185–186, 190–191, 196, 197–198,
    201, 203, 204–210, 211–232, 250–251,
    252–253, 256, 258
    tensions between defendants in, 161
    verdict in, 256–258
    Warren, Jacob's testimony in, 189,
    243–248, 254
Radio City Music Hall, Trippie's
    performance at, 78
Rap-A-Lot Records, 71, 77, 80, 81, 83, 212
    need for retaliation against, 77
    robbery of artist, 86
    Tekashi robbing of, 116
Rap music, 181–182
    attempt to show criminality at
    racketeering trial, 187

Rap on Trial: Race, Lyrics, and Guilt in America
(Dennis and Nielson), 187
Rappers, fight against police abuse and, 173–174
Rap, relationship between boxing and, 91
Rap songs, as offensive in racketeering trial,
184–185
Rap stars, successes and failures of, 3
Rap videos, playing of, in racketeering trial,
181–182, 184–185, 186, 187–188
Rebold, Jonathan, as attorney in racketeering case,
189, 191–195
"Red Barz," 226
Red Hook, 53, 54
"Red Stuy," 40, 41, 51
Righteous P, 8, 280
    choice of jobs for, 10
    desire to manage rappers, 8
    efforts to raise bail for Danny, 16
    help for Danny and, 17
    as manager of group, 13
    mention of, in racketeering case, 204
    negotiations with Epic Records, 24
    as rap name for Rogers, Peter A., 9
    as Scumgang crew member, 47
Rikers Island Jail
    formation of Nine Trey Gangsta Bloods in, 31
    Hernandez, Daniel, sentencing to, 16–17
    Latin Kings as force in, 31, 32
    Nine Trey's purpose in, 31–32
Rivera, Jorge. See Jorge
Robbery, bragging on social media and, 87
Roc Nation, 284
Rodriguez, Steven "ASAP Yams," 66, 67
Rogers, Junius. *See also* Zilla Kami
    interest in using Danny to get Hispanic
        audience, 11
    Zilla Kami as rap name of, 9
Rogers, Peter A. *See* Righteous P
"Rollin Stones," 12
Ro Murda, 78–79, 82
    arrest of, 155–156
    Barclays Center fight and, 93
    emptying of magazine of bullets at July 16

cookout, 158
    guilty plea of, 177
    Nuke's robbery of, 87–88, 116, 137, 177, 182,
        215, 216, 240, 248, 249
    pulling of gun on, 89
    release from prison, 69–70
    renouncing of Nine Trey by, 259
    sentence for, 259
Rose, Justin, 17

S
Santana, Edwin, as president of New Jersey
    chapter of East Coast Investigators
    Association, 152
Saraiyah, 111, 125
    birth of, 17
Schlosser, Christopher, 23, 45–46
    viral videos of, 18–19
    work with Danny, 18–22
"Scumbag69" hashtag, 15
Scumgang, 9–10, 12, 13, 17, 22–23, 28, 79, 260
    sentencing of Tekashi and, 260
    style of, 10–11
    Trippie's plan of re-uniting, 24
Scumlord D!zzy, 13, 79–80, 81, 86
    backpack from This Is 50 robbery, 137
    This Is 50 robbery and, 214–215
    ties with Crips, 17, 18
"Scummo," release of, by D!zzy, 79–80
"Scums," 12–13
Seqo Billy, 29, 30, 40, 45, 46, 288
    aunt of, 34
    desire to get Danny more in tune with
        urban community, 43
    dislike of Tekashi's trolling, 55
    first meeting with Tekashi, 41
    intelligence of, 64
    lack of charges against, 205
    as member of Nine Trey, 205
    mention of, in racketeering case, 204–205
    as rap moniker, 31
    songs from, 44
    video shooting and, 44

"Set Trippin," 64, 65
  release of, 91
Shadow Group, 126
Sha, kidnapping of Tekashi and, 114, 115, 116
Sheehan, Maureen, 16, 57
  arrest of Tekashi, 14–15, 16
Shotti, 50–51, 55–56, 78–79, 84–85, 287
  assault weapon of, 137
  Barclays Center fight and, 93, 94, 95–96
  birth and childhood of, 35
  in car chase, 54
  claim to be CEO of Tr3yway Entertainment, 127
  conflict between Harv and, 138
  control over Tekashi's career, 69
  control over the term "Treyway," 65
  crimes and arrests of, 36–40
  in Death Row Records sweatshirt, 124
  as defendant in racketeering case, 151, 161–162, 163, 164, 183, 197, 211, 216, 233–234, 246
  desire for revenge, 130, 131
  drug use and, 36–69
  education of, 36
  efforts to keep Lazzaro, Lance, from Tekashi's case, 165–166
  effort to save face, 76–77
  "fake management role " of, 212
  family of, 35–36
  in federal prison in Pennsylvania, 289
  as felon, 65
  firing on people in downtown Brooklyn, 273
  first meeting of Tekashi 6ix9ine, 35
  as fugitive, 39
  gang rank of, 62
  as gang sponsor, 51
  Harv and, 73–74, 188
  hostility between Tekashi and, 165
  on instability of Tekashi, 65–66
  interest in getting gun, 88
  internal rift in Nine Trey family and, 55
  Jorge's efforts to calm down, 84–85
  kidnapping of Tekashi and, 122
  lack of social media presence, 65
  Leemon, Scott, as attorney for, 155, 161–162

  legal options for, 162
  lying by, 225–226
  meeting with judge, 154–155
  meetup between Harv and, 103–104
  at Mets game, 87–88
  monologue of, on Tekashi, 129–130
  motto of, 152
  move to Crown Heights, Brooklyn, 36
  near-constant contact with Tekashi, 110
  as a Nine Trey member, 35
  phone call with Mel Murda, 144–145
  pistol-whipping by, 92–93
  pre-fight publicity and, 92–93
  in racketeering trial, 183–184
  recovery of phone, 156
  running of cosmetics company by, 39
  Sara and, 143, 226, 281
  sentence for, 259
  switching of roles with Tekashi, 288
  Tekashi and, 61–62, 75, 76–77, 84–85
  TMZ appearance of, 145
  as tough guide, 69
  at video shoot, 44
  violence and, 53, 70, 131–132
  visibility of, 77
  "We don't fold, we don't bend, we don't break" motto of, 187
  worldview of, 71
"Shotti move," 40, 237
6ix9ine, xv
  Kanye's desire to meet, 135
"69 Scrum Cartel," 11
"Skyy Daniels," 80, 81, 82–83, 264–265
"Skyy Lyfe," 80
Smith, Will, 91
Smollett, Jussie, 197
"Smurf Line," 137, 138
"Smurf Village," 48, 100, 137, 138, 200, 241
Snipknot, 9
Snitching
  prohibition against in hip-hop, 172
  prohibition of, by Nine Trey's 31 rules, 15,
  by Tekashi, 171–172, 173, 219, 281

21 Savage on, 174
Snoop Dogg on snitching, 174
Snow Billy, 56, 212
Sobande, Solomon, 107–108
Sosmula, 28
SoundCloud, 11, 19, 23
    press coverage of, xv
Springsteen, Bruce, song about Murder
    Incorporated, 274
Stay Fresh Grill, 8, 268
"STD Gang," 21
Stokes, Milo, 26
"Stoopid," 137
Strainge Entertainment, 25–26
Strange Music, 25–26
"Street code," 281
"Street Lineup," 32–33
Street people, 17
"Street Stories," 157
Sugarcubes, 25
Summer Jam, 105–106, 126
Summit Rooftop Lounge, 75–76
"Superviolate" conversation in racketeering case,
    224
SXSW show, 76

T
Tadoe, 97–98
Take That, 25
Tati at sentencing of Tekashi, 270
TattleTales, 3
    Billboard ranking of, 282–283
    failure of, 3–4
    release of, 282–283
Tay Milly, Danny's concerns about, 13–14, 15
Tekashi. *See also* Hernandez, Daniel
    abuse of Sara by, 126
    account of kidnapping, 129
    acting like rich rapper, 130
    advocacy of Nine Trey, 14
    arrest of, 14–15
    attack on Chicago rappers, 134
    attack on Trippie Redd, 51

attempt at aerial shot, 58–59
beef between Chief Keef and, 100–101
beefing and, 108, 133
beef with Trippie Redd, 47
Blood ties and, 48
Blue Diamond and, 106–107
bragging on Instagram by, 221–222
on *Breakfast club*, 143
calling names by King, Chris, 55
canceling of tour, 143
in car chase, 54
as celebrity, 56–57, 91
charges of, 153–154
chart performance of, 133
cheating on Sara by, 281
clash with Prince, J., 71–72
as cooperating witness in racketeering
    case, xv–xvi, 166–169, 183–184, 185–186,
    190–191, 194, 196, 197–198, 201, 203,
    204–210, 211–232, 250–251, 252–253, 256,
    258
crime spree of, 264
Crippy's efforts to keep safe, 84
Cuban Doll and, 96–97
as cult figure, 209
decisionmaking within Nine Trey
    structure, 62
desire to be hands-on in his image
    making, 111–112
desire to stay on top and, 109
details of previous criminal history in
    sentencing of, 261
domestic abuse charges against, 136,
    179–181
effect of disorganization of, on Rivera's
    pocketbook, 105
efforts to mollify Harv, 74–75
efforts to talk sense into Shotti, 84–85
European tour of, 108, 109, 125
as fabulist, 229
as fan of heavy music, 9
filming of videos by, 110–111, 143
Florio, Dawn, and, 168

at Foxwoods Resort Casino, 147
as full-fledged member of Blood, 57
gang connections of, 51
Grainge, Elliot, as new label head, 46
growth in popularity of, 132
guilty plea of, in racketeering case, 168, 172, 260
Harv as bodyguard of, 56
Harv's possession of jewelry, 130
Harv's protection of, 188
Harv's selling of jewelry, 129, 178
hatred engendered by, 71
hospital prank of, 229
hostility between Shotti and, 165
house confinement of, 278
Houston incident and, 71–86
illegal recording of testimony of, 218–219
incarceration of, in Queens private prison, 261–262
insistence on remaining in Bushwick, 130
instability of, 65–66
Instagram account of, 156
internal rift in Nine Trey family and, 55
interview with *Mass Appeal*, 59
issues with Casanova, 91, 216
jewelry of, 117, 124, 129, 130, 134, 144, 229, 231, 239, 246, 254, 280, 290
job in making money for the gang, 132
kidnapping of, 111, 115, 116, 120, 121, 122, 123, 124, 125, 126, 129, 132, 139, 154, 172, 177, 178, 179, 190, 193, 194, 201, 217, 218, 1967
lack of organization in career, 67
law enforcement shadowing of, 147
Lazzaro, Lance, as lawyer for, 141, 153–154, 164, 174
legitimacy for, 111
letters in support of, 263
letter written to Engelmayer by, 263
lying by, 66–67
making of real money by, 62
making payments to Shotti and Harv, 62
Martinez, Angie's interview of, 128, 129, 231, 234, 238
meeting with booking agent, 146–147
meeting with judge, 154–155

as member of the Bloods, 57
in Metropolitan Detention Center, 171
at Mets game, 87–88
need for attention as motivation for, 62–63, 287–288
need for bulletproof truck, 130
nightly ritual with jewelry, 111
Nine Trey as out to get, 165
as not part of gang, 154
Nwandu, Angelica's interview of, 136
offer of money to get Harv, 179
ostentatious public appearances of, 290
overall lack of deference to Prince family, 72
at overseas festivals, 132
paranoia of, 108
payments to the gang, 61
on people stealing his gig money, 144
performance at Yams Day concert, 66
performance of "Gummo," 63
plea deal of, 140–141
posting on Instagram by, 133
post-prison career of, 289
post sentence monologue of, 280–281
pre-fight publicity and, 92
priming of to cooperate, 152–153
rainbow hair of, 43, 63, 64, 66, 71, 72, 86, 101, 133, 225, 241, 271, 285
rap beef of, 63
rap lyrics and videos of, 186
recordings of, 67
release of, 282–285
removal from Bureau of Prisons custody, 171
rising stardom of, 62
Rivera, Jorge, as driver for, 69
robbing of Rap-A-Lot by, 116
seizure of phone, 156
sentence of, in private jail, 277–278
sentencing of, 260, 261–276
sharing of record label with Trippie Redd, 26–27
Shotti and, 51, 69, 75, 76–77, 110, 129–130, 28

shows in U.S., 132

snitching by, 171–172, 173, 219, 260, 281

on stage presence of, 132–133

sudden stardom in, 193–194

Summer Jam and, 105–106

symbiotic relationship with Nine Trey, 274

take-no-prisoners attitude of, 71

taking of, to Homeland Security Investigations, 146

as target to rival Nine Trey factions, 130

tattoos of, 36, 71, 84, 88, 123, 124, 304

testimony of, 261

This Is 50 robbery and, 88

tickets for Barclays Center fight and, 93

treatment of, after arrest in racketeering case, 171–172

Trey Nine treatment of, 281

as troller, 141, 229, 263–264

turn to speak at sentencing of, 268–270

use of gang as "personal hit squad," 55

use of social media and, 108

at video shoot, 68

violence and, 143

visit to Dubai, 136–137

wearing of Jordans by, 60

wearing of Reebok Instapump Fury sneakers by, 60

weighing of legal options and, 162

West's gifting unreleased version of Yeezy Boost 700 sneakers, 135–136

willingness to take on impossible foes, 71

would-be casino trip of, 152

"Tekashiiii69," 14

10K Projects, 26

This Is 50, 50 Cent, 80, 82, 86

This Is 50 robbery, 87, 88, 90–91, 214, 233, 248, 260–261

Scumlord Dizzy's backpack from, 137

sentence for gang member committing, 259

Tiesha, kidnapping of Tekashi and, 113

Treyway, 200

adoption as catchphrase, 51

Shotti's control over, 65

The Trey Way, 41

Treyway Entertainment, 175–176

TriBeCa neighborhood, 50

Trippie Redd, 22, 30, 98

affiliation with Five-Nine Brims, 34

assault on, at Gansevoort Hotel, 54–55, 192, 207, 212, 260–261, 273

attack on, 287

beef with Tekashi, 47

dissing of Danny by, 27, 28

"Gummo" and, 185

Harv's punching of, 54–55

Instagram Live spat with, 97

mocking of, 63

move to Los Angeles, 26

music of, 22

performance at Radio City Music Hall, 78

plan of re-uniting Scumgang, 24

sharing of record label with Tekashi, 26–27

shooting of video by, 53

Tekashi's attack on, 51

Trolling, 55, 141, 225, 229, 263–264

"Trollz," 284

Tr3yway

need to brand, 65

pop-up shop for, 135

Tr3yway Entertainment, 56, 65, 92

creation of, 126

Tr3yway Records, 41

21 Savage, 50

on snitching, 174

2 Chainz, 133

Tyree, Garland, 40–41

Tyson, Mike, 91

U

United Blood Nations

comparison to Kappa Kappa Psi, 196

formation of, 31–32

United States of America v. Aljermiah Mack a/k/a "Nuke," and Anthony Ellison a/k/a "Harv." See Racketeering case/trial

United States Sentencing Guidelines, 5K1 letter
    and, 167, 191, 253, 260

Universal Music Group International, 25

Untouchable Gorilla Stone Nation, 34

V

Vargas, Jessie, 92

W

Walter, Faheem "Crippy." See "Crippy"

Warren, Jacob
    Tekashi's thanking of, 282
    testimony in racketeering case, 189, 243–248, 254

Wattley, Rachel "Jade," 279

Wattley, Sarah, 279

"Wavy Line," 137

Weekend Festival, Tekashi at, in Helsinki, 132

West, Kanye, 105
    desire to meet 6ix9ine, 135
    DJ Pharris interview of, 134, 135
    gifting of Tekashi an unreleased version of
        Yeezy Boost 700 sneakers, 135–136
    Tekashi's filming of video with, 143

White, Frank
    Nuke's robbery and, 90
    as prison leader of Nine Trey, 247
    trial of, 252

"Without Me," 127

"World Wide Lineup," 32

X

XXXTentacion, 29, 107–108
    murder of, 108, 109, 125

Y

Yaksha, 12, 25
    Danny and, 12, 25, 45
    as label, 18

Yams Day brawl, 212, 213

Yams Day concert, Tekashi's performance at, 66

YG, 133, 134, 287

Z

Zarrab, Reza, removal from Bureau of
    Prisons custody, 171

ZillaKami, 18, 22, 26, 30, 57, 280
    Danny's stealing of money from, 25
    duets of Danny with, 18
    efforts to raise bail for Danny, 16
    negotiations with Epic Records, 24
    as rap name for Rogers, Junius, 9
    release of paperwork from 2015 arrest, 57
    as Scumgang crew member, 47
    tension between Danny and, 27

COMPLEX SHAWN SETARO DUMMY BOY TEKASHI 6IX 9INE AND THE NINE TREY GANGSTA BLOODS COMPLEX SHAWN SETARO

DUMMY BOY TEKASHI 6IX 9INE AND THE NINE TREY GANGSTA BLOODS COMPLEX SHAWN SETARO DUMMY BOY TEKASHI 6IX 9INE AND THE NINE TREY GANGSTA BLOODS

COMPLEX SHAWN SETARO DUMMY BOY TEKASHI 6IX 9INE AND THE NINE TREY GANGSTA BLOODS COMPLEX SHAWN SETARO

DUMMY BOY TEKASHI 6IX 9INE AND THE NINE TREY GANGSTA BLOODS COMPLEX SHAWN SETARO DUMMY BOY TEKASHI 6IX 9INE AND THE NINE TREY GANGSTA BLOODS

COMPLEX SHAWN SETARO DUMMY BOY TEKASHI 6IX 9INE AND THE NINE TREY GANGSTA BLOODS COMPLEX SHAWN SETARO

DUMMY BOY TEKASHI 6IX 9INE AND THE NINE TREY GANGSTA BLOODS COMPLEX SHAWN SETARO DUMMY BOY TEKASHI 6IX 9INE AND THE NINE TREY GANGSTA BLOODS

COMPLEX SHAWN SETARO DUMMY BOY TEKASHI 6IX 9INE AND THE NINE TREY GANGSTA BLOODS COMPLEX SHAWN SETARO

DUMMY BOY TEKASHI 6IX 9INE AND THE NINE TREY GANGSTA BLOODS COMPLEX SHAWN SETARO DUMMY BOY TEKASHI 6IX 9INE AND THE NINE TREY GANGSTA BLOODS

COMPLEX SHAWN SETARO DUMMY BOY TEKASHI 6IX 9INE AND THE NINE TREY GANGSTA BLOODS COMPLEX SHAWN SETARO

DUMMY BOY TEKASHI 6IX 9INE AND THE NINE TREY GANGSTA BLOODS COMPLEX SHAWN SETARO DUMMY BOY TEKASHI 6IX 9INE AND THE NINE TREY GANGSTA BLOODS

COMPLEX SHAWN SETARO DUMMY BOY TEKASHI 6IX 9INE AND THE NINE TREY GANGSTA BLOODS COMPLEX SHAWN SETARO

DUMMY BOY TEKASHI 6IX 9INE AND THE NINE TREY GANGSTA BLOODS COMPLEX SHAWN SETARO DUMMY BOY TEKASHI 6IX 9INE AND THE NINE TREY GANGSTA BLOODS

COMPLEX SHAWN SETARO DUMMY BOY TEKASHI 6IX 9INE AND THE NINE TREY GANGSTA BLOODS COMPLEX SHAWN SETARO

DUMMY BOY TEKASHI 6IX 9INE AND THE NINE TREY GANGSTA BLOODS COMPLEX SHAWN SETARO DUMMY BOY TEKASHI 6IX 9INE AND THE NINE TREY GANGSTA BLOODS

COMPLEX SHAWN SETARO DUMMY BOY TEKASHI 6IX 9INE AND THE NINE TREY GANGSTA BLOODS COMPLEX SHAWN SETARO